DIGITAL DIPLOMACY

DIGITAL DIPLOMACY

Conversations on Innovation in Foreign Policy

Andreas Sandre

ROWMAN & LITTLEFIELD
Lanham • Boulder • New York • London

Published by Rowman & Littlefield
A wholly owned subsidiary of The Rowman & Littlefield Publishing Group, Inc.
4501 Forbes Boulevard, Suite 200, Lanham, Maryland 20706
www.rowman.com

Unit A, Whitacre Mews, 26-34 Stannary Street, London SE11 4AB

British Library Cataloguing in Publication Information Available

Library of Congress Cataloging-in-Publication Data

Library of Congress Cataloging-in-Publication Data Available

ISBN 978-1-4422-3635-6 (cloth : alk. paper)—ISBN 978-1-4422-3912-8 (pbk. : alk. paper)—ISBN 978-1-4422-3636-3 (electronic)

♾™ The paper used in this publication meets the minimum requirements of American National Standard for Information Sciences Permanence of Paper for Printed Library Materials, ANSI/NISO Z39.48-1992.

Printed in the United States of America

CONTENTS

FOREWORD

Claudio Bisogniero, Ambassador of Italy to the United States

We often forget about the many implications of diplomacy and foreign policy in our daily lives. It is not just about national interests and how governments relate to each other. It's also about the way people interact around the world, across borders, continents, languages, and customs. It is also about security, rights, opportunities, and growth; about giving a voice to the voiceless; about our heritage and our future.

In the twenty-first century, diplomacy and foreign policy have even greater implications, as we're now citizens of an ever more complex and interconnected world.

Technology is all around us: cell phones will soon outnumber the global population; Internet-connected devices are in the billions; apps and mobile technologies are making our lives easier, whether it's for accessing government services, banking, or consuming information, in real-time and on-demand.

The foreign policy community has been adjusting slowly and somewhat inconsistently. While social media platforms like Twitter and Facebook have contributed to a way forward, technology is still a Pandora's Box for many. It is still being perceived with some fear. We fear possible failures. We fear the unknown. But nothing happens overnight. Since the very first bit of data was transmitted over the Internet in the late 1960s, it took us a while to get comfortable with the way technology has changed the way we communicate.

Today, the Internet is part of our daily routine—and so are social media. Twitter has long entered my daily life. It is a way to learn, listen, and engage. It is not just a microphone but a megaphone that connects me with millions of Italians and Americans. But Twitter is only part of how the digital age has impacted diplomacy. That is why, at the Embassy of Italy in Washington, we created a Digital Diplomacy Series, seminars aimed at better understanding the new dynamics of foreign policy in the twenty-first century. Not only to nurture a dialogue around innovation, but also to bring innovative ideas to the table and explore best practices, new products, and platforms, and better ways to embrace technology.

Italy's presidency of the Council of the European Union in the second semester of 2014 showed the importance of technology in the policy process. The challenge was not limited to exploiting technology's high potential in every sector of activity, but also as a source of growth and stability.

As part of our foreign policy priorities, Italy's EU presidency pushed for the digitalization of Europe's entire economy and public services across the board, as the key to unlocking the next decade of growth and innovation. We focused on key priority areas including e-skills and jobs; rethinking "digital" to favor economic development; trust and security for digital citizenship; the digital service infrastructures, cloud computing, open and big data value chains; and the digitalization of the public sector as an enabler for Europe's competitiveness.

Today's foreign policy is as much about digital citizenship as it is about digital government and digital economy. It is about understanding who the players are and how to interact with them. It is as much about local communities as it is about the international arena.

With this backdrop, this book is very timely. It gives a very detailed picture of how digital diplomacy has evolved during the years and where it's heading. I invite everyone—ambassadors, diplomats, government officials, communicators, teachers, students—to share it, tweet it, Facebook it, Google+ it. But most of all, I invite the reader to use it as a way to start a dialogue about our own future as more informed, responsible, involved, participatory, engaged citizens of the world. This is, after all, what innovation in foreign policy is all about.

PREFACE

Naked Diplomacy

Tom Fletcher, British Ambassador to Lebanon

Andreas Sandre is doing vital work to drag diplomacy into the twenty-first century, and I urge you to read his conclusions on how innovation can reshape our business.

Members of the iGeneration have more opportunity than any generation before to understand their world, to engage with their world, and to shape their world. In the ten years since 9/11, that world has been transformed more by American geeks in dorms than Al Qaeda operatives in caves.

It was citizens who took the technology and turned it into something extraordinary. In years to come, people will say that the most powerful weapon in the Middle East was not sarin gas or Iran's bomb, but the smartphone. We have seen the power of the best of old ideas allied with the best of new technology: regimes can ban the iPhone, but iFreedom will get through in the end.

This new context changes everything. Increasingly, it matters less what a Minister or diplomat says is "our policy" on an issue—it matters what the users of Google, Facebook, or Twitter decide it is. As the rock star of digital diplomacy, Alec Ross, says—networks are replacing hierarchies.

Diplomacy is Darwinian. We evolved when sea routes opened up, empires rose and fell, the telephone came along. Some said you could replace the FCO with the fax. Well, we saw the fax off, and the telegram. Now we have to prove that you can't replace the foreign office with Wikipedia and Skype.

Equipped with the right kit, and the right courage, diplomats should be among pioneers of this terrain. We're already writers, advocates, and analysts. We must now become digital interventionists.

Jamie Oliver, as the Naked Chef, pared back cooking to the essentials. The Naked Diplomat has a smartphone to protect his modesty, but also the skills that have always been essential to the role: an open mind, political savvy, and a thick skin. He will learn the language of this new terrain in the way he has learnt Chinese or Arabic.

Set piece events are being replaced by more fluid, open interaction with the people whose interests we are there to represent. I ask colleagues who are not convinced about the power of these tools to imagine a reception with all their key contacts. You would not delegate it, stand quietly in a corner, or shout platitudes about warm bilateral relations. You would be in the mix, exchanging information. With or without the Ferrero Rocher.

Some practical examples. We're aiming to use online dating technology to link UK producers with one of the world's most powerful trading networks—the Lebanese diaspora. Crisis/contingency preparation now relies increasingly on social media. We judge that it is not now worth doing a speech unless it is reaching, via social media, over one thousand people. We've done a virtual dinner, live-streamed to involve thousands of Lebanese, and the first "tweet up" between an ambassador and a prime minister. One of our blog posts reached one in ten Lebanese citizens.

But the most important thing social media does for us is that, for the first time, it gives us the means to influence the countries we work in on a massive scale, not just through elites. This is exciting, challenging, and subversive. Getting it wrong could start a war: imagine if a diplomat tweeted a link to an offensive anti-Islam film. Getting it right has the potential to rewrite the diplomatic rulebook. A digital démarche, involving tens of thousands, will be more effective than the traditional démarche.

I think, like the best traditional diplomacy, iDiplomacy comes down to authenticity, engagement, and purpose. It is raw and human. People are more likely to read your material if they know something about you.

We need to interact, not transmit. Our followers will be a mix of the influential, curious, eccentric, and hostile.

The Internet brings nonstate actors into the conversation. That's part of the point. Once they're in, they can't be ignored. Diplomacy is action not reportage, so tweets should be about changing the world, not just describing how it looks. What makes my country richer? What makes my country more secure?

Of course social media can't replace diplomacy. We still need secrets, and direct conversations, however many of us become what the *Economist* calls "Tweeting Talleyrands." We have to recognize the limits. This is just one tool among many. Just like a clever telegram, the pithy tweet does not matter more than the action it describes. The message matters more than the medium.

Many of us have made mistakes on social media, but the biggest mistake is not to be on it.

This is happening all around us, with or without diplomats. It presents threats as well as opportunities. But so did the printing press, the telephone, air travel. Now that anyone can be a diplomat, we have to show that you can't live without diplomats.

We need to seize our smartphones.

ACKNOWLEDGMENTS

Andreas Sandre

This book is the result of almost two years of work, research, and traveling. I wouldn't have been able to bring it to life without the encouragement and understanding of Glenn Carter, who has been present and supportive all throughout the process, and my editor at Rowman & Littlefield, Marie-Claire Antoine, who passionately guided me from the first proposal to the final publication of the book. I would like to express the deepest appreciation to my boss, Italian Ambassador to the United States Claudio Bisogniero, and the former spokesperson of the Embassy of Italy in Washington, DC, Luca Gori. A special thank you also to my editorial assistants who helped me at different stages throughout the process, Monica Fourmann, Daniel Loufman, and Shelby Robinson; and to my nonresident interns in the early stages of the book, David Folley and Scott Limbrick. The support and insight of all the experts I interviewed for the book was invaluable, and I can't thank them enough for offering me their time and expertise (in alphabetical order): Alain Brian Bergant, Vincenzo Cosenza, Stéphane Dujarric, Tom Fletcher, Charles Firestone, Kim Ghattas, Teddy Goff, Alexander Howard, Joi Ito, Robert Kelley, Matthias Lüfkens, Nick Martin, Chris Messina, Adrian Monck, Macon Phillips, JR Reagan, Gianni Riotta, Alec Ross, Carne Ross, Arturo Sarukhan, Marietje Schaake, Petrit Selimi, Deborah Seward, Anne-Marie Slaughter, Timotej Šooš, Lara Stein, David Thorne, Lance Ulanoff, Aleem Walji. Scheduling interviews was not easy, and I wouldn't have been able to arrange all my travels and meetings without the help and collaboration of the following people:

Alan Jarus, Julie Snell-James, and Chaitanya Sonar at the United Nations; Bruno Giussani and Melody Serafino at TED; Kelsey Bacon, Jackie Ball-GullJee, Peter Martin, Sandy Polu, Rena Seaholm, and Stephanie Suttons at the US Department of State; Zach Duffy at Precision Strategies; Ellen Hoffman, Alexandra Kahn, and Danielle Nadeau at the Massachusetts Institute of Technology's MediaLab; TJ Thomander at TechChange; Natalie Montelongo at Podesta Group; Jane Norris and Shaqualla Howell at Deloitte and Touche; Gillian Schreiber at Independent Diplomat; Gjeneza Budima at the Ministry of Foreign Affairs of Kosovo; Hana Passen at the New America Foundation; Melle van Dijk and Willem Steketee at the European Parliament, Office of MEP Marietje Schaake; Hallie Applebaum, Jose Manuel Bassat, Vinod Beri, Nagat Dawaji, Arathi Sundaravadanan, and Rachel Winter Jones at the World Bank. In the making of this book I met and contacted many people. Many have helped me point to the right direction in my research, including: Suzanne Flinchbaugh; Stefania Piffanelli; Joakim Eskil Edvardsson Reimar, Tobias Nillson, and Charlotta Ozaki Macias at the Ministry of Foreign Affairs of Sweden; Kristin Lee at Microsoft; Beth Noveck, Stefaan Verhulst, and Lauren Yu at the GovLab of New York University; Helen Clark and Christina LoNigro at the United Nations Development Fund; Oliver Money at the International Rescue Committee; Catherine Castro and Hasan Salim Patel at Al Jazeera America; Claire Diaz-Ortiz, Katie Stanton, Gabriel Stricker, Alexandra Valasek, and Karen Wickre at Twitter; Niki Christoff Fenwick at Google; Sarah Foster at the Council on Foreign Relations; Lynn Fox and Oren Remeika at Klout; Annie Augustine at The New Republic; Pat Zindulka at the Aspen Institute. Finally, I want to thank all the diplomats, digital diplomacy practitioners, communications professionals, and journalists who have showed support for my work from the very beginning. A special thank you to Stefano Baldi of the Italian Diplomatic Institute and Jovan Kurbalija of DiploFoundation, who guided me through the publication of *Twitter for Diplomats* in 2013; to the Digital Diplomacy Coalition in Washington, DC, Yeni Diplomasi in Turkey, and all the participants at the 2014 Stockholm Initiative on Digital Diplomacy for their dedication in nurturing the dialogue around digital diplomacy.

INTRODUCTION

The Road to Diplomacy 3.0

Andreas Sandre

For a video introduction to the book, scan the QR code or visit: http://goo.gl/0gfRny

Foreign policy and diplomacy have been changing and reinventing themselves since their very beginning, from their primordial origins in sixth-century China, where they were closely connected to war and military strategy, to modern-day diplomacy.

From wars to peace treaties, invasions to summits, and even Twitter town halls and tweetups, throughout the centuries diplomacy has evolved constantly. Its evolution, however, is more evident in the tools used and its focus and priorities, rather than in its definition and core aspects. War has changed as well—as are its tools. Both war and diplomacy still relate to how states interact with each other; how they negotiate deals; how they regulate their relations with outside entities—mostly other sovereign states; how they survive through a set of laws and conventions, of which the diplomatic corps and the military are usually the most well-known and elitist appendices.

QR codes are inserted throughout the book. Each QR code, when scanned, will bring up to a video with clips of each interview.

Today's diplomatic environment is solidly anchored to its legal eco-system within the international community. However, technology seems to be having an impact on the way diplomacy is conducted as well as on the emergence of new, less traditional players.

Technology per se is not the cause, but rather the effect. When we look at the historical evolution of diplomacy and foreign policy, for centuries it centered on states sending and receiving emissaries, establishing legations or embassies, and formalizing bilateral and multilateral agreements on the most diverse of issues. Where technology had—and still has—a large initial impact is in the speed of how the information flows. When Thomas Jefferson[1] and his predecessor Benjamin Franklin[2] were sent to France as ambassadors of the United States, messages could take months before reaching their final destination—from the president's cabinet to the embassy in Paris, and back. Ambassadors and diplomats have always embraced the traditional way of practicing diplomacy and receiving instructions from their home capitals. It still happens today, just like in Jefferson and Franklin's time. The modernization of the postal service and the invention of the wireless telegraph in the late 1800s—and later the telephone and fax—sped up communications but didn't affect the interaction of diplomats outside of the elitist world of foreign affairs. We then have to wait until the widespread use of email—and later the Internet—to observe a more prominent effect on diplomacy, the way it's conducted, and how it affects regular people.

Back in 1994, US President Bill Clinton sent his first official email[3] to a foreign head of government, Swedish Prime Minister Carl Bildt. It read:

> *Dear Carl:*
> *I appreciate your support for my decision to end the trade embargo on Vietnam and thank you for all that Sweden has done on the question of the POW/MIA's.*
> *I share your enthusiasm for the potential of emerging communications technologies. This demonstration of electronic communications is an important step toward building a global information superhighway.*
> *Sincerely,*
> *BILL*

The email was Clinton's response to an email by Bildt:

Dear Bill,

Apart from testing this connection on the global Internet system, I want to congratulate you on your decision to end the trade embargo on Vietnam. I am planning to go to Vietnam in April and will certainly use the occasion to take up the question of the MIA's. From the Swedish side we have tried to be helpful on this issue in the past, and we will continue to use the contacts we might have.

Sweden is—as you know—one of the leading countries in the world in the field of telecommunications, and it is only appropriate that we should be among the first to use the Internet also for political contacts and communications around the globe.

Yours,

CARL

The brief email exchange between the two leaders, Clinton and Bildt, focused in part on how the Internet was changing the political and foreign policy arena and communications around the world. The technology element in this new course for diplomacy and politics was also clear in a more recent statement by Clinton: "Every day, technological innovations are giving people around the world new opportunities to shape their own destinies," he said,[4] reminding us how technology has affected the most traditional aspect of diplomacy, meaning its government-to-government nature. Fast forward twenty years from that first email between Clinton and Bildt: in December 2014, President Barack Obama, already the world leader most followed on social media, partnered with code.org to kick-off a campaign to push for code literacy. "If we want America to stay on the cutting edge, we need young Americans like you to master the tools and technology that will change the way we do just about everything," he said[5] at the launch of the annual Computer Science Education Week. Obama, who during the event wrote a simple program thus becoming the first US president ever to code, is among the many politicians in the US who have been pushing for code literacy, including former mayor of New York, Michael Bloomberg.

Thanks to technology and digital tools, diplomacy has been partially democratized so as to include more voices. That also opened the way to different personifications of power and influence. This transformation is happening very fast and seems to affect the very DNA of traditional diplomacy. New nonstate actors are emerging quite rapidly, reshaping the international landscape and forcing foreign policy practitioners to rebalance their focus so as to accommodate new priorities, engage with civil society, and open the process.

The core of diplomacy, outside of technology, remains a close eco-system of laws and official relations which make the practice of diplomacy sustainable and at times organic. However, it doesn't make diplomacy prone to changes and adaptation cycles, in particular in today's digital and participatory age. While diplomacy's core hasn't changed much, it has certainly grown and expanded to understand the potential of technology. It has dynamically altered the space in which diplomacy operates to account for—rather than to include—more players. However, it has not changed. It hasn't changed from the way Sun Tzu described it in 500 BC in his *The Art of War*, where the need to know oneself and your enemy was key to any intervention outside of your borders; where rapidity and deception were the ingredients for taking your opponent by surprise. While diplomacy then was about war and not about peace, it was about evaluating one another's strengths and weaknesses in order for the ruler to act—or react—accordingly. Niccoló Machiavelli's sixteenth-century morality of power highlighted in *The Prince*, although through the lens of national politics and internal af-fairs, clearly shows the need for diplomatic strategy when it comes to war and conquest. They become ingredients to the survival of a state's sovereignty. Both the *Art of War* and *The Prince* can be very useful in understanding even today's power dynamics, where a state exercises power through diplomacy or military strategy.

Sun Tzu and Machiavelli were certainly not familiar with cyber-warfare and twenty-first-century policy making, but they laid out a clear path for the government to follow in terms of preserving its sovereign identity, knowing all the players, crafting alliances and partnerships, and understanding the paradigm of risk—where action carries more value than reaction.

Machiavelli went even further in his analysis. He writes: "It ought to be remembered that there is nothing more difficult to take in hand, more perilous to conduct, or more uncertain in its success, than to take the lead in the introduction of a new order of things, because the innovator has for enemies all those who have done well under the old conditions, and lukewarm defenders in those who may do well under the new. This coolness arises partly from fear of the opponents, who have the laws on their side, and partly from the incredulity of men, who do not readily believe in new things until they have had a long experience of them."[6] Surprisingly enough, the sixteenth-century Machiavellian ruler needed to be an innovator. This is quite a familiar concept in today's world where innovation is the 'salt and pepper' of every sector, from diplomacy to the economy, and beyond. Innovation has become the *mot-du-jour* for everybody, for foreign ministers and ambassadors as well.

Innovation in Machiavelli's time is different from today. And while innovation today is hard to define—especially in the government and foreign policy realms—it usually entails disruption. Innovation is about doing things differently; it is about changing institutions, disrupting the system, and reforming processes. Innovators have to disrupt the current systems to find new solutions to old—and new—problems. Innovation means thinking outside the box and looking into the unknown. Indeed, the task of the innovator—in government and in the private sector—is to make the unknown known and better understood, and certainly to find the most efficient way to achieve goals.

Seen through the lens of disruption, innovation in government is a hard commodity to come by, even if it is now part of the bureaucratic jargon. But is it really part of the bureaucratic and policy process? Hardly so.

Economist Umair Haque[7] puts it quite well when he calls 'unnovation' what most of us would call 'innovation.' He writes: "Most innovation, well, isn't: it is 'unnovation,' or innovation that fails to create authentic, meaningful value."[8] While his definition of true innovation implies the creation of authentic, meaningful value—a concept that works well in the private sector—in the public sector the value lies in the end user, and that is the citizen. The goal is then to create a veritable ecosystem for innovation, in which ideas become a true vessel to nurture innovative processes that really create authentic, meaningful value—in Faque's words—for all citizens.

It all comes down to the power of ideas—not to just technology, not the money needed to achieve our goals, not to the process itself. It comes down to all of us—diplomats, politicians, civil society, and citizens—becoming champions for ideas, even when they seem too disruptive, or even too simple to achieve our goals.

Prime Minister Matteo Renzi of Italy put ideas at the center of the Italian presidency of the Council of the European Union in the second semester of 2014.[9] *"Tristo è quel discepolo che non avanza il suo maestro,"* Renzi said, quoting Leonardo Da Vinci (which translates: "Sad is that disciple who does not surpass his master") and emphasizing the importance of ideas, innovation, and creativity in everything we do, from government to the arts. "Europe will be saved by ideas," he continued, highlighting his plan to change Europe in a more digital and cohesive entity that puts citizens first. Renzi's presidency was in fact the first truly digital presidency of the Council of the European Union, according to Neelie Kroes, then vice president of the European Commission in charge for the Digital Agenda.[10] But Kroes also warned: "If we want to be a strong continent, rich in innovation and jobs, we need to be on the right side of technology history. It's not people like me who are going to provide this innovation. Governments and policy makers aren't best equipped to come up with these ideas. But we can ensure that public rules and regulations and, yes, financial investment, all support and stimulate that innovation."

Government has an important role to play as, in this new environment, technology has become a facilitator for innovation, including in foreign policy. It might not produce innovation, but it helps ideas better circulate and move between spaces and sectors. This is where Twitter, Facebook, and other social media tools have played an important role in complementing traditional diplomacy and making it more inclusive, more participatory—thanks mostly to the power derived from the reach social media allows its users.

"The potentially global reach of social media networks is among their defining characteristics," says the World Economic Forum.[11] "For the first time in history, it is as easy to video-chat and share everyday news with friends on the other side of the planet as with friends in the same city."

Social media channels have been generally showing a continued strong growth over the last few years, with top social platforms adding more than 135 million new users in the course of 2013—monthly-active users—according to digital agency We Are Social's 2014 Social, Digital and Mobile Worldwide report.[12] North America tops the ranking in terms of social media penetration by region (56 percent); but Western Europe, Central and Eastern Europe, Central and South America, East and Southeast Asia, and the Middle East are all at or above the average (26 percent). Facebook remains the largest with over 1 billion active users around the world, followed by China's QQ, at around 800 million active users, and QZone, at over 600 million. WhatsApp, bought by Facebook in early 2014, Google+, and Twitter are all in a range between 250 and 400 million active users.

In the African continent, while social media use is still below the average, the Internet has witnessed a sustained increase in adoption rates, with penetration currently pegged at 16 percent and more than 167 million active users across the continent. Said Tolu Ogunlesi, a renowned Nigerian political commentator and journalist: "In the early 90s, the government took control of almost everything, but now social media has changed everything. People have been able to speak up and pursue causes against governments."[13]

While censorship has its effect on Africa's Internet and social media landscape, the continent is going digital, according to a 2013 report by McKingsey and Company.[14] The study shows that Africa's iGDP (which measures the Internet's contribution to the overall Gross Domestic Product) remains low, at 1.1 percent—just over half the levels seen in other emerging economies. But there is significant variation among individual countries: Senegal and Kenya, though not the continent's largest economies, have Africa's highest iGDPs, and governments in both countries have made concerted efforts to stimulate Internet demand.

"Evidence of what is to come can already be seen in Africa's major cities, where consumers have greater disposable income, more than half have Internet-capable devices, and 3G networks are up and running," the reports states. "Significant infrastructure investment—for example, increased access to mobile broadband, fibre-optic cable connections to households, and power-supply expansion—combined with the rapid spread of low-cost smartphones and tablets, has enabled millions of Africans to connect for the first time. There is a growing wave of innovation as entrepreneurs and large corporations alike launch new web-based ventures."

Somewhat different is the situation in Asia. For instance, when it comes to China, home of some of the largest social media tools in terms of users, its social media environment is characteristically its own. Behind the *Great Firewall* of China—as some call it—lays an ecosystem driven by cultural circumstances and censorship as well as a focus on images and a mix of public and private postings that are more likely to escape the censors.

China, together with Cuba and Iran, remain among the most restrictive countries in terms of Internet freedom and the use of social media platforms. According to Freedom House's 2013 *Freedom of the Net* report,[15] of the sixty countries evaluated, China is one of the fourteen countries with systematic censorship, bans, and filters in effect, coupled with laws and measures to restrict free speech online. The number of countries increases to twenty-nine—almost half of the total analyzed— when it comes to governments that have applied blocks to suppress certain types of political and social content. "The global number of censored websites has increased, while Internet users in various countries have been arrested, tortured, and killed over the information they posted online," the report says.

In a space where censorship and propaganda seem to be rampant, where countries are trying to increase their control over any online activity, commonalities among users still exist, no matter if you're in China, in Europe, North America, or elsewhere.

"It [. . .] appears that social media is now an engrained part of the lives of people across different demographic groups," reads We Are Social's 2014 analysis. "This increased ubiquity may result in some changes to the specific demographic bases of individual platforms, but even if people's habits are changing, it appears that people are moving from one social platform to another, rather than deserting social media in its entirety," the report continues.

In other words, the social interactions created on online platforms are becoming almost a self-sustaining space. It is a space that, at times, is even able to withstand restrictions and repressive tactics by governments—as is the case of Turkey. It happened in the spring 2014, when then Prime Minister Recep Tayyip Erdoğan banned Twitter following the circulation of leaked recordings that implicated him and members of his inner circle in irregularities and corruption allegations.[16] While users were quickly able to find alternative ways to access the platform— via mobile text messages and simple technical bypass tools like Google DNS,[17] and virtual private networks (VPNs),[18] or anonymous browsing tools like Tor[19]—the debate that generated around the ban crossed international boundaries and helped the Turkish online community overcome the obstacle as a group.

Censorship and monitoring of social media are one side of what Hillary Clinton calls "the dark side of the digital revolution." In her memoir about her four years as US Secretary of State, she writes: "The same qualities that made the Internet a force for unprecedented progress—in its openness, in its leveling effect, its reach and speed—also enabled wrongdoing on an unprecedented scale."[20] This is when technology becomes both an opportunity to bring change, but also one of the biggest challenges the international community has ever faced. "Terrorists and extremist groups use the Internet to incite hate, recruit members, and plot and carry out attacks," Clinton says. "Human traffickers lure new victims into modern-day slavery. Child pornographers exploit children. Hackers break into financial institutions, retailers, cell-phone networks, and personal email accounts. Criminal gangs as well as nations are building offensive cyber warfare and industrial espionage capabilities."[21]

The technology and social media space—as dynamic, dangerous, and complex as it can be—is certainly very challenging, but it represents for governments new, exciting opportunities. In the past few years, part of diplomacy's focus has been to harness social media networks to increase the reach. It is an effort that goes under the name of digital diplomacy, ediplomacy, or social media diplomacy. However, much of it is still about broadcasting messages. Governments have been flooding social media with Facebook pages, Twitter profiles, YouTube channels, Instagram accounts, and the like. Some have been better at it than others. Some, including the United States[22] and the United Kingdom,[23] have invested heavily in training and people; some others have relied on new strategies, like Sweden, for example. Under the leadership of foreign minister Carl Bildt,[24] the Swedish diplomatic apparatus, instead of growing its social media presence organically, decided to ask all its embassies to open both Facebook and Twitter accounts in an effort to exponentially increase the country's reach.[25]

But even countries that have grown in their use of digital platforms are still struggling to adjust their presence and learn how to better integrate their articulate, vast social media presence into their foreign policy priorities. They're still struggling to identify nongovernment actors quickly. One of the problems revolves around the ability of governments to really listen to what is happening out there. The implementation of a social media program that allows governments to listen to and understand their audiences should be a top priority. But is it? How can governments move beyond simple sentiment analysis to a position where social data can provide valuable insight in the crafting of a veritable digital diplomacy presence as a tool to actuate a country's foreign policy agendas? The question remains open, as many governments still don't understand the full value of their presence on social media. It's not just about numbers and analytics; it's about learning the new dynamics within social media, and outside of them.

"Policy makers can quickly assess public opinion on draft policies to better gauge the potential impact on citizens, actively pull the ideas of citizens into the government innovation process, or use social media to provide citizens with lifesaving information during emergencies," says Ines Mergel, associate professor of public administration and international affairs at the Maxwell School of Citizenship and Public Affairs, Syracuse University.[26] "Big data collection and analysis are for many government organizations still unchartered waters. It is important to understand how to make sense of the massive amount of data that is produced on social media every day, especially in response to formal government updates."

An area of interest and great successes is the development sector—in terms of supporting all efforts in situations of natural catastrophes as well as in achieving a country's sustainable development goals. In this context, technology holds tremendous potential to improve public services and to enhance broad stakeholder involvement in public service, nationally and internationally.

According to the 2014 United Nations e-Government Survey,[27] countries in all regions of the world are increasing their investments on information and communications technologies (ICTs) to complement their development programs. They're tools that are proven to enhance public participation in decision making; remove access to services rendered by the government and by international governmental and nongovernmental entities; and contribute to good governance and effective public management.

An area of development in which governments have been very active is disaster management and disaster risk reduction—where government and the international community play the critical coordination role—

particularly by harnessing mobile technologies. First, new programs have been crafted to forecast, map, and mobilize—as well as to raise awareness and give more access to information and data. Secondly, mobile and open-source technologies have been very helpful in terms of coordinating the response and rescue operations, as it was the case of Haiti in the aftermath of the 2010 earthquake that affected three million people and killed around 150,000 people.

Since Haiti, a lot has been accomplished. In Bangladesh, for example, one of the most vulnerable nations in terms of climate change, floods, cyclones, and other major natural disasters, the government has collaborated with the international community to develop an SMS-based disaster warning system. Developed within the country's broader National ICT Policy, the program revolves around disaster warning and management technologies: remote sensing for disaster management and mitigation; web-based environmental clearance certification system; cell phone/SMS-based targeted warning systems; Geographic Information System (GIS)-based systems to monitor flood and cyclone shelters (including equitable distribution in vulnerable areas); relief management and postdisaster activities monitoring.

Bangladesh's efforts show how technology can be an important tool for policy makers and the international foreign policy agenda. Technology has a lot of potential if governments understand it, learn to harness it properly, and look beyond the simple use of technology to really transform the way they operate and interact with all stakeholders. But the road ahead is long and steep, starting from the simple understanding of social media dynamics—let alone of larger technology programs and open-source platforms.

This book aims at analyzing the evolution of digital diplomacy as a complementary tool to traditional diplomacy. It aims at understanding the Diplomacy 2.0 movement—as some have labelled it—and how governments have been modeling around it. It is reflected in how foreign ministers and ambassadors tweet and blog today, how everyday citizens can participate into the process and even influence it.

The book, however, is also about the new foreign policy space that technology and digital diplomacy have contributed to craft within the diplomatic realm; as well as outside of it. It's a space inhabited by a plurality of players, both from government and from civil society, and a plurality of networks of players. It's a space that struggles to transform and adapt itself to new challenges. It's a space where power and influence have acquired new forms. It's a space where connections, partnerships, and collaborations play an important role. I call this space Diplomacy 3.0,[28] a space where technology and tradition meet; where nodes and links are components of networks that transcend government as we know it; where all actors interact and collaborate.

Diplomacy 3.0 is not about technology or innovation. It looks beyond the use of social media. Diplomacy 3.0 is about the evolution of foreign policy into a networked environment where state and nonstate are horizontally interacting with each other; where parts of networks interact with other parts of networks, including government agencies, local governmental entities, and their spin-offs. It is a space where power is dispersed and dependent on how connected you are.

Diplomacy 3.0 is shaping itself as a true startup environment, in which disruption shall not have a negative connotation. It is aimed at hacking and reinventing diplomacy while creating organic, collaborative ways to actuate your foreign policy priorities. The January 2014 meeting of the Stockholm Initiative on Digital Diplomacy (SIDD),[29] hosted by then Swedish foreign minister Bildt, certainly helped the foreign policy community face the new dynamics of diplomacy and better understand the road ahead. It helped us evolve from 140 characters to a myriad of opportunities embedded in the very nature of the digital era and of the networked world. And while we have not yet outgrown Twitter and Facebook—still key ingredients for any government's digital strategy— foreign policy is trying to move onto the direction of Diplomacy 3.0. We're on the right path toward a modern diplomacy that fits our hyperconnected, networked, super-speed, media-centric, volatile world.

"By bringing together an international group of people at the forefront of digital diplomacy in Stockholm, we hope to pave the way for stronger networks and new methods for the diplomacy of the future," said Bildt.[30] "The idea is to further investigate the implications for future diplomacy of a growing culture of digital participation, and to look into what will be required of the diplomats of tomorrow—nobody has the answers yet, but it will certainly involve collaboration and learning from each other."

The Arab Spring is possibly the first instance where a new sense of global hyperconnectivity—while not absent before—became more evident. From the town of Sidi Bouzid, where the 2010 Tunisian Revolution originated, the protests and demonstrations spread out to social networks and in neighboring countries like Egypt, Libya, Yemen, and Syria—with repercussions that we still see today. It certainly represented a wake-up moment for the foreign policy community around the world in terms of digital awareness, as well as social and economic interactions in the digital age. Also, social media exponentially increased a complicated web of interactions where a new, very visible actor clearly emerged on the international stage: the Arab people. Thanks to mobile technologies, they rapidly organized in networks and communities, while reshaping their own future through grassroots organizing and growing networks of people and civil society organizations. In the case of the Aragb uprisings, the role of social media tools certainly accelerated the process, rather than caused it.

A 2012 study by the Pew Research Center[31] suggests that in that instance faith in social media wasn't misplaced—users in Lebanon, Tunisia, Egypt, and Jordan still take to social networks to discuss politics at nearly twice the rate of their Western counterparts.

"Expressing opinions about politics, community issues and religion is particularly common in the Arab world," reads the Pew report. "For instance, in Egypt and Tunisia, two nations at the heart of the Arab Spring, more than 6 in 10 social networkers share their views about politics online. In contrast, across 20 of the nations surveyed, a median of only 34 percent post their political opinions. Similarly, in Egypt, Tunisia, Lebanon and Jordan, more than seven-in-ten share views on community issues, compared with a cross-national median of just 46 percent."

Since the Arab Spring movements, the foreign policy community has understood that in today's world conventional diplomacy alone is not sufficient. Digital or social media diplomacy are not sufficient either. New ideas are needed.

Since the first SIDD meeting in Stockholm, a new wave of collaboration has appeared and has affected all aspects of digital diplomacy and communication. That was quite clear in the preceding of the 2014 general elections in Ukraine, followed the wave of demonstrations and civil unrest that brought to the collapse of President Viktor Yanukovych's[32] government and the subsequent secession crisis in the Crimea region. During the Brussels leg of US President Barack Obama's trip to Europe in March 2014, the US Department of State launched the #unitedforukraine campaign on social media, coordinating the efforts with European partners.

"Over the last several days, the United States, Europe and our partners around the world have been united in defense of these ideals and united in support of the Ukrainian people," President Obama said in his address in Brussels. [33] "Together, we've condemned Russia's invasion of Ukraine and rejected the legitimacy of the Crimean referendum. Together, we have isolated Russia politically, suspending it from the G-8 nations and downgrading our bilateral ties. Together, we are imposing costs through sanctions that have left a mark on Russia and those accountable for its actions," he continued.

The hashtag #unitedforukraine put a social media spin to the concepts highlighted in Obama's speech. "Our goal with this campaign and everything else we're doing is to make sure the world knows what is happening, what is the truth and making sure people come together, again, and are united for Ukraine," said State Department Deputy spokeswoman Marie Harf in a briefing. [34]

Thanks to the coordination efforts, the hashtag went viral but not without problems, as Russia took to Twitter[35] to try to hijack the campaign and use the hashtag in its communications with its own spin. The experience certainly shows how we still have a long way to go to move beyond the tool, and craft strategies and best practices that are sustainable and waterproofed. But it is a first step in the right direction, toward a diplomacy open to collaborative ideas.

Hashtag diplomacy and hashtag activism go hand by hand, as it was the case with the #bringbackourgirls campaign to draw attention to the kidnapping of nearly three hundred schoolgirls in Nigeria in April 2014. After exploding on Twitter, the campaign went viral on many different platforms and made its way first to the White House—First Lady Michelle Obama posted a photo in the style of a sefie, [36] on Twitter[37] and Facebook[38] the day after President Obama said the United States was sending a team to Nigeria to assist in finding the missing girls[39] —and later even to the World Cup in Brazil,[40] the most watched sporting event in the world, with an estimated global viewership surpassing the 2010 record of 3.2 billion people[41] through television sets and live streaming on computers and mobiles. During games played by the Nigerian national team, posters with the hashtag #bringbackourgirls were popping up at every game.

"Hashtag activism will not save the more than 200 Nigerian school-girls abducted by terrorist group Boko Haram," says Ben Scott, senior advisor to the Open Technology Institute at the New America Founda-tion and Director of the European Digital Agenda program at the Stif-tung Neue Verantwortung in Berlin.[42] "But the #bringbackourgirls hashtag is not meaningless, as some of its critics contend. Hashtag acti-vism is a gateway between politics and popular culture, a platform to educate the ignorant and draw attention to the operation of power in the world. And when it shines a spotlight on a burning crisis in Africa that has been raging for years, that matters."

The foreign policy community has to look now beyond hashtags and viral campaigns. The challenges of the future are numerous and ever growing, not just in numbers but also in terms of complexities related to the rising global integration, interdependencies, and interconnectivity. The focus should now be placed not on the tools per se but rather on sustainability of the current technology ecosystem and on increasing international policy cooperation and coordination, especially in areas like foreign policy, trade, innovation, and the environment.

While Diplomacy 3.0 is just a name, a label, a symbol, it represents a way forward. The foreign policy community needs a collaborative road-map to emerge from the current stall in digital diplomacy. The past ten years have been very exciting for the digital diplomacy agenda, which has gone through many transformations, labels, tools, phases, and cri-ses. From a small task force incubated in 2002 by then–US Secretary of State Colin Powell to what his successor Condoleezza Rice championed as "Transformational diplomacy,"[43] to the era of "21st Century State-craft"[44] of Hillary Clinton and Alec Ross. Inside and outside Washing-ton, what we call digital diplomacy has expanded into very effective programs, involving new partners, regional and nonstate actors, and the public as well. It has evolved into crowdsourcing capabilities, mapping technologies, and big data. This is what British Ambassador to Lebanon Tom Fletcher calls "Naked Diplomacy;" what Philip Seib of the Univer-sity of Southern California's Center on Public Diplomacy brands as "Real-Time Diplomacy."[45] However, this evolution is still mostly cen-tered on the use of social media tools, rather than on a discussion to the future of diplomacy.

Thanks to the many diplomats, practitioners, and experts—from government and from the private sector—who agreed to be part of my project, this book aims at becoming a tool to understand what direction diplomacy is moving toward. I call it Diplomacy 3.0, but you can simply call it diplomacy. It is, after all, what diplomacy is today, where it's heading, and how it's shaping its future, and ours as global citizens.

NOTES

1. Thomas Jefferson was the second US representative to France, appointed in 1785 with the title of Minister Plenipotentiary. While minister to France, he negotiated a commercial treaty with Prussia (1785) and the Consular Convention with France (1788). He terminated his ambassadorial post in Paris in 1789 to become the first secretary of state, serving from March 22, 1790, to December 31, 1793. As secretary of state, Jefferson's approach to foreign affairs was limited by Washington's preference for neutrality regarding the war between Britain and France. He was the third President of the United States, from March 4, 1801 to March 4, 1809.

2. Benjamin Franklin was the first US representative to France, appointed in 1778 with the title Minister Plenipotentiary. During his post in Paris, which he left in 1785, he was commissioned by President George Washington to negotiate a treaty with Sweden, which was signed at Paris, April 3, 1783.

3. The American Presidency Project, electronic mail message to Prime Minister Carl Bildt of Sweden, February 5, 1994, http://www.presidency.ucsb.edu/ws/?pid=49664.

4. In his review of the book *The New Digital Age: Reshaping the Future of People, Nations and Business* (Alfred A. Knopf, 2013), Bill Clinton writes: "Every day, technological innovations are giving people around the world new opportunities to shape their own destinies. In this fascinating book, Eric Schmidt and Jared Cohen draw upon their unique experiences to show us a future of rising incomes, growing participation, and a genuine sense of community—if we make the right choices today." The book was authored by Eric Schmidt, chairman, Google Inc., and Jared Cohen, director of Google Ideas and adjunct senior fellow at the Council on Foreign Relations, Council of Foreign Relations, The New Digital Age, http://www.cfr.org/technology-and-foreign-policy/new-digital-age/p30507.

5. Kint Finley, "Obama Becomes First President to Write a Computer Program." *Wired*. Last updated December 8, 2014. http://www.wired.com/2014/12/obama-becomes-first-president-write-computer-program.

6. Chapter 6 of *The Prince* is titled: *Concerning New Principalities Which Are Acquired by One's Own Arms and Ability*. Niccoló Machiavelli, *The*

Prince, translated by W. K. Marriott (Salt Lake City: The Project Gutenberg, 2006). Kindle e-book.

7. Umair Haque is Director of Havas Media Labs (http://www.havasmedia.com/) and author of *Betterness: Economics for Humans* and *The New Capitalist Manifesto: Building a Disruptively Better Business*. He is ranked one of the world's most influential management thinkers by Thinkers50.

8. Umair Haque, "Is Your Innovation Really Unnovation?," *Harvard Business Review* (blog), May 27, 2009, http://blogs.hbr.org/2009/05/unnovation/.

9. Italian Presidency of the Council of the European Union, Twitter post, July 9, 2014, 9:35 a.m., https://twitter.com/IT2014EU/status/486866175021056000.

10. European Commission, Speech by Neelie Kroes, Vice President of the European Commission responsible for the Digital Agenda, at Digital Venice on Italian leadership for a connected continent, http://europa.eu/rapid/press-release_SPEECH-14-534_en.htm.

11. Hu Yong and Takeshi Natsuno, "Asia Loves Facebook, Latin America Loves WhatsApp," *World Economic Forum* (blog), June 18, 2014, http://forumblog.org/2014/06/social-media-worldwide/.

12. Simon Kemp, "Social, Digital and Mobile Worldwide in 2014," *We Are Social* (blog), January 9, 2014, http://wearesocial.net/blog/2014/01/social-digital-mobile-worldwide-2014/.

13. Ehidiamhen Okpamen, Niyi Aderibigbe, Temitope Bolade, Douglas Imaralu, and Chinedu Agbatuka, "#AFRICA–Inside the Continent's New $14bn Social Media Industry," Ventures, last updated June 20, 2014, http://www.ventures-africa.com/2014/06/africa-inside-the-continents-new-14-billion-social-media-industry/.

14. James Manyika, Armando Cabral, Lohini Moodley, Suraj Moraje, Safroadu Yeboah-Amankwah, Michael Chui, and Jerry Anthonyrajah, "Lions Go Digital: The Internet's Transformative Potential in Africa," McKinsey and Company, last updated November 2013, http://www.mckinsey.com/insights/high_tech_telecoms_internet/lions_go_digital_the_internets_transformative_potential_in_africa.

15. Sanja Kelly, Mai Truong, Madeline Earp, Laura Reed, Adrian Shabaz, and Ashley Greco-Stoner, *Freedom of the Net*, Washington, DC: Freedom House, 2013, http://freedomhouse.org/sites/default/files/resources/FOTN%202013_Full%20Report_0.pdf.

16. The Turkish government blocked Twitter from March 20, 2014, to April 3, 2014. It lifted the ban a day after the country's highest court ruled that the ban violated freedom of expression.

17. Google Public DNS is a free, global domain name system (DNS) resolution service that you can use as an alternative to your current DNS provider.

The DNS protocol is an important part of the web's infrastructure, serving as the Internet's phone book: every time you visit a website, your computer performs a DNS lookup. Complex pages often require multiple DNS lookups before they start loading, so your computer may be performing hundreds of lookups a day.

18. A virtual private network (VPN) extends a private network across a public network, such as the Internet. It enables a computer to send and receive data across shared or public networks as if it is directly connected to the private network, while benefiting from the functionality, security, and management policies of the private network. A VPN is created by establishing a virtual point-to-point connection through the use of dedicated connections, virtual tunneling protocols, or traffic encryptions.

19. Tor (https://www.torproject.org/) is free software and an open network that helps you defend against traffic analysis, a form of network surveillance that threatens personal freedom and privacy, confidential business activities and relationships, and state security.

20. Hillary Clinton, *Hard Choices* (New York: Simon and Schuster, 2014), 547.

21. Clinton, *Hard Choices*, 547.

22. Most of the digital diplomacy work of the US Department of State—excluding those connected to its consular activity—goes through the Under Secretary for Public Diplomacy and Public Affairs, its Bureau of Public Affairs, and its Bureau of International Information Programs (IIP). The latter is the State Department's foreign-facing public diplomacy communications bureau. IIP provides and supports the places, content, and infrastructure needed for sustained conversations with foreign audiences to build America's reputation abroad. It supports both physical and virtual places, including over seven hundred American Spaces around the world, as well as a growing social media community that numbers over twelve million followers.

23. The British Foreign Office (FCO) has a very detailed digital diplomacy strategy that covers the implications of digital for the UK overall diplomatic work around the world, as well as their services to the British public. The FCO's digital strategy is available online at http://blogs.fco.gov.uk/digitaldiplomacy/, including blog posts, case studies, best practices, and social media presence.

24. Carl Bildt has been the Minister of Foreign Affairs of Sweden since 2006.

25. Bildt announced the new strategy on February 13, 2013, in his address at the Parliament Debate on Foreign Affairs in the Riksdag, Stockholm. Carl Bildt, *Statement of Government Policy in the Parliamentary Debate on Foreign*

Affairs (Stockholm: Regeringskansliet, February 13, 2013), http://www.government.se/content/1/c6/20/90/53/c7791e9a.pdf.

26. Ines Mergel, "Assessing the Impact of Government Social Media Interactions," Brookings Institution, last updated June 10, 2014, http://www.brookings.edu/blogs/techtank/posts/2014/06/23-government-social-media-interactions.

27. Haiyan Qian, and Vincenzo Acquaro, *United Nations e-Government Survey 2014* (New York: United Nations, 2014).

28. Andreas Sandre, "Diplomacy 3.0 Starts in Stockholm," *The Huffington Post*, January 15, 2014, last updated May 17, 2014, http://www.huffingtonpost.com/andreas-sandre/digital-diplomacy-stockholm_b_4592691.html.

29. The Stockholm Initiative on Digital Diplomacy (SIDD) was the first major international meeting about digital diplomacy. It was held in Stockholm, Sweden, from January 16 to 17, 2014. It was convened by Swedish Foreign Minister Carl Bildt and the Swedish Foreign Ministry. It was attended by some twenty diplomats and experts to produce concrete, feasible solutions for the diplomacy of the future, as well as to create a truly sustainable and collaborative ecosystem for digital diplomacy.

30. Sandre, "Diplomacy 3.0 Starts in Stockholm."

31. Andrew Kohut, Richard Wike, Juliana Menasce Horowitz, Katie Simmons, Jacob Poushter, Cathy Barker, James Bell, Bruce Stokes, and Elizabeth Mueller Gross, *Social Networking Popular across Globe: Arab Publics Most Likely to Express Political Views Online* (Washington, DC: Pew Research Center, 2012), http://www.pewglobal.org/files/2012/12/Pew-Global-Attitudes-Project-Technology-Report-FINAL-December-12-2012.pdf.

32. Viktor Yanukovych served as the fourth President of the Ukraine from February 2010 until February 2014, a year before his presidential term of office was set to expire.

33. Barack Obama, "Remarks by the President in Address to European Youth," Brussels: The White House, March 26, 2014, http://www.whitehouse.gov/the-press-office/2014/03/26/remarks-president-address-european-youth.

34. Mary Harf, daily press briefing, Washington DC: United States Department of State, March 26, 2014, http://www.state.gov/r/pa/prs/dpb/2014/03/223978.htm.

35. On April 2014, Russia's Ministry of Foreign Affairs sent out the following tweet: "Russia surprised by US, Ukraine misinterpreting Geneva agreement #UnitedForUkraine." Ministry of Foreign Affairs of Russia (MFA Russia), Twitter post, April 23, 2014, 12:44 p.m., https://twitter.com/mfa_russia/statuses/459009929227931648.

36. A selfie is a self-portrait photograph, typically taken with a smartphone and shared on social media platforms.

37. Michelle, Obama, Twitter post, May 7, 2014, 5:03 p.m., https://twitter.com/FLOTUS/statuses/464148654354628608.

38. The White House, Facebook post, last updated May 7, 2014, 6:24 p.m., https://www.facebook.com/photo.php?fbid=10152473948824238.

39. David Hudson, "U.S. to Help Nigeria in the Search for Kidnapped Girls," *The White House* (blog), last updated May 7, 2014, 3:34 p.m., http://www.whitehouse.gov/blog/2014/05/07/us-will-send-military-and-law-enforcement-officials-nigeria-help-rescue-missing-girl.

40. Bhas Kunju, "Bring Back Our Girls Campaign Makes World Cup Appearance," Goal.com, last updated June 23, 2014, 12:14 a.m., http://www.goal.com/en-sg/news/3999/world-cup-2014/2014/06/23/4904548/bring-back-our-girls-campaign-makes-world-cup-appearance.

41. KantarSprt, *2010 FIFA World Cup South Africa: Television Audience Report*, London: FIFA, July 2011, http://www.fifa.com/mm/document/affederation/tv/01/47/32/73/2010fifaworldcupsouthafricatvaudiencereport.pdf.

42. Ben Scott, "#WhyHashtagActivismMatters," *The Weekly Wonk* (blog), last updated May 15, 2014, http://weeklywonk.newamerica.net/articles/whyhashtagactivismmatters/.

43. Condoleezza Rice, *Transformational Diplomacy*, Washington, DC: United States Department of State, January 18, 2006, http://2001-2009.state.gov/secretary/rm/2006/59306.htm.

44. United States Department of State, *21st Century Statecraft*, http://www.state.gov/statecraft/.

45. Philip Seib is a professor of journalism, public diplomacy, and international relations at the University of Southern California. He is author or editor of numerous books, including *Real-Time Diplomacy Politics and Power in the Social Media Era* (Palgrave Macmillan, 2012). He served as director of USC's Center on Public Diplomacy from 2009 to 2013.

I

Traditional vs. Innovative

I

TWENTY-FIRST CENTURY STATECRAFT

A conversation with Alec J. Ross, Senior Advisor for Innovation to the US Secretary of State (2009–2013)

To view clips
from the conversation
with Alec Ross
scan the QR code
or visit:
http://goo.gl/hyMrY8

Under US President Barack Obama and US Secretary of State Hillary Clinton's stewardship, innovation has certainly started to become one of the main focuses of American foreign policy. Innovation, however, is not easy to define. It can take different shapes and forms, especially when it comes to its application in diplomacy and international affairs. You've often referred to innovation as one of America's great assets. What is innovation and how has the US State Department applied it to its foreign policy agenda?

I define innovation as the creation of new products or processes that allow for the continuous realization of the future. It is imagining and inventing the future. In our statecraft at the US State Department and in the Obama administration's foreign policy, part of what we've tried to do in creating this twenty-first-century statecraft[1] agenda is not throw out the old diplomacy but build on traditional forms of diplomacy to account for the networks, the technologies, and the demographics of the twenty-first century.

Now, social media is the part of this that gets all the attention. But it is actually far broader than that. The question for us is how we respond to old foreign policy challenges while using new tools and new approaches in order to execute those goals.

Innovation has always been a hallmark of the United States. If you think about the founding of our country, everyone who came to the United States was trying to innovate their own future. There was a lot of risk inherent for anybody coming here, and in those terms you can certainly define our society as a pioneering society. The pioneers literally got on wagons and drove west into unknown territories. America has always been a place that has had a higher acceptance of risk than most societies, and we haven't punished risk or punished failure that came from risk as some other societies do. It's in part because there's no 'royalty' in America, there's no blue blood running through anybody's veins in the United States. If you were a royal, you wouldn't be here. There is a willingness to try new things in the United States that I find does not exist to that degree in many other places. There's no reason not to apply this new diplomacy in the same way it's applied in all the other aspects of our lives.

Winston Churchill well described the interaction between tradition and innovation in a speech to the Royal Academy of Arts in 1953: [2] *"Without tradition, art is a flock of sheep without a shepherd. Without innovation, it is a corpse." Churchill believed that "a love of tradition has never weakened a nation, indeed it has strengthened nations in their hour of peril; but the new view must come, the world must roll forward," as he emphasized in his address to the House of Commons in 1944.* [3] *Diplomacy is without doubt a product of tradition, often very ceremonial and hierarchical in nature. How would you describe the interaction between tradition and innovation in the digital age?*

There's actually some inherent conflict between tradition and innovation. A lot of the ceremonial aspects of diplomacy are necessary, but many of them are also out of time and mostly useless. People who have spent thirty, forty, fifty years and come to love that aspect of diplomacy, often have come to love the tradition for its own sake, as opposed to for its utility.

Many of the traditions in diplomacy made sense back in the day, when you would hand over paper with a wax seal and this was the way that formal communications took place. Communication has changed in the last two or three hundred years, and if our diplomatic communications don't change then they become an anachronism. There's a challenge for the diplomatic world generally, juxtaposed against the intelligence and military worlds, to stay relevant and to stay—hopefully—dominant. Because you don't want to lead all the time with intelligence or with the military, and the intelligence services and the military services are always very innovative. Not only do they keep up with the times, but they often get ahead. So, when our diplomats continue to work in a world of wax seals, what they do is lose relevance; they lose power, and the importance of the intelligence and the military services increases because the diplomats are viewed as those people who are sipping tea and doing things that don't matter. Now, I'm not averse to tradition: I was a medieval history major, studied at Università di Bologna, and I like and respect those aspects of tradition that help make our diplomacy more binding, but I don't like that aspect of diplomacy that makes it slow or that confines it to very few.

The second part of the question refers to hierarchies in diplomacy. One of the things that most constrains the effectiveness of diplomacy generally is its excessively hierarchical nature. The idea that people in their thirties and forties are, more often than not, not in power in diplomatic contexts to me is absurd. The global economy is being imagined, invented, and commercialized by people under the age of forty, and for the foreign policy world to completely write off people for decades of their professional lives because of their youth to me is stupid, for lack of a more diplomatic word.

Second, an excessive reliance on hierarchy creates systems of extreme conformity, because the way that people rise up in traditional hierarchies is through conformity and understanding how they gain this play within a given ministry. Being good at playing the bureaucratic, hierarchical game does not necessarily mean you are a good steward of your country's foreign policy interests. The traditional hierarchical system in foreign ministries is very bad for it, and I think that it is good in this respect for innovation to test the centuries-long tradition of excessive hierarchy.

When we talk about generations, when we think about people in power today—leaders mostly in their fifties to late sixties—do you think there is a fear of technology?

Fear of technology comes from the unknown. I don't think you have to be young to understand technology. What I do think is that younger people tend to have grown up in a world more immersed with technology, so they take to it more naturally. While there are a lot of people in their sixties and seventies who are very sharp when it comes to the use of technology, there are a lot of others who are not. What they're threatened by is two things: first of all, the fact that they don't understand it and that this seems to give them an inherent disadvantage against their younger peers; secondly, the loss of control.

As I've said many times before, the twenty-first century is a terrible time to be a control freak. The kind of control that diplomats could have had ten, fifteen, thirty years ago is not as possible today. So to engage this world is to understand it and accept that the kind of control that existed in more traditional media and communications spaces does not exist today. So some people, even though that control is gone, close their eyes and imagine that it's still there. I think that's the second thing that creates the change.

Tools like Twitter and Facebook have certainly changed the way we see the world, the way governments talk to each other, to their citizens, and to foreign audiences. Have they made America's voice louder abroad, especially in countries where the United States is perceived as hostile?

I don't know if it's made our voices louder or not. It's made citizens' voices louder—American citizens and citizens of the other 195 countries on planet Earth. However, I don't know that it's made the American government's voice louder. In part because even though the United States is the leader in pioneering the use of social media in government, I still think the American government is not as good as the American people. In addition, the American government is certainly not necessarily as good as foreign publics in making its voice heard. So when I think of the voices that have risen, at least from my perception of the last five years during the Obama administration, I think more of it is amplifying the voices of citizens. And while I include American citizens, it more often than not includes the citizens of foreign publics as well. So what I see with social media is a largely diminished voice by government and an enhanced voice by publics.

In the early 1800s, John Marshall, a former secretary of state and the longest-serving chief justice in the history of the Supreme Court, wrote: "To listen well is as powerful a means of communication and influence as to talk well." Marshall, whose impact on American constitutional law is peerless, was known for bringing men together. He was able to manage a congenial court with seldom any bickering. Two hundred years later, in the era of Twitter and Facebook, to be able to "listen well" is as important as ever. Are social media tools making it easier or rather more difficult for world leaders to listen to their publics?

I think it's making it much easier for world leaders to hear their publics. I told all of the ambassadors and foreign leaders that I trained: "Remember, you only have one mouth, but you have two ears." I think it makes it easier to listen, but it doesn't mean they want to hear it, nor they like what they hear. This is part of what comes with a loss of control because of social media. Instead of people in suits and ties speaking to you to your face very politely, people who will never shake the hand of a president, a prime minister, a foreign minister, or an ambassador can now communicate with high-ranking officials without engaging with them face to face. They have this inner mediating force—technology—which to them creates some distance, so it makes it easier to hear them, but it doesn't necessarily make the communications more polite or something that you want to hear.

I have found—over the past couple of years I've been my own experiment in this regard—when you show people that you're listening, you don't have to show that you agree with them. If you show that you're listening, then more often than not this produces a measure of goodwill. Now, there are exceptions to this. There are trolls, and often I don't respond to individual people. More often than not I respond to the themes and concerns that are articulated by people whom I'm listening to. You have to be smart about who you respond to individually because you don't want to feed the trolls. By the same token, I think that it makes you smarter. I think it's better for leaders to get feedback from people other than their peers.

In August 2013, then Swedish foreign minister Carl Bildt used Twitter to invite his British counterpart to visit Sweden.[4] *His counterpart Foreign Secretary William Hague promptly replied, "I will be delighted to visit."*[5] *Skeptics doubt whether the two foreign ministers compiled those tweets personally.*

They use Twitter themselves. I know personally that Hague thumbs it into his device. He personally types away on his iPad. I've been with Bildt when he's checked his Twitter replies, when he's looked at his stream. Hague does this all personally; I've spoken with his advisors and said, "Well maybe you guys can do this, that" and what they say is, "Oh no, he does it himself!"

Innovation is often associated solely with social media. But there's much more to that, including mobile technologies, now so widespread that in the African continent more people have access to mobile phones than to clean drinking water. The data on mobile communications are quite astonishing. According to the 2013 edition of the Ericsson Mobility Report,[6] *total mobile subscriptions exceeded 6.4 billion by the first quarter of 2013, and they are expected to reach 9.1 billion by 2018, with almost half being smartphone, due to reach 4.5 billion by the end of 2018. Mobile subscriptions are also increasing for PCs, mobile routers, and tablets that use larger screen sizes. They are expected to grow from 300 million in 2012 to around 850 million in 2018, exceeding the number of fixed broadband subscriptions. Are mobile technologies the future of foreign policy?*

I don't think mobile technologies are the future of foreign policy, but I do think they are going to grow in importance as tools in the diplomatic toolbox.

There are vast swathes of the Earth that were historically isolated in Africa, South America, and Central Asia. The big disruption created by mobility is that those places are no longer isolated. And what does this mean? Most obviously it means that they can be a part of the communications that take place, but from my standpoint it actually is most relevant from a development context, from an economics standpoint. It means that people are going from the economics of the market of the village square to larger and more efficient regional markets.

Another important side of the diplomatic world is development, and where I think of mobile as being most important and most impactful is in the development world. The World Bank study that gets the most attention has shown that for every 10 percent increase in mobile subscriptions there is a corresponding increase of 0.8 percent in Gross Domestic Product (GDP). And the study ascribes causality, so it says *because* of the 10 percent increase in mobile subscriptions there is a 0.8 percent increase in GDP. So what that says to me is that it takes places that were outside of the economic mainstream and now makes them accessible in ways they weren't before.

I tell the story—I've told the story many times before and maybe you've heard it, but I'm going to continue telling it—about a friend of mine who worked at the World Bank, and she's travelled for years to this little village in Togo, a small country in West Africa with per capita GDP of less than eight hundred Euros a year. For years she always travelled to this village, and she would buy a toy for her son Yusef from a kid standing on the street corner. She did this for years, and one of the recent times that she went back and visited this young man, he said, "Madam, in the future when you know you're coming to my country and you know you're coming to my village, don't just buy one of the two or three toys I have on display. E-mail me ahead of time and let me know if you would like me to have something specific waiting for you here. And if you have a smartphone like me you can take a picture of an image, send the image to me here in my village in Togo, and I'll make something for your son that looks exactly like this image." The point of this is that when the teenage tin toymaker in Togo is now connecting to the global marketplace, through increasingly ubiquitous and powerful mobile networks, the world is not changing—the world is changed. It takes us places that we thought of as dark and isolated and hopeless, and it has brought much more economic opportunity to those places.

Technology has certainly given governments new and improved opportunities in terms of policy making and public diplomacy. That's true also for governments in countries in which human

rights and civil liberties are far from being fully enjoyed by all
citizens. What is the dark side of the digital era?

I think there are a number of dark aspects to technology.

To paraphrase my former boss Hillary Clinton, our information networks are like nuclear power and they can be used to fuel a city or
destroy it.[7] The technology itself is value neutral, it's inanimate. It takes
on the values and intentions of the users, so it can be used for bad as
easily as it can be used for good. One of the obvious ways in which it's
been used for bad is, as network technologies have grown more sophisticated, it is increasingly the case that governments will use them to
monitor peaceful political dissent.

If you look in the Gulf, if you look in Iran, if you look at big parts of
the world, governments are becoming increasingly sophisticated with
regard to using the Net and data as a way of identifying people who
disagree with them and then punishing that dissent. The United States
has gotten a lot of attention for its use of network technologies to surveil
people for counterterrorism.

The distinction I made between that and the use of these technologies elsewhere is I have not yet seen an example of where—and there
may be an example, I just haven't heard of it yet—where the PRISM
program[8] and others have been used for something other than counter-
terrorism. Whereas in the Gulf, in China, in dozens of other countries,
what governments are looking for are people who disagree with them
politically and are exercising their universal rights, but it's against the
law to believe in a religion other than Islam or to hold a political belief
that's different than the monarch, and they arrest them for that. So the
technologies can be used for good or for ill.

The other thing that scares me about the technologies is in regard to
my role as a parent. I'm the father of a ten-year-old and a six-year-old,
and I'm personally very glad there wasn't Facebook when I was in
university. I had a lot of fun when I was in university, and I'm glad that
there aren't hundreds of digital pictures out there floating of the good
times that I had when I was having good clean fun in university. But still
I see pictures of me drinking out of a beer hose. The other thing that
I'm worried about is that it becomes much more difficult for young
people growing up digital, who are being young, to have their youthful
indiscretions become part of their documentable past. If it becomes

part of their eternal present, then that is very worrisome. I understand that norms can shift and things that were not acceptable in the past might become more acceptable in the future, but nevertheless as a parent it irks me. Because when I think about people who are sixteen, seventeen, eighteen, nineteen years old, you make mistakes. You do things when you're eighteen that you wouldn't do when you're twenty-eight, thirty-eight, forty-eight, fifty-eight, or sixty-eight, and I think that there's some virtue in youthful indiscretions being a part of one's past and not a part of one's present, and technology makes that very difficult.

It's like parents giving their children full, unsupervised access to the Internet and technologies . . . using the Internet to explore things that sometimes they shouldn't explore.

When I was a kid, the kinds of information and images that I could have accessed as a kid are nothing compared with anything anybody with a web browser can get today. I think that's worrisome. I don't believe that we should throttle back people's rights because of it, but it does present challenges, and the people who I think this principally poses challenges to are parents. I think parents should play the most prominent role in this.

In a key speech on Internet freedom, Secretary Clinton said: "The spread of information networks is forming a new nervous system for our planet. When something happens in Haiti or Hunan, the rest of us learn about it in real time—from real people. [. . .] Now, in many respects, information has never been so free. There are more ways to spread more ideas to more people than at any moment in history. And even in authoritarian countries, information networks are helping people discover new facts and making governments more accountable."[9] It was January 2010, and only eleven months later, the Arab Spring seeded in the Algerian town of Sid Bouzid, later spreading to the rest of the Arab world.[10] But social media and technology were not the cause, but rather a means, making information more available. Since then much has changed in terms of Internet freedom and power in the digital era. How free would you say is information today?

I think that it's hard to keep information under lock and key. I think that Wikileaks showed that. I think that the Edward Snowden revelations[11] with PRISM revealed that it is very, very hard to keep information buried in a more networked world.

With developments in recent years, information has only become increasingly free. That doesn't mean that that is always in the interests of—say—the United States. This is part linked to the loss of control I've talked about earlier. With all of this information, with the oceans of information that is out there, you lose control over things that you want to have control over, and this presents challenges to the traditional hierarchies, including the US government.

When Hillary Clinton first gave her speech on January 21, 2010, it was viewed as this little obscure piece of foreign policy, and now it's something quite bigger. When she first gave that speech, people were like, "What is she doing giving a speech about freedom on the Internet?", and now I think it's obvious to people. Hillary Clinton doesn't often get credit for being someone who can see very far into the future, but in this case clearly she proved that she could see around the corner; she did know that this was something that maybe was not of major importance in the past but was going to be very important in the future. Internet freedom is going to be something that is increasingly contested around the world. It's going to stay at the grown-ups table of foreign policy and be something that's battled over and battled over and battled over, especially as you see the position of certain countries like Russia harden and get more difficult.

In your four years as Hillary Clinton's senior adviser for innovation, you had the privilege to travel the world and sit down with countless presidents, prime ministers, foreign ministers, and ambassadors. You also trained countless ambassadors and the future generations of diplomats. What has been your advice to them in order to help their governments fully embrace a digital approach to policy?

I could answer that question over the course of an hour, but I'll give you a couple of bullet points.

The first is that whether you like it or not, diplomacy is changing. You can change with it, or the change can take place without you. This is an inevitability. You can get as frustrated as you want about it, you can say it's bad, you can say it's degrading diplomacy. Too bad. The world is going to change with you, or it's going to change without you. That's thing one.

Two: you've got to understand that the people who are relevant today are far more numerous than people who were relevant to you as a diplomat in the past, or as a president or prime minister. It used to be the case that when an American diplomat went to a country, he or she had a list of the two hundred people who mattered in a country. When an American diplomat went to the embassy in Rome, there was a list of the two hundred Italians who mattered, and all of the effort of the embassy was to influence and make connections with these two hundred people. That's not the case anymore. The two hundred people still matter, but so do the other sixty million people in the country. So the second thing is that, in the parlance of diplomacy, you have to broaden your interlocutors. You cannot just talk to generals, CEOs, and government representatives. You have to have some sort of face to the public because the public matters. One of the reasons I think the United States was slow to understand what was happening in Egypt during the first stage of that revolution was because we were doing traditional diplomatic engagement. "Oh, well the generals said this, well the ministers said this, this influential businessman said that," but you didn't have your ear to the street. So our statecraft has to have more streetcraft. Our statecraft has to recognize the increased power and the increased relevance of people who do not walk down corridors of power.

The third point is that change can happen much faster now. Things that would have once taken years now often can take months. Things that would have taken months can take days. And so the pace of diplomacy is much, much faster than it once was. This is something that people have to adjust to—you know it's not the case that you put a letter in the mail and you wait and somebody reads it, they wait a couple of days, a letter is written, it's put back in the post with a diplomatic pouch, and it comes back. The pace of diplomacy has changed. It's a much faster race now.

What did you learn during your years with Hillary Clinton and how—if at all—has she changed your perception of the world and of American politics?

The single most important take-away I had from working at Hillary Clinton's elbow was the fact that the disempowerment of women is still a massive unresolved issue. For all the other things that I could say, it still remains the case that through much of the world women do two-thirds of the work for one-third of the pay and own less than 2 percent of the businesses and properties. This is something that I was struck by. There is such systematic disenfranchisement of women—and not just in the Arab world—certainly in the Arab world, but also in Europe, also in the United States. We sometimes create these popular figures out of women and think because there's one woman who's very popular and well known that the problem of incorporating and empowering women is solved. It's not. And it's very, very frequent that I will go to a meeting and I will sit down at the long mahogany table, and there will be one or two women at a table of fifteen or sixteen men. So the single most important thing I think she highlighted for me is that we need to change that. We need to change that not just for issues of fairness. It's not just about equity, it's also in our interests from a security standpoint and an economic standpoint. Nothing can do more to stimulate our economy than reducing the barriers to full participation by women, and I think that if you look at the security problems we have around the world, the problems have overwhelmingly been created by men. Women are natural peacemakers and community-builders. That's not to say all of them, but I think that they can play an important and prominent role in peace-making processes that they historically have been largely excluded from.

Do you think that technology is helping women? If we take an example—for instance, Anne-Marie Slaughter—I remember meeting her for the first time in 2006. At the time I was working on a documentary on women at the United Nations after then–Secretary-General Kofi Annan said: "The world is ready for a woman secretary-general." Back then, you couldn't see many women within the UN inner circles. In the summer 2012, Professor Slaughter famously wrote an article in **The Atlantic** *on equal opportunities for women titled "Why Women Can't Still Have It All."* [12] *The article went all over the world thanks to the Internet,* *with millions of hits. Do you think digital technologies are helping the cause of women?*

I hope so, I think so. Part of the problem with the Internet and with these digital mediums is that moderate voices often are drowned out by loud voices. And so I question whether the moderate voices of women are benefiting or not.

What's next with Alec Ross? You worked with Barack Obama, you work with Hillary Clinton, you started your own startup before joining the administration, and you were a teacher at the beginning of your career. What's going to be next?

The big thing that I'm doing right now is writing a book.

I'm writing a book about the future of globalization. I think most people understood the nature of globalization from 1990 to 2010, but I think that very little has been written about globalization for the everyday person in 2010 to 2025.

It's also good for me to detach myself a little from politics. I never thought of myself as a politician; I came into it because of Obama, but as a practical matter since 2007, over six years, my life was dominated by Barack Obama and Hillary Clinton. While I have an enormous amount of affection for Barack Obama and Hillary Clinton, I also think it's good to go back to the life of the entrepreneur, of startups, of innovation and the private sector. So I'm joining boards of directors of startups. I'm taking a lot of the kind of advice that I've given over the past number of years to government leaders and I'm going back to my entrepreneurial roots. So going forward, what I really want to do is have a blend. I want to have a blend of continuing to keep my hands on and stay relevant in policy circles, but also help guide and nurture the startup and the innovation ecosystems in the United States and also abroad.

NOTES

1. United States Department of State, *21st Century Statecraft*, accessed June 12, 2014, http://www.state.gov/statecraft/.

2. Royal Academy of Arts Archive, *Transcripts of Annual Dinner Speeches 1953*, RAA/SEC/25/5/4.

3. Commons and Lords Hansard, *Debate on the Address: HC Deb 29 November 1944 vol. 406 cc9-56*, accessed October 4, 2013, http://hansard.millbanksystems.com/commons/1944/nov/29/debate-on-the-address#S5CV0406P0_19441129_HOC_52.

4. Carl Bildt, Twitter post, August 9, 2013, 4:21 a.m., https://twitter.com/carlbildt/status/365749692673425412.

5. William Hague, Twitter post, August 9, 2013, 4:45 a.m., https://twitter.com/WilliamJHague/status/365755800951599104.

6. Ericsson, *Ericsson Mobility Report*, accessed July 22, 2013, http://www.ericsson.com/mobility-report.

7. Hillary Clinton, "Remarks on Internet Freedom," Washington, DC: United States Department of State, January 21, 2010, http://www.state.gov/secretary/20092013clinton/rm/2010/01/135519.htm.

8. The top-secret PRISM program allows the US intelligence community to gain access from nine Internet companies to a wide range of digital information, including e-mails and stored data, on foreign targets operating outside the United States. "NSA Slides Explain the PRISM Data-Collection Program," *Washington Post*, last modified July 10, 2013, http://www.washingtonpost.com/wp-srv/special/politics/prism-collection-documents/.

9. Hillary Clinton, "Remarks on Internet Freedom," Washington, DC: United States Department of State, January 21, 2010, http://www.state.gov/secretary/20092013clinton/rm/2010/01/135519.htm.

10. Garry Blight, Sheila Pulham, and Paul Torpey, "Arab Spring: An Interactive Timeline of Middle East Protests," *Guardian*, last modified January 5, 2012, http://www.theguardian.com/world/interactive/2011/mar/22/middle-east-protest-interactive-timeline.

11. Joshua Eaton and Ben Piven, "Timeline of Edward Snowden's Revelations," Al Jazeera, accessed June 9, 2014, http://america.aljazeera.com/articles/multimedia/timeline-edward-snowden-revelations.html.

12. Anne-Marie Slaughter, "Why Women Still Can't Have It All," *The Atlantic*, last modified June 13, 2012, http://www.theatlantic.com/magazine/archive/2012/07/why-women-still-cant-have-it-all/309020/.

2

THE ARAB SPRING OF DIPLOMACY

A conversation with Charles Firestone, Executive Director, Communications and Society Program, The Aspen Institute

To view clips
from the conversation
with Charles Firestone
scan the QR code
or visit:
http://goo.gl/vyADaj

In 2012, the Aspen Institute Communications and Society Program convened its first annual Aspen Institute Dialogue on Diplomacy and Technology[1] *to create an open dialogue on the evolution of traditional diplomacy in the twenty-first century. In your introduction, you said: "In the period leading up to the overthrow of political authorities in the Middle East, young activists used social media to spread dissident discourse, organize protests and transmit live footage of revolutions across the world. Simultaneously, stubborn autocrats clung to political survival tactics by blocking their citizens' access to social media sites like Twitter and Facebook in order to disrupt the gathering momentum of a networked people determined to change their governments."*[2] *We all agree, social media was not the deciding force of these revolutionary movements. But indeed, they were a key factor and played an important role, in particular when it came to organizing the protests. Since the first uprising in the Tunisian city of Sidi Bouz-*

id in December 2010, many other countries have gone through the same protests, and social media is increasingly becoming more of a factor in many countries.

In the beginning, the role of social media in the Arab Spring was very much that of an enabler, a tool. You needed the leaders; you needed the movements to get things going. Social media added to the information that people had and it added to their organizing abilities, better amplification of messages, and their ability to show the world what was happening minute by minute, tweet by tweet. A self-immolation in Tunisia went pretty much unnoticed when only twenty-eight thousand of the country's population subscribed to Facebook, but it was entirely different when that number was close to two million.

Since then, we've seen that social media have become a lot more penetrated. More people have the tools. You have, therefore, more information abundance, a little less novelty in it. You're seeing more and more the tools in the Middle East being the same tools that are being used everywhere else, which are for listening. We get the radar of Twitter, where people are learning what's happening by Twitter, bumps or peaks. You have more opportunity to express yourself—as a citizen but also as a government. What we've seen is the divergence of views and parties. It's not always the most positive result that you might like. In fact, during and following the Arab Spring, young activists used social media to spread dissident discourse, shape narratives, and broadcast live footage of revolutions across the world. Simultaneously, repressive governments and stubborn autocrats clung to political survival tactics by blocking their citizens' access online in order to disrupt the gathering momentum of a networked people determined to change their governments.

I don't ascribe now any super role for social media in the Arab world as opposed to when the Spring first sprung—when we all focused on the importance of Facebook as an organizing tool. Now it's one more tool that everybody has. I think it is just more of an enhancement of how it's been used, not only in the Arab world, but everywhere else.

What we have observed is also how the concept of leadership was affected. We're having a harder time identifying leaders. There are so many voices out there. There's not one single leader. It's harder for one leader to step forward and be seen and recognized and followed. You're following how many people on Twitter? You're hearing how many voices?

In the attention economy—if that's what we have—the ability to get attention is a real asset, as attention is the real scarcity with the over-abundance of information. Attention has always been an asset of leader-ship. Technology and social media are now tools for leaders to get that much needed attention. But they also represent a big challenge, as it's not easy to crack the thick layer of noise on the Internet and catch the attention of your audience, your constituencies. It's extremely hard and I'm not sure how that's going to play out ultimately.

Another consideration is about demographic shifts. In the Arab world, countries have a disproportionately large youth population. Those are the people who tend to be more active, in politics and else-where. Therefore, they tend to have a greater role. In this environment, social media allows for greater transparency. But greater transparency is also leading to greater volatility. It's making it harder to identify the leaders. While the tools make young people able to empower them-selves, they make it more difficult to identify followership.

How do you turn that transparency into trust?

Transparency does help with trust because people can now see if some-thing's wrong. We see this all over. The great example, I think, is in China where you're seeing local leaders exposed. There's always been corruption at various levels, but now that corruption is being exposed and exacerbated. That exposition is being shown all over and, there-fore—if there are consequences, that is, if officials are made account-able—people can trust more of what's happening because they can really see what's happening. Transparency has become a great tool for enhancing trust.

Transparency, however, has its other side, which is that a lot more is exposed. That affects trust in government. And frankly, I think this is going to go in a sort of sine curve of trends. First people will say, "Oh, they're all corrupt." Then they're going to say, "Hey, we're weeding out the corrupt ones." And then we can trust more. I think those are just natural cycles. You're going to see in any place where you have in-creased transparency a cycle of trust that will maybe go down at the beginning and then increase. You need people to trust in, and it's not just the media. All of these points about leadership, about organization, about empowerment, it takes the people; it's not the technology. The people use the technology. Technology is the tool.

Also, trust and authenticity are very much interrelated. How authentic is what you see in the media? In the last decade, authenticity has become an issue. We've seen it in Syria with the YouTube videos on the regime's use of chemical weapons against their own citizens in 2013. While we didn't know at the very beginning whether those videos and photos were fakes or doctored in some way, the administration reacted even before investigators started gathering additional evidence on the ground.

Diplomacy is slowly adapting to social and demographic shifts that social media has accelerated, not just in the Middle East. Governments have been using social media to reach beyond their traditional reach and beyond borders, while interacting with all new players, including citizens, corporations, foundations, and networks. Challenges are new, but the practice of diplomacy is, however, deeply grounded in tradition, with bilateral and multi-lateral closed-door meetings, negotiations, and diplomatic norms. Traditional diplomacy has certainly not become obsolete, but needs to learn how to complement tradition with innovation, technology, and social media. How's the foreign policy community embracing changes?

The foreign policy community is not known for its advances.

One of the things that came up in our Aspen Dialogue on Diplomacy and Technology is that there's a risk adversity. There's a culture against risk, particularly in diplomacy. You can't make mistakes in government generally, let alone in diplomacy. There's not a lot of tolerance for that. There is in business, where you can fail or you can have a bad product. It's all part of the process. But not in government: if you make a mistake in politics or in diplomacy, somebody usually wants your head. You could be fired, and there could be a lot worse consequences at times.

Innovation implies a tolerance of risk if you're going to innovate. But that is a barrier in foreign policy. It's not going to be a culture that's welcoming a lot of innovation. However, there are obviously attempts. Many ambassadors and embassies are now using social media as a way to innovate their public diplomacy efforts. Hopefully, they understand that there will be mistakes. And there will be failures. But there seems to be a lot more risk tolerance, at least in the Twitter sphere.

Now, one area of innovation relates around new ideas and how governments can become more innovative to analyze problems and find sustainable solutions to them. And that is contests, where governments go out to a large number of people and see who comes up with the best solution to a given problem. There are a number of organizations that do that—in businesses and perhaps in the nonprofit sector. But do you see diplomacy doing it? That just isn't in the government nature to go out to the general public, in particular when it comes to help overcome problems and finding solutions. On the other hand, you might see them starting to listen to more ideas. I could see more ideas getting into the realm.

Technology is also a tool for innovation. So, how can technology be integrated into the highly institutionalized diplomatic realm? While technological tools and advances could facilitate more transparent communication between the diplomatic community and private sector, the world's foreign ministries may not always have the cultural, procedural, or institutional disposition to effectively integrate them into policy. Technology may enlighten diplomats about public opinion, but diplomatic institutions still lack protocol in absorbing this information.

The advances in social media and technology and the wave of citizen involvement in both internal and external state affairs— derived from the Arab Spring and the debate around a more participatory digital age—have heightened the need to take a closer look at the very nature of government and democracy. What's your take?

There are essentially four types of democracy at play here: representational democracy allows people to voice their opinions on many things, but the votes are made by the representatives duly elected by the people; direct democracy would have the people vote on all major actions, such as we see with ballot initiatives or directly in town meetings; communitarian democracy describes smaller communities that deal with matters of concern to the group in a rough consensus—this is great for the community but not always for "outsiders"; and pluralistic democracy sees a play among the various interests vying for power in the representative democratic arena.

The role of technology changes the dynamic of each. First, one needs access to the Internet in order to be an effective citizen in the modern demos. So in places where access is limited, usually due to financial constraints, the poor have less say in both the decision making and in influence. With those who do have access, the tendency on the net is to move toward direct democracy. Movements such as the Stop SOPA and PIPA legislation evidenced a willingness of the "netizens" to flex their opinions and their power. This tendency toward direct democracy then puts pressure on the representatives to vote or act according to the wishes of the vocal majority. The good news is that representatives and officials are more visible and accountable than ever. The bad news is that sometimes we want representatives to take unpopular positions to advance a longer-term interest. And we always have to be protective of minority rights.

The trends of the uses of technology, then, are that transparency and visibility lead to accountability and ultimately trust, that the opportunity to be heard will in the long run lessen the frustration of those with minority positions and allow in some cases for those opinions to emerge to majority positions, and that eventually the power of the person will outweigh the power of the purse. But as for that last point, it will take quite a while to get there, and much damage may come in the meantime from undue influence of money shaping opinion in the media and the Net.

Indeed, the shifts we have observed in the nature of democracy and of the democratic process have significant policy implications for incorporating the tools of technology into policy, including ways to advance access to communications technology while creating a new protocol to apply it effectively. But our policy priorities have to adjust to a different environment, denoted by what I described as a shift from representational democracy to direct democracy. The tendency toward direct democracy generates difficulties in compromise and reconciliation, thus possibly hindering long-term decision making.

So, how should officials in the diplomatic realm advocate how democracies work? Government officials should deconstruct the impact of the Internet on the government and focus on the broader work of helping other countries adopt technology tools and a culture of innovation that can enhance the way governments—as well as the foreign policy community—address policy and issues.

In this new environment, where democracy itself has been impacted, how would you describe the diplomat of the future? How do you see the role of an ambassador evolving?

Well, the ambassador certainly has to be well connected in electronic media. First of all, ambassadors of the future should be the ambassadors of the past in that they have to be smart, open people who learn the country in which they are posted—all the traditional diplomatic skills needed to be successful in the job. Technology hasn't minimized the traditional skills of a diplomat: influence, ability to persuade, attractiveness in their country. That's all I think a given. On top of that, the ambassador now has to be basically a media star. Ambassadors should be able to communicate in an effective way to that public in the country that they're the ambassadors to. That's not just getting on a news show. That's now getting on social media and using it in such a way that they get a following and that they're interesting—not just talking about what they had for breakfast. Also, at the same time, being an effective listener is of key importance. That again is the skill of a diplomat, but in the digital era, even that has changed. Using social media can be a radar system to help determine influences within the country.

I like to think of the technology as tools. In the end, you need wisdom and leadership, you need a good, well-trained diplomat. You can't substitute the technology for those skills. Those are human qualities.

We should look at how and if technology has made a change not only in degree but also in kind. In other words, is there a new diplomacy? To explain that in a word, I've coined the label 'netpolitik.' On one side you have the global liberalism, and on the other you have the realpolitik, or politics and diplomacy based on power and governance. Neither adequately describes the world of today.

My thought is that the operative organizational form of our era is the network, and we have to understand network behaviors and principles. It's like behavioral flocking. What President George W. Bush called the "Coalition of the Willing,"[3] I think was the right concept. I don't think he did it right. The willing were pulled along. But, I think there will be more and more coalitions of the willing. In this scenario, the diplomat of the future has to understand networks; understand how to influence them and how to operate them. That will be a key skill going forward. You will see global networks of media networks, but you will also see diplomatic networks and citizen networks—like the Green Party— across borders. You're going to see things that will erase borders around ideas and around networks, which will influence the practice of diplomacy going forward. That may be a change in the nature of diplomacy as opposed to just a tool for a diplomat.

NOTES

1. The inaugural Aspen Institute Dialogue on Diplomacy and Technology (ADDTech) took place July 8–10, 2012, in Aspen, Colorado. As of 2014, the dialogue is at its third edition. The Dialogue convenes and engages leaders from the worlds of diplomacy, democracy, and technology to determine how new technologies might transform diplomacy.

2. Clifton Martin and Laura Jagla, *Integrating Diplomacy and Social Media: A Report of the First Annual Aspen Institute Dialogue on Diplomacy and Technology*, Washington, DC: The Aspen Institute, 2013, http://csreports. aspeninstitute.org/documents/IntegratingDIPLOMACY.pdf.

3. President Bush first coined the term "Coalition of the Willing" during a joint news conference with Czech President Vaclav Havel just ahead of a NATO summit in Prague. The summit brought seven former Eastern bloc nations into the alliance, including the Czech Republic. The White House, Office of the Press Secretary, "President Bush, President Havel Discuss Iraq, NATO," last updated November 20, 2002, http://georgewbush-whitehouse. archives.gov/news/releases/2002/11/20021120-1.html.

3

FROM A SKEPTIC'S POINT OF VIEW

A conversation with Carne Ross, Founder and Executive Director, Independent Diplomat

To view clips from the conversation with Carne Ross scan the QR code or visit: http://goo.gl/pAM0bV

In January 2013, you tweeted: "Getting very bored with the rubbish talked about 'ediplomacy' when fundamental nature of diplomacy has barely been affected by technology."[1] You went on, saying: "It is not innovation that is changing diplomacy, which in truth is changing little, it is slow decline of states."[2] Can you elaborate on that, beyond 140 characters?

Technology is not dramatically changing the fundamental nature of foreign affairs. The fundamental nature of classical diplomacy rests in the relations between governments, and that is still largely a private business. For instance, here at the United Nations in New York, the press is not allowed in to negotiations whether for General Assembly resolutions negotiations or for Security Council discussions. Diplomats don't come out and tweet—or don't tweet—what's going on while they're at the negotiating table. In that respect, the fundamentally untransparent nature of diplomacy has certainly not changed.

Twitter and Facebook can basically be considered new forms, new tools of propaganda for governments; it is not a two-way conversation between governments, nor a dialogue with their audiences. It is another form of one-way communication, propaganda, where governments say exactly the same things they used to say: instead of doing it the old way, they do it with a tweet. At times you can, however, observe a kind of patina of "personalness" about it and a minister, politician, or diplomat will say something slightly personal, but never do they really engage in personal revelations. For example, US Secretary of State John Kerry doesn't come out of talks in Moscow about Syria and say "God, Lavrov gave me a real hard time, what am I going to do?" Instead, one of his flunkies will more formally tweet about "Progress in US–Russia talks on Syria"—or something banal or boring along those lines.

It's notable to me that—I don't know how to say this politely—most of the important foreign ministers and diplomats don't tweet or, if they do, they just have some official do it for them. In the process, that essentially idiosyncratic and personal quality of social media is lost. Alec Ross—or somebody like him—at a conference I attended once claimed that Hillary Clinton sat down and looked at a selection of tweets every morning when she was Secretary of State to help judge policy. I can only imagine that's total nonsense. The idea that Twitter is some kind of neutral indicator of reactions to a country's action is completely ludicrous: (a) people who are using Twitter are a very particular subset of the population; and (b) the sort of issues that people get obsessed with on Twitter are not necessarily the important ones. I'm sure Secretary Clinton was driven by what governments are always driven by, which is this kind of rather manufactured idea of what the national interests are—and that is a term you will see in the United States a lot, and it is one that effuses policy making in the State Department or the White House.

It would be nice to think that technology might break it down, but I don't see it happening. Instead, what I think might break it down is that states are in decline. States have less and less sovereign power over things that matter to their populations whether it is the climate, the economy, or indeed their own security. All of these things have become globalized, and national governments have lost control of all of them. Global agreements and cooperation have not brought these things properly under control. There is a collective phenomenon that national governments are declining in importance, and I think that is a much more significant development than the so-called ediplomacy.

When Ambassador Susan Rice was at the United Nations as US Permanent Representative, she claimed to have tweeted from behind closed doors. There's a famous Twitter conversation between her and the Russian foreign minister when the Security Council was discussion a resolution on Syria. [3]

Nonsense. Susan Rice actually made it more difficult for the press to report on the Security Council's work. She physically kept journalists further away. They were penned up in this awful little sort of cattle pen.

You don't know what it was like in the old days: it was a lot better. The Security Council has actually become less transparent. In theory, it's become more open with more open meetings; but in actuality, the real business of the Council is all done behind closed doors, increasingly by the permanent five alone with communications between them mostly done at meetings in their own permanent missions. In this respect, the Security Council has got certainly worse. The idea that Susan Rice has made it more transparent by tweeting from its chamber is completely and utterly misleading.

Would you describe yourself as a pessimist or rather a skeptic when it comes to digital diplomacy and the use of social media in foreign policy? Or just like an observer, from a person who was behind closed doors before and is now working as a less traditional diplomat?

Whether I am a skeptic or pessimist doesn't really matter. What matters is the efficacy of the system, which I think has become less effective. The reason is certainly not the failure of technology to open it up, but the fact that it doesn't include citizens. A much more serious deficit than transparency—which is in itself a serious deficit—is that by and large, diplomatic bodies do not include the people who are most affected by their decisions. That to me is a much more serious problem: the Security Council, for example, will sit and discuss Somalia or Sudan without of course ever listening to actual Somalis. They might listen to their own representative government of Sudan, but they won't actually listen to all the Sudanese. It is the practice to ignore the people most affected and not give them any chance to voice their opinions about the future of their own country. In my view, that separation of diplomacy from actualities is a very serious problem, and ediplomacy is just a camouflage for the continuation of that closed practice.

In a July 2013 profile on you, BuzzFeed described you as "perhaps the leading representative in the United States of stateless people and would-be states, and has created a new line of work in helping marginalized groups and semi-states learn how to conduct traditional diplomacy."[4] *What's diplomacy in the twenty-first century?*

I am a bit wary of all this kind of semantic discussion of what diplomacy is. As I said before, to me it is still what it always was: government-to-government relations and negotiations about their priorities. I don't think that practice has changed.

You can argue that Bono talking about poverty or Burma is a form of diplomacy—I personally don't regard that as that. I believe it's just a different form of engagement, and calling it diplomacy is really to confuse matters. I don't want to be snobbish—and say, "Oh that's not diplomacy." It has certainly got its own value, but that's not diplomacy. Likewise, individuals tweeting from Tahrir Square is a very interesting, and perhaps positive, development. Though, it's not diplomacy. It is a way of getting news that is more disaggregated. Certainly, what you are seeing with global communications is a more direct contact between people. Again, I don't see that as diplomacy.

In your 2011 **The Leaderless Revolution** *you write: "When large numbers of people make decisions for themselves, the results are remarkable: everyone's views are heard, policies take all interests into account (as all lasting policy must), and are thus fairer. Facts and science are respected over opinion. Decision making becomes transparent (and thus less corrupt), respectful and less partisan—people who participate in decisions tend to stick to them. More responsibility and trust in society can only come about by giving real decision-making responsibility, they tend to behave irresponsibly, and sometimes violently. Happily, the converse is also* *true—give people power and responsibility, and they tend to use it more wisely—and peacefully."*[5] *Has social media any role in leadership?*

In *The Leaderless Revolution* I talk about the emergence of horizontal organizations and self-government. Certainly, social media is helping those horizontal organizations to be more visible and potentially more powerful. It is absolutely a very significant phenomenon. But social media is not a political phenomenon in its own right. It is not democratizing in its own right.

Horizontal people-to-people organizations still have to take power back from governments. So far, they only detain a limited amount of power. It's not this infinite thing. Governments try to control most of our affairs. If we are to take control over them, there has to actually be a switch of government's control. Just tweeting or Facebooking is not that switch. It is a form of mass communication—which is per se very exciting—but it is not yet that political shift we need. What it is, though, is the possibility that that political shift might happen. And social media is uniquely powerful in helping groups, organizations, and movements organize themselves, whether it is Occupy Wall Street, or the initial protesters against the Mubarak regime in Egypt. Social media has proven itself to be extraordinarily important for that purpose. But social media has not proven to be a challenge to more traditional hierarchical institutions, which still unhappily dominate our affairs. The Egypt revolution is a very striking example: it began through a mass movement loosely organized through social media, and then it was eventually coopted by two particular groups, the first being the Muslim Brotherhood. It was a highly, traditionally organized group not using social media—it was organized in a very traditional local way; it was representing a very traditional power structure. But then, of course, they themselves were usurped by an even more traditional organized hierarchy—namely, the Egyptian military.

Let's talk about Syria. Social media emerged as one of the key forms of evidence in the case for intervention in Syria. "No one disputes that chemical weapons were used in Syria," US President Barack Obama said in his address to the Nation on September 10, 2013.[6] *"The world saw thousands of videos, cell phone pictures, and social media accounts from the attack, and humanitarian organizations told stories of hospitals packed with people who had symptoms of poison gas," he continued. A few weeks earlier, US Secretary of State John Kerry cited the role of social media when he said: "Last night after speaking with foreign ministers from around the world about the gravity of this situation, I went back and I watched the videos, the videos that anybody can watch in the social media, and I watched them one more gut-wrenching time. It is really hard to express in words the human suffering that they lay out before us."[7] Is that a new direction for foreign policy or just Internet-inspired rhetoric?*

I don't think it is just rhetoric. I think it's a new form of information and newsgathering. It's aggregated, more spread out, more comprehensive. The intervention in Kosovo—which predates social media—was, to a large extent, triggered by suggestions of war crimes by the Serbs in Kosovo—in particular, the Račak massacre—but was of course widely reported in the international press. And that was one of the things the United States and the United Kingdom used to justify the military intervention in Kosovo. The arguments haven't necessarily changed. However, what has changed is the medium. This is of course significant, but I don't see it as necessarily transformative.

Social media has become a tool for governments to establish and nurture a dialogue with their audiences. "If we are going to have a dialogue—as opposed to I am going to talk at you and you are going to talk at me—then you have to sense that I am listening," writes Anne-Marie Slaughter, president of the New America Foundation, in the Journal of Law and International Affairs *of the* Pennsylvania State University.[8] *"If you sense that I am willing to be persuaded, you will be much more willing to be persuaded yourself. Leadership in this context often requires a willingness to change your own mind, to alter your own preferences within the broad parameters of the common mission." Going back to what you said about leadership, how do you think leadership has changed in foreign policy? And certainly related to that: is charisma still part of the political discourse?*

It is very difficult to generalize about an individual quality like leadership. What is depressing is how little real leadership we see today; how few world leaders are able to articulate the complexities of today's world in a way that is persuasive. I don't see anybody out there, in the most senior positions—presidents or foreign ministers—capable of doing this. They all seem trapped by their domestic circumstances, locked in rhetorical discourses that are very much national rather than international. They're depressingly narrow-minded about the way they pursue their foreign policy goals.

Yes, Barack Obama is capable of lofty rhetoric but his seems very much a twentieth-century form of rhetoric: its grand phraseology, its sort of neat aphorisms. It is not personal. It is not persuasive. It fails Anne-Marie Slaughter's test of making it seem that he is persuadable. To me, Obama doesn't seem persuadable at all. He seems almost like a much more old-fashioned leader, delivering the sermon from on high to the rest of us poor mortals. In fact, in a way, he could be seen as a regression from earlier more personal presidential styles.

I am not pessimistic about it, but the lack of global leadership that we see today is evident. The world is facing terrible, difficult, complicated problems, and we're not seeing them properly grasped.

What to me is the most fundamental quality of leadership is something that hasn't really changed, which is that we tend to trust people who demonstrate, through their own actions, the qualities that we admire. That is why we find them more convincing. For instance, using once again Bono as an example, I believe he is completely unconvincing talking about poverty. He is one of the world's richest men. He flies business jets. His band—which is technically a business—has been accused of massive tax evasion in his own country of Ireland. These are hardly the actions of a responsible global citizen in any way, whether it is dumping carbon into the atmosphere or avoiding your social obligations to others. In that sense, this is not leadership. What is more convincing is the sort of leadership that Gandhi showed, where he demonstrated through his own life the courage, through nonviolence and political acts, and took considerable personal sacrifice and risks to achieve his political goals. Seeing people standing up to us at Davos, preaching to us about the world, doesn't quite cut it.

Partnerships and grassroots networks are also becoming preva-
lent in foreign policy. It is the idea behind the TechCamp program
at the US State Department, an effort to galvanize the technology
community to assist civil society organizations across the globe by
providing capabilities, resources, and assistance to harness the
latest technological advances in order to build their digital capac-
ity. Similarly, the European Commission in Brussels has imple-
mented programs—and provided funds and grants—to encourage
partnerships between governments, local authorities, and non-
state actors to get more involved in development issues. "There is
a higher degree of public skepticism about the importance and
appropriateness of public/private partnerships," said Brian Jack-
son, assistant chair at the Public/Private Partnership Council, at a
conference in May 2013.[9] *"Because of the financial crisis and the*
bailouts that followed, the public is taking an increasingly jaun-
diced look at government and business working together and won-
dering if they are really working in the best interests of the tax-
payer." What's your take on that?

For instance, the 2008 banking crisis revealed a picture of government that was basically operating at the behest of banks—that is pretty much a universal phenomenon. The kind of rhetoric in public–private partnerships is widely seen as what it really is: pure rhetoric. The examples of this rather corrupt relationship between the two are legion, and I think they evidently fuel the collective skepticism of what we used to call democracy. The representative democracy, somewhere between the wishes of the people and those of the institutions, has been corrupted. Polls asking people about their trust in institutions indicate a steady decline in people's trust.

As a former diplomat—and a nontraditional diplomat now—what
would be your advice to the future generations of diplomats?

My views have moved a long way since the days I worked for the government. I find much greater joy, fulfillment, and inspiration in spontaneous political movements like Occupy Wall Street. My world is a weird one because I flipped between the UN Security Council and basements of scruffy churches in Brooklyn where I discuss radical financial reform with people who really care about it.

You know all too often, in diplomacy diplomats divorce themselves from their own feelings and personal convictions. They are asked to do things they don't believe in. When I was a diplomat, I convinced myself that it was a profound and important activity that satisfied me. Only when I left, I realized that it wasn't true. It was sometimes important, but it was inauthentic, and it didn't respond to my political or personal concerns.

If you are a very political person who cares and wants to change the world, then it can be very frustrating to be a diplomat, because you don't really have much agency. The paradox is that governments have their own power. In small governments, in modern, open countries, things are changing. There are young people who are different from old-fashioned diplomats. They are culturally different. Things are being a bit more open, and the younger generation is a bit biased. One of the curious things about them is that they like Edward Snowden. They seem to demonstrate far less loyalty to their own state and far more to values like stopping repression, trying to support democracy, the environment, human rights. That is a real change.

So to care about what you do and being honest to yourself?

Yes. Keep track of your emotions, of your principles, of your conscience. If you lose track of it, ask others to remind you, your family, and your friends. That's not easy though. It's far easy to lose yourself and be divorced from what you thought you believed in. In a world where you have to do what you're told, where you have to be loyal to the system, and where everybody around you is doing the same, it's sometimes difficult to be the one who says: "Actually, this is not right." In fact, it's very difficult to be that one—I know that myself. It doesn't mean mine was necessarily a bad experience: I learned a lot and, at times, enjoyed it a great deal.

NOTES

1. Carne Ross, Twitter post, January 9, 2013, 12:47 p.m., https://twitter.com/carneross/status/289065873749196800.

2. Carne Ross, Twitter post, January 9, 2013, 3:23 p.m., https://twitter.com/carneross/status/289105069964664832.

3. Susan Rice, Twitter post, February 4, 2012, 12:49 p.m., https://twitter.com/AmbassadorRice/status/165854588216414208. Susan Rice, Twitter post, February 6, 2012, 4:36 p.m., https://twitter.com/AmbassadorRice/status/166636416216997889. Ministry of Foreign Affairs of Russia (MFA Russia), Twitter post, February 6, 2012, 6:35 a.m., https://twitter.com/mfa_russia/statuses/166485247180017664.

4. Rosie Gray, "How Carne Ross Created a New Kind of Diplomacy," BuzzFeed, last updated July 9, 2013, 11:47 a.m., http://www.buzzfeed.com/rosiegray/how-carne-ross-created-a-new-kind-of-diplomacy.

5. Carne Ross, *The Leaderless Revolution: How Ordinary People Can Take Power and Change Politics in the 21st Century.* New York: Simon and Schuster, 2011.

6. The White House, Office of the Press Secretary, "Remarks by the President in Address to the Nation on Syria," last updated September 10, 2013, http://www.whitehouse.gov/the-press-office/2013/09/10/remarks-president-address-nation-syria.

7. John Kerry, "Remarks on Syria," Washington, DC: United States State Department, 2013, http://www.state.gov/secretary/remarks/2013/08/213503.htm.

8. Anne-Marie Slaughter, "Remarks, The Big Picture: Beyond Hot Spots and Crises in Our Interconnected World," University Park: Pennsylvania State University's *Journal of Law and International Affairs* 286 (2012), http://elibrary.law.psu.edu/jlia/vol1/iss2/5.

9. Ron Nyren, "Public Private Partnership Outlook," UrbanLand, last updated May 3, 2013, http://urbanland.uli.org/economy-markets-trends/public-private-partnership-outlook/.

4

THE CLINTON REVOLUTION

A conversation with Kim Ghattas, BBC State Department
Correspondent, and author of *The Secretary: A Journey
with Hillary Clinton from Beirut to the
Hearth of American Power*

In your latest book The Secretary: A Journey with Hillary Clinton
from Beirut to the Heart of American Power,[1] *you described
yourself as "a liberal, moderate secular Lebanese woman with a
Dutch mother." You write: "In a country where many looked to
Iran and Syria for guidance, I was more at home in the other half
of the country, the pro-Western, pro-American camp. Yet, I had
often felt let down by the United States, whether the president was
a Democrat or a Republican." Very early in the book, describing
your sentiments after the election of Barack Obama, and the nom-
ination of Hillary Clinton as the president's "envoy to the
world"—to use your own words—you write: "I struggled to rec-
oncile my positive impression of this country, its people, and its
diplomats, with the confusion and frustration I often felt in the
face of American foreign policy." Has Clinton's approach to
foreign policy changed your perspective?*

To some extent, yes. Hillary Clinton was very keen to explain foreign
policy to the average person. And that includes me. I may be a journalist, and I may be travelling with her everywhere, but I am there to ask
the questions that friends and family and acquaintances around the
world have about America's foreign policy. I always found that she was

very willing to answer those questions in a very candid way, keeping in mind of course that there were some things that she couldn't say because of classified documents and information. Diplomats know that. Whatever question I asked her she usually tried to answer as openly as possible and be very frank about things. It was an approach that she also took when she had town hall meetings in India, or Pakistan, in Iraq or in China. She was quite open and candid in a way that I wish other American officials had been in the past—or even today. It's not given to everyone to speak in those terms. She was always trying to translate the diplo-talk for the laypeople and everyone who is affected by American foreign policy.

Obviously, when I was writing the book, I was also reflecting on my thoughts and my confusions as a young Lebanese in Beirut who's not yet a journalist—when you grow up and mature, you certainly understand more. I came to the United States in 2008 at the age of thirty-one with already a better understanding about how the world worked. But in the course of the four years that I travelled with Hillary Clinton and with her staff—her direct staff and the senior aides at the State Department were very approachable as well—having this front-row seat to the making of American diplomacy, sometimes very much in front of my eyes, on the plane, when they were trying to figure out what to do on the next stop, that also helped me understand better what American foreign policy was about, how it was made. The proximity to the making of those decisions allows you to understand them better. I'm very aware that I was in a very unique position, and that is why I decided to write the book—so that I could share what I had seen in a way, bringing the reader into the American foreign policy machine, trying to demystify it. But also to explain that foreign policy, whether it's in Italy, Lebanon, or the United States, is made by real people, real human beings who do not have all the answers or the facts; they're trying to do the best that they can.

That said, it doesn't mean you agree with everything that they do. As a journalist, I'm reporting those policies and decisions, but for the people on the receiving end of American foreign policy, or those who are watching it play out, you can agree or disagree. It certainly changes your perspective in a way that you're able to better understand the dynamics of diplomacy. You may still feel disappointed. Some people in Syria—or in Lebanon even—may feel disappointed, as President Obama has not decided to conduct a military strike. Perhaps they understand why. I can understand the process that led to this decision—through my contacts in the administration, at the State Department, at the White House—but as a private citizen it's up to me to agree or disagree. Understanding it, however, helps you to come to terms with it.

Since the very beginning, the Obama administration—as Clinton always tried to make clear—was reaching out to the world "not only to suit-wearing officials sitting in ministries but to people as well" as you put it in your book. Social media has certainly been key in the administration's efforts to connect with the people, what Anne-Marie Slaughter has referred to a "pivot to the people."[2] How has Clinton harnessed social media tools?

Hillary Clinton had a lot of people around her using social media. She encouraged them to use social tools. She hired an advisor for technology and innovation. There was a real push at the State Department to start using tools like Facebook and Twitter to make American diplomacy and diplomats more accessible. It was about accessibility. When you're accessible, it's easier to understand, it's easier to have an exchange. And I have watched many exchanges between American and foreign diplomats as they try to explain a position that the United States has taken or try to clarify the wrong impression that people might have about Washington's foreign policy. In countries like Egypt, for example, where social media has gone wrong occasionally as used by American officials, tools like Twitter can produce positive outcomes and certainly a better understanding about American positions. When people are able to tweet directly to the embassy and ask, for example, why the US ambassador has met with a certain official, then the embassy has the ability to reply, address the question, and clarify if that meeting has never happened or the information is not based on credible information.

Clinton went beyond just using social media to make this pivot to the people, she met with people face to face. It's not enough to be on Twitter. You have to really engage with the real people, whether in person, in town hall meetings, interviews across the world, interactive meetings from the studio at the State Department with millions connected through television, social media, or other platforms. She really tried to be very accessible, and she encouraged her staff and diplomats to do the same.

It's very difficult to quantify the result and the impact. But let me give you the example of Clinton's trip to Pakistan, where she engaged in a lot of people-to-people diplomacy. Over the course of a couple of days, she did television interviews, town halls with students, tribal leaders, and a variety of groups. When she first arrived, the tone of the local media was really acerbic, very acrimonious and critical. By the time she left, the newspapers' headlines were softer. They showed a newly found respect and dialogue with the United States—and ultimately with her—because she agreed to sit down with the real people and answer all the questions they threw at her. "You abandoned us in the past, why?," somebody asked. "You're not giving us enough cooperation money," somebody else stated. She allowed people to be angry and responded with respect and addressed their concerns. When you address people's concerns so clearly and frankly, you're definitely able to move beyond the issue and build up a dialogue.

You certainly had a privileged view of US foreign policy during Clinton's four years as secretary of state. Like many other State Department correspondents, you traveled thousands of miles with her and her close staff. What do you think was Clinton's personal relationship with social media and what do you think it is now, only a few months after she opened her personal Twitter profile?

I am not sure what her personal relation with social media was when she was at the State Department. She did not tweet herself and actually opened her own Twitter account only after she left as secretary of state. While she embraced the idea, she didn't necessarily feel she needed to do it herself. During her tenure at the State Department she certainly warmed up more and more to the idea of doing it herself, and during the process she famously interacted with Adam Smith and Stacy Lamb, the creators of the Tumblr blog "Texts from Hillary."[3] She has quite a good sense of humor, and that made her able to engage with people at any level and see the benefits, making her even more approachable to people. Isn't that what social media is all about? Certainly, for a politician who had troubles on the campaign trails in 2008 for not being approachable and likable, she seemed during her years as secretary of state to transcend that to some extent. Social media helped show her in a very different light. Does she use Twitter herself or her staff tweets for her now that she's on Twitter? I'm not privy to how she uses social media today, in her private life. But I have a sense she's behind the bio she has on her Twitter profile.[4]

Were digital tools also a double-edged sword for Hillary Clinton as the incidents in Cairo show us?[5]

When it comes to Cairo, whether you're a diplomat or a journalist, you rely on people's common sense and initiative—that is, after all, the whole point of social media. If you're looking to approve every tweet that comes out from diplomats, or by any company employee, you are stifling the process and the idea of what social media is all about, which is to engage with people in real time. Mistakes happen and people have to retract their tweets or apologize. We've seen people having to resign from their positions because they sent out the wrong tweet. There is a certain spontaneity about Twitter, and even if you're a seasoned diplomat or a journalist, you can be carried away by the instantaneity of it. There are crucial moments in which it is better to check back with your home base and see what is better to say or not say. The whole point of Twitter is to be personal: there's no point for me to only tweet links to my articles or for diplomats to only put out official statements. We need to be engaging and personable, but at times it becomes difficult to tip in to that, so much so that a diplomat can become too engaging and too personable while forgetting about the talking points.

You write: "I also saw a clear dissonance between the reality of American power, whether hard, smart, or soft, and what people believed was in America's power to achieve. The sometimes bizarrely optimistic attitudes of American officials themselves and their belief in their own ability to get things done only fed that perception. It had always been so, but now American influence was being challenged in unprecedented ways in a world spinning faster than ever before." The very concept of power has certainly changed in the twenty-first century and—as you put it—in the twenty-first century "America could no longer walk into a room and make demands; it had to build connections first."[6] *What is power in the digital age?*

In many ways power remains the same: armies, money, resources, how big you are. The United States remains very powerful in that way. But power is also much more diffuse, it's much harder to exercise, to hold on to. Also, many new players are emerging, from multinationals, money makers, networks. Because it's more diffuse, power is in a way more precious, because it's also about the perception of power—the perception that you still are everywhere and everything is still under control. Hillary Clinton was acutely aware of the new dynamics of power. She travelled a lot around the world to assert the presence of the United States, to dispel any notion that the United States was in retreat. In that, she was very successful. If you look back at the end of 2008 when she accepted the job offered by President Barack Obama, and later confirmed in 2009, there was a perception that the United States was in decline, and the financial crisis very much added to that perception. However, after she got on a plane and travelled to 112 countries in an effort to show that the United States was there, she helped change that perception. Since she's left office, things have changed again somewhat.

Power in the digital age is also about the narrative. Social media helps you feed that narrative. If you control it and if you flood the airwaves, you can add to the perception that you're still powerful and in control. When you talk about power, the way you portray yourself on social media very much plays into that in the twenty-first century.

New nonstate players have emerged, partly thanks to a more innovative approach to foreign policy, and certainly in the wake of social media popularity and increasing usership around the world. Clinton has always highlighted the role of grassroots organizations and partnerships, even more now in her role at the Clinton Foundation and the Clinton Global Initiative.

It goes back to the people-to-people diplomacy and to the realization by the current administration that power is more diffuse, that the United States is not the only superpower anymore—even though it remains the largest—that people have more power, more so than before, and certainly amplified through social media. In this day and age, it becomes very important to deal with entities beyond states.

When Clinton was at the State Department, she was very keen to connect with nongovernmental organizations, with companies' CEOs, with United Nations agencies, but also with countries that are not necessarily considered among the big power players. She spearheaded many multilateral initiatives, minilateral ones with regional groups—whether with Asian nations working on the lower Mekong, or with Turkey on counter-terrorism, or with the UN working on women's health and gender balance, with celebrity chefs to raise awareness on the clean cookstove initiative.

To some extent, none of that is new. But she felt it was important to her as secretary of state to focus on the efficacy of partnerships and not just on traditional diplomacy. She always believed in the need to empower people in a way that they can become the solution to their own problems: it's not enough to work top to bottom. Her view was that it's also important to work from the bottom up.

Her approach was not new or groundbreaking. It was certainly a much more focused effort to make it one of her priorities for the American foreign policy. Even when she was criticized, she felt it was very much part of her portfolio as secretary of state to move beyond traditional diplomacy and deals signed behind closed doors. It was her way to blend soft power into smart power.

As a State Department correspondent for BBC, you experienced a different side of Clinton and her style: "I'd seen firsthand how Clinton schmoozed. I'd watched her position herself at the heart of the world's community of foreign policy deciders and experts and become the connector. Just as Washington sat at the heart of a web of connections tying it to the world, Hillary was a center of gravity to herself. From the day she took office, she had worked hard to be available to her counterparts, both because she believed in being accessible but also because availability was political capital."[7] You elaborated on accessibility and personability earlier. With that perspective in mind, do you think social media has changed the nature of traditional diplomacy and traditional politics, or rather complemented both?

They work in parallel. You still have to sit down behind closed doors and worked out a deal. There's no social media tools that can substitute for that.

At the same time, you have the Iranian president who, the minute he gets off the phone with President Obama for the very first conversation between the two countries in more than thirty years, goes to Twitter and tweets about his conversation with the American president. The impact of that tweet is enormous. You cannot underestimate that! While the conversation the two leaders had on the phone—and any other future conversations they will have—is still part of the very traditional diplomatic process, you can certainly amplify it and shape the narrative by taking to social media and expressing yourself with tools like Twitter. The fact that President Rouhani took to Twitter certainly added a dimension of hopefulness and showed him as a pragmatic, modern leader. You have critics saying it was just a ploy. However, the tweet that he sent out and the exchanges that followed, including the one with Twitter cofounder Jack Dorsey,[8] fed that narrative of hope and allowed the message to circulate and resonate with people. Obama used the more traditional mean of a television message after the phone call, but for Rouhani—as he immediately boarded his plane back to Iran—it would have taken hours to comment about it if he had waited until he landed. He did it immediately with a simple tweet. That fed the momentum that something was moving, that more was in motion between the two countries.

To answer your question, while they're still separate, traditional and less traditional diplomacy are both needed, and they certainly feed off each other.

As for Rouhani, his message was indeed amplified, but only to the Western world, as Iranians are still excluded from any online interaction or information.

And that was exactly the question that Jack Dorsey asked Rouhani in his tweet. But imagine all the Iranians who are able to go around the online barricades and restrictions imposed by the regime. Imagine the Iranian diaspora abroad. Or even all those in the Arab world who are not too keen about the *rapprochement* between the United States and the Iranian government. That single tweet made things a little bit more transparent.

That is something I mention at the end of my book, when I describe the gap between what America says and what America does. That gap is getting smaller as it is more difficult to hide anything or to keep it from the public. Whether it's because of social media or the determination of reporters to scavenge for sources to expose possible wrongdoings—the NSA, Guantanamo, or Abu Ghraib are some of the examples—we are more aware of our surroundings, including what governments are doing.

In your description of Clinton's trip to China, you write: "Kissinger had stayed here [Diaoyutai State Guesthouse] in 1971 when he had established the first direct contact with Communist China in over twenty years. Before the age of Twitter and the twenty-four-hour news cycle, Kissinger had slipped out of Pakistan unnoticed, leaving reporters behind, to make his secret trip and pull off his diplomatic coup."[9] It's a completely different picture from May 2012, when, hours before the official announcement that President Barack Obama had landed in Kabul, Afghanistan, for a surprise visit, the media—both social and electronic—were already buzzing with reports about the trip.

Do you think social media and the new real-time news cycle can be detrimental to traditional diplomacy?

I do. As a journalist, I think it's fantastic that we are able to report on everything, see everything, be everywhere. There is simply no way today for a secretary of state to have a secret visit to any country—it's just not possible. As a journalist, as someone who wants to keep government official to account, to shed light on what governments are doing, and bring information to citizens, that's a great thing. But I do understand that for a diplomat it can be very frustrating. Diplomats always say that diplomacy does not flourish in the limelight as sometimes you need a little bit of space, a little bit of darkness to move toward a deal. Look at the backchannel that the United States opened to Iran in 2012 with secret meetings in Oman. It's possible to keep that a secret only because those who were involved aren't very public officials. Whatever conversation Secretary of State John Kerry and his Iranian counterpart had in New York, on the sideline of the 2013 UN General Assembly, it was behind closed doors. We were able to report on the fact that the meeting had happened but not necessarily on the specifics of what it was discussed. What we knew was only what sources from the two camps told us. If you want to give diplomacy a chance, as a diplomat, sometimes you have to let the two sides go back to their principals and to some extent manage their domestic audiences separately. President Rouhani has many adversaries in Iran who are against any level of *rapprochement* with the United States. It becomes very difficult to do so if every single conversation with the Americans is reported in details in the media all over the world. As journalists, it's our job to do that and report on everything, and that creates a natural tension between the media on one hand, and diplomats and government officials on the other. In particular, when it comes to diplomacy and the interaction between countries, I do have some sympathy for diplomats as they try to engage in very sensitive negotiations that have an international impact. Those are difficulties that they didn't have to take into account in the past. That said, there are also a lot of advantages, including more transparency, more openness, and certainly the ability of journalists today to be better aware of what is happening behind closed doors and what the world needs to know about.

There's something, however, that diplomats and officials sometimes forget when they are weary about sharing information with the media or explaining the context. Talking strictly about diplomacy—and not about intelligence or intelligence gathering, which is a whole different debate—when officials are not willing to share information, that leaves a hole that is going to be filled by someone else's narrative. There's a real difference in the quality of what journalists are able to report to their audiences depending on what officials are able or willing to share. When we can't get the context of a particular decision or action, then they run the risk to get criticized. Of course, government officials also try to spin you and sell their story, but when there's no communication at all, then the gap can be filled by whomever, and whatever narrative; often to the detriment of what diplomats are trying to achieve.

What's your personal relation with social media, both as a private citizen, and as a journalist? Has Hillary Clinton affected the way you see and use social media?

At the BBC we try to be very innovative with the way we report news, and we've always been multimedia with television, radio, and online platforms. We're very much out there using these tools. For me it was just a natural process to use social media. I don't think Hillary Clinton had an impact on it, but obviously the more people around you use it, the more you want to engage on those tools.

I have to say that it does take a lot of time, and there are times where I wish I could turn it off. You need to find that right balance between staying connected and letting information come to you but also stepping back and switching it off so that you can still look at the big picture, connect all the dots, and not get drowned in all the details.

I remember covering the Egyptian revolution, during which I gained the most followers in the shortest period of time. I was on air every hour, sometimes even more. In between takes, I was tweeting, reporting in real time what I was learning from diplomats and government officials. It's that kind of information that people want, that they're really hungry for. It helps them understand the context as well as the official narrative that governments are putting out. Foreign policy, after all, is not a machine with clear goals and clear paths to implement them. Foreign policy keeps changing, negotiators often have to go back to the drawing table to redesign a strategy. It's real time, it's real people at work carrying out foreign policy. They too make mistakes and have often to come up with back up plans. This is the kind of information that the public wants and that they mostly engage with.

NOTES

1. Kim Ghattas, *The Secretary: A Journey with Hillary Clinton from Beirut to the Heart of American Power* (New York: Times Books, 2013).

2. Anne-Marie Slaughter, "A Pivot to the People," Project Syndicate, last updated March 20, 2012, http://www.project-syndicate.org/commentary/a-pivot-to-the-people.

3. Adam Smith and Stacy Lamb, "Texts from Hillary," *Texts from Hillary* (blog), http://textsfromhillaryclinton.tumblr.com/.

4. "Wife, Mom, Lawyer, Women and Kids Advocate, FLOAR, FLOTUS, US Senator, SecState, Author, Dog Owner, Hair Icon, Pantsuit Aficionado,

Glass Ceiling Cracker, TBD. . ." Hillary Clinton, "Twitter profile," https:// twitter.com/HillaryClinton.

5. Max Fisher, "The U.S. Embassy to Egypt's Oddly Informal Twitter Feed," *The Atlantic*. Published September 13, 2012. http://www.theatlantic. com/international/archive/2012/09/the-us-embassy-to-egypts-oddly-informal-twitter-feed/262331.

6. Ghattas, *The Secretary*, 115.

7. Ghattas, *The Secretary*, 197.

8. Jack Dorsey, Twitter post, October 1, 2013, 11:00 a.m., https://twitter. com/jack/status/385056531269427201. Hassan Rouhani, Twitter post, October 1, 2013, 4:24 p.m., https://twitter.com/HassanRouhani/status/38513817482285 0560. Jack Dorsey, Twitter post, October 1, 2013, 6:34 p.m., https://twitter. com/jack/statuses/385170855380000769.

9. Ghattas, *The Secretary*, 46–47.

5

THE PILLARS OF DIGITAL DIPLOMACY

A conversation with Macon Phillips, Coordinator,
International Information Programs,
US Department of State

To view clips
from the conversation
with Macon Phillips
scan the QR code
or visit:
http://goo.gl/BCIWMp

On January 20, 2009, you posted the first blog entry of the newly launched whitehouse.gov right after the inauguration of President Barack Obama.[1] *In your blog post, you highlighted the guiding principles of the new administration's digital presence—a new strategy aimed to "put citizens first," to use your own words. The new media efforts center around three priorities: communication, transparency, and participation.*

We came into work every day at the White House with those three goals in mind. To some extent, those three priorities still inform my thinking in the State Department.

The first was communication. When you think about communication you have to think in terms of amplification of your message. Technology is changing how and where people get information. It's really important that we were making sure the White House and the president have a presence in new communities and these new sites. One of the ways I sum that up is by saying that my mother is probably the only person who has whitehouse.gov as their homepage. We really have to look at where people were going to get information.

The second priority, in terms of accessibility and transparency, certainly flowed from the president's commitment to an open government, to a government that is accountable to people. As we got into the work, we also realized it meant accessibility in terms of making complex topics, complex policies more accessible, explaining the context for regular people who weren't following these issues on a day-to-day basis. We realized that people might be discovering and learning about those issues through social media or through search engines like Google, or even landing on one of the whitehouse.gov pages. That involved relying a lot on graphic design, copy-writing, and videos to really explain issues.

The final element is about participation. To me it's certainly the most exciting but also the most challenging in terms of changing the way government works. It is about looking at how technology can give people a voice in their government; how we can be a responsive government; and how we can be in touch with what people really care about. We had a number of efforts to do that: from We The People,[2] the petitioning system we developed; to frequent online chats to address the concerns of the public.

Can the same strategy be applied to foreign policy and serve as a base on how to engage foreign audiences and address the new challenges of a hyperconnected world? Or should it be expanded in order to work with foreigners and the plethora of nonstate actors that is reshaping the foreign policy arena in the twenty-first century?

I think part of what makes me excited about the work here in the State Department is the complexity of the challenge that this work presents: every country. Every audience is a puzzle. That's a puzzle informed by a number of factors: technology and how it has impacted that society; the culture of that society in terms of their engagement; the US foreign policy goals vis-à-vis that country or that audience.

It's hard to answer your question uniformly, but of course that's what makes this an interesting line of work. I do think those three goals of amplification and communication, of accessibility of complex topics, and of genuine engagement—not just in terms of word-of-mouth marketing—inform our work here at the State Department, coupled with elements of responsiveness and collaboration.

It's often hard to measure your success in terms of digital strategies. In a blog titled "Diplomacy in the Cloud," US Ambassador to the UK Matthew Barzun proposes[3] *a wearable band to measure the soft power of the United States abroad. "The hot trend now is wearable tech, like Google Glass and Jawbone bracelets," he writes. "What if we designed a gadget that could measure our activities as diplomats?"*[4] *It might be a crazy idea, but it certainly shows how hard it is to measure how successful we are abroad with our digital strategy. How would you define success in digital diplomacy?*

I think it is challenging to define success for a concept as broad as digital diplomacy because there are so many different scenarios depending on our goals and our audiences. That said, I think success in digital diplomacy can be measured in certain ways that you can't otherwise. To understand the audience that you're reaching, you can really look at the demographics of the kinds of people you're speaking with. Even metrics as fundamental as loyalty—or "does a person that I reach with this program return to use this content or these services again?"—really give you an indication to what extent that person values your work. It's certainly something we looked at in the White House. I think it's sort of a core question about whether you're relevant to that person.

Ultimately, the public diplomacy and digital diplomacy aspects have to flow from policy goals that are measurable, and that oftentimes can be a challenge. Policies have to have a goal: for instance, if we were interested in promoting entrepreneurship in a country, how are we going to know that it worked? Once we have a specific goal to achieve, then we can really come up with the digital aspect of our strategy. It's important to put this back in a context. A lot of the energy for digital diplomacy, at least in the United States, comes from what we see in the political space and campaigns, on all sides. If you take into consideration President Obama's campaigns, those campaigns came about from business goals, from campaign goals like voter turnout, fundraising, etc. Those are really quantifiable metrics that created a framework for the digital work to really hook into. Those kinds of metrics are things we need to develop in our foreign policy goals as well.

Communication, transparency, and participation are objective priorities—you can straightforwardly include them in any strategy. I believe personability and charisma are also two important factors—though more subjective—for the success of a communications strategy, let alone in the digital realm. While staffers and strategists can always work on enhancing the personability of a leader or a whole government, charisma is becoming scarcer and scarcer. Somebody who might seem charismatic to his or her constituents might not be to foreign audiences . . . and certainly not to all audiences around the world. What's your take?

I don't think it's important at all that people behind those tools are charismatic (laughs). Obviously the most basic requirement to have an interesting Twitter account is to be an interesting person. And some of the times, at least in my experience, there have been people who wanted to be really active on Twitter or Facebook in a sort of personal capacity, and it just didn't work because they're not interesting. That has been one of the strengths I think that President Obama has. He's fundamentally someone who's not only funny and smart, but also someone who does a lot of interesting things, starting from his defining experience in his professional life as a community organizer in Chicago—long before the Internet. Because of his experience, Obama fundamentally approaches these types of opportunities from the standpoint of community. Similarly, I think Secretary of State John Kerry has seen firsthand the transformative power of technology in foreign policy. His approach to social media reflects a respect for the growing power of these tools. But Kerry is also a funny guy. When French President François Hollande was in Washington for his first official visit to the White House, Secretary Kerry tweeted in French[5] all day—little touches like that, I think, are really nice.

At the end of the day, is it really important if the president or the secretary of state write their own tweets? Is it important that you present yourself personally on Twitter, Facebook, or any other social media?

I think that's up for each person to decide. I think that the power of the president or the secretary's voice is something that can be quite helpful in digital diplomacy. However, it's certainly something you don't want to overuse. At the same time, it's sometimes the best way to show a personal side or to really speak in a very direct way on key occasions.

While strategy is key in digital diplomacy, the art of persuasion is still a big part of the process. Digital diplomacy, as an integral part of traditional and public diplomacy, aims at reaching out to audiences and exercises that "soft power." In Joseph Nye's words, "the ability to get what you want through attraction rather than coercion or payments."[6] How do you describe persuasion in the digital era?

Persuasion in the digital era is a very interesting concept. One of the things that I've been thinking a lot about and spending a lot of time processing is this trend that we're seeing of a decline in the public's trust in institutions. It is a worldwide trend. Certainly, in the United States it is met with a growing rise in people's trust in people like themselves. At the same time, you're seeing an explosion of networks. When you think about those trends, you start to realize that influence oftentimes is best exerted from people who are like each other. That isn't really a new concept, but when you apply it to foreign policy, it really underscores the value of finding these interlocutors who can help facilitate the kind of conversation you want to have. Fundamentally, I think we've moved beyond "I tell you something and hope you believe it." It's more that I influence the conversation that hopefully an audience will find to be reasonable because of who is participating in it. Those outcomes hopefully are part of where I want to be, but it's just not as direct as it used to be.

In the foreign policy arena we keep highlighting how new media technologies can help us make citizens around the world, foreign audiences, groups, and networks become part of the diplomatic process. It's that participatory quality that we talked about before. Often when we talk about digital diplomacy, participation and engagement are always part of the equation. However, when you look at what countries are doing around the world, sometimes it's just a hint of inclusion, a hint of participation. Most of it is still broadcasting. Do you see concrete progress toward this goal or at times do we sort of oversell digital initiatives?

I totally agree that there's a profound and important difference between using social media as a way to engage and collaborate with the public and to genuinely discuss things with the public versus using social media as a complementary way to broadcast out your messages. I don't think they're mutually exclusive by any means. I don't think just having a broadcast outlet for information is bad in and of itself. But, it's certainly something to avoid—having people think that just by broadcasting their media, they're actually really achieving the full potential of what's possible. Fundamentally, these tools have to flow from a policy approach that does bake in public engagement as part of the path. If policy makers aren't truly looking for public engagement, they're probably better off just broadcasting messages. What you're seeing at the State Department and in the US government—generally led by the president or the secretary—is very exciting. Look at public engagement as a way to answer foreign policy goals. Once you do that, social media is a very clear path to do so. However, this is still a new concept, and I think in many ways it's a radical concept from an organizational culture standpoint. So, patience is important. We're not going to be as nimble as a twenty-person startup in a tech sector, but at the same time I think we can expect that kind of change—and really push for that kind of change.

Do you think it's important for an outsider to understand the machine behind our governments and how that machine works? Or is it important to make it simpler?

Simplicity is a huge part of that. The more burdens you put on a person to decipher your organization in order to have a meaningful interaction with that person, the worse you do. This is not just about digital diplomacy; this is directly transferrable to things like citizen services here in the United States—absolutely something we spend a lot of time on. Citizens are paying us to make these services work for them. As a result, they need to be simple so that they're better utilized.

When I think about the State Department, I view it less as a functional division—who does what, so to speak. One of the things that's really remarkable about the State Department—and it's unlike any other organization in the US government—is that we operate offices in pretty much every country around the world. In those places where we don't have an office, we have a virtual presence. That is fabulous when you think of relevance, when you think of being able to put messages out and have interactions that are culturally attuned, that are refined, that really work on that puzzle that I mentioned earlier, composed by every country's own characteristics, every audiences' own characteristics. We have the assets and the human capital, super smart Foreign Service officers and civil servants. We even have foreign, locally employed civil staff who know how these cultures work to sort of facilitate that kind of public engagement that can be tailored for each audience.

"When I ran for this office, I pledged to make government more open and accountable to its citizens," President Obama said when the platform was first announced.[7] "That's what the new We the People feature on whitehouse.gov is all about—giving Americans a direct line to the White House on the issues and concerns that matter most to them." Indeed, one of the most popular digital initiatives you ran while at the White House is the We the People petition, launched in September 2011. Today, it counts more than five million users, over ten million signatures, and its source code has been public since the summer of 2012, with a new API released in November 2013. Can you talk about that a little bit and how that same experience can be applied to foreign policy, for instance? Creating a platform where you really see how people can get engaged and participate in the process?

We the People is one of my favorite projects from my time at the White House. Certainly something I've put a lot of my own heart and soul into. We the People is basically a platform that allows anyone to create a petition, and if a certain number of signatures is reached, then the government responds. We've seen over eleven million people using the system.

One of the most important things about We the People that few people know about is that we survey people who receive a response.

Typically our responses are not, "Hey that's a great idea. We're going to go do that." Oftentimes, it's a chance for us to address issues that people really care about and make sure we're clear about where we stand. Sometimes, we have acted on those petitions because there was an issue we weren't thinking about or they made an argument that made a lot of sense. On one issue of gun control, we actually got a petition with a lot of people who opposed the president's views and felt strongly about some things that weren't true about his approach. We responded directly to them and laid out his arguments. We also asked people who received that response to tell us about that experience, and 80 percent said they would create another petition or sign another petition. This kind of response tells me—back to that point of loyalty—that they'd do it again, that they felt like it was relevant. Also, 30 percent responded saying that they learned something new through the process. When you apply that math to a petition that got over one hundred thousand signatures, you're now having thirty thousand people tell you that they learned something new about the president's position. I guarantee you that we are NOT talking to a lot of those people on a day-to-day basis in the traditional media landscape. So, for us to be able to have that kind of interaction with our critics that demonstrates our genuine commitment to listening to them, but also the importance of making sure the facts are out there and then to have them respond and say they value that, to me that's a step forward. There are certainly many more steps to take, but I think this is a very promising platform.

In terms of foreign policy, how can you bring that same experience so that you can see exactly how people interact with each other and with their government just like We the People? For instance, former US Ambassador to Italy David Thorne, now a special advisor to Secretary Kerry, worked on a digital economy forum in Italy that brought together the public and private sectors, startups, entrepreneurs, and citizens. He's now creating a package here at the State Department so that every US embassy can apply that same experience in the country where they are. That's a visible platform, a visible step forward in terms of engaging with the people and making them part of the process. How can a brand as popular as We the People be applied to foreign policy?

I think fundamentally it starts with really being responsive and listening to what people are telling you, and what they care about. When you think about entrepreneurship, for example, you have to appreciate that the kinds of challenges you might see in Italy are different than maybe the ones you see in Argentina, or the ones you see in Vietnam. As a result, it's really important that public engagement is built into our economic statecraft efforts so that we're not trying to apply a cookie-cutter approach everywhere. It's important that we really are putting an understanding of people's needs, people's concerns first in terms of how we develop that policy. Ultimately, it will be more successful on behalf of the American people and on behalf of the State Department. That kind of empathy, that kind of responsiveness is made so much easier with these new technologies, but ultimately has to be connected to the policy work.

NOTES

1. Macon Phillips, "Change Has Come to WhiteHouse.gov," *The White House* (blog), last updated January 20, 2009, 12:01 p.m., http://www.whitehouse.gov/blog/2009/01/20/change-has-come-whitehousegov.

2. The White House, "We the People: Your Voice in Our Government," https://petitions.whitehouse.gov/.

3. Matthew Barzun, "Diplomacy in the Cloud," *Matthew Barzun* (blog), last updated February 10, 2014, http://matthewbarzun.tumblr.com/post/76233037602/diplomacy-in-the-cloud.

4. Matthew Barzun, "Diplomacy in the Cloud," *Matthew Barzun* (blog), last updated February 10, 2014, http://matthewbarzun.tumblr.com/post/76233037602/diplomacy-in-the-cloud.

5. John Kerry, Twitter post, February 11, 2014, 5:12 p.m., https://twitter.com/JohnKerry/status/433362824413200384.

6. Joseph S. Nye, *Soft Power: The Means to Success in World Politics* (Cambridge, MA: PublicAffairs, 2004).

7. The White House, Office of the Press Secretary, "White House Announces We the People," http://www.whitehouse.gov/the-press-office/2011/09/01/white-house-announces-we-people.

6

LET'S TALK STRATEGY

A conversation with Teddy Goff, Digital Director,
Obama 2012

To view clips
from the conversation
with Teddy Goff
scan the QR code
or visit:
http://goo.gl/8dtThb

*When it comes to communications, you've often referred to a very
simple three-word equation to base your strategy: don't be lame.*

Users have a lot more choices than they had before, and as they become
accustomed to this ever-expanding set of choices, they become more
discerning. Often, they develop higher expectations. They don't have to
sit through stuff they don't like any longer.

Having worked on the practitioner side for a long time, for both
political campaigns and brands, I think anybody who has done communications for a living can attest that most of the time your job is to look
out for your company's priorities: a certain deadline, a department's
plan, or an angry boss. That sort of dynamic gets reflected in the actual
program that gets put out to users. The fact of the matter is that users
don't care. The final user has no idea about a possible division between
this or that department, or a deadline, or even an angry boss. What
users want is interesting content. If they are not getting it, they have no

reason to stick around. The Internet plays an important role in this as users can click elsewhere, as content online is growing exponentially.

What we try to do on a campaign—certainly what I've tried to do with all other clients I've worked with—is figure out what are the issues that people care about and what sort of policy abstraction turns audiences off because either they don't understand it or because they consider it Washington nonsense. The key, whether for a campaign or for a government addressing its citizens or a foreign audience, is to communicate policies and priorities in a way that they are seen by the public as important issues that affect their lives. The reason we don't like politics in the first place is often because it's perceived mainly as rhetoric.

In a **Washington Post** *article, Fabio Rojas, an associate professor of sociology at Indiana University, wrote: "We no longer passively watch our leaders on television and register our opinions on Election Day. Modern politics happens when somebody comments on Twitter or links to a campaign through Facebook. In our hyper-networked world, anyone can say anything, and it can be read by millions."[1] He went on by arguing that political and campaign professionals might soon be out of work as "new research in computer science, sociology, and political science shows that data extracted from social media platforms yield accurate measurements of public opinion." How accurate can social media be, especially considering the complexities of political communications in times of crisis and scandals?*

Let me address the first part of that question: it's absolutely true that ordinary people have a lot more levels and a lot more ways to affect politics than they used to. Ten years ago, if I was steamed about something that was going on in Washington—other than talking to my five to ten best friends until they decided to stop listening to me—there was really nothing more that I could do. That's obviously not the case anymore.

As for the accuracy of listening, I think it's somewhat accurate and it can be somewhat misleading. I don't think social media listening obviates the need for good strategists or for the public for more qualitative than quantitative thinking. Social media tends to adapt to certain kinds of cradle. It tends to attract people who feel very strongly about something one way or another. It's a good way to get engaged on elite opinion, what reporters are thinking or what partisans on one side of the issue think. A lot of the time, people not commenting or not expressing their opinions online are actually those you try to win over.

Because social media rewards quick decision making and quick opinion-formation, because people are just reacting to things as they are happening, it becomes a key ingredient for a great dynamic and a fun place to hang out. However, it's not necessarily the best way for a campaign or a brand or a country to figure out what people are really thinking about things, what their opinions are. The flash decisions that people make, the ways in which they are trying to be funnier or comment on current events can be very different to what they are actually thinking when they think things through. When you go back to the issue and talk to people in a focus group or a more casual setting, you realize that most people have pretty nuanced views about things. Most people are pretty thoughtful about things, and they are doing their best at figuring out what to believe and how to respond. In this regard, social media can be too blunt of an instrument to get across those nuances, because you are trying to consolidate all of your thoughts into one short, small snippet.

Social media is certainly an important tool, both on the communication and the measurement sides. I don't think, however, it obviates the need for other kinds of measurements, opinion research focus groups, or other ways to study a people sentiment, in particular when you look at a longer term than the immediate social media reaction.

Because platforms like Twitter and Facebook can be good indicators of the audience sentiment—at least in absolute terms—how much should social media weigh on your communications strategy?

You have to separate the measurement side from the program side.

On the measurement side, social media tools are getting better. I don't think they're quite at a point where they are going to be a central part of informing in an overall communication strategy. They may inform a social strategy, which is part of a communication strategy, but I don't think there are many world leaders, candidates, CEOs, saying, "Let's stop focus grouping, let's stop polling, let's just look at social sentiments." One, because who is on social—that extensive system that makes people you know come to quick decisions and try to articulate them in a very short way—but also on a tactical level, the tools aren't great yet. Digital tools aren't perfect ways to figure out actual sentiment.

On the program side of a communication strategy, I think social is an excruciatingly important part of what organizations are doing. It's only going to grow. I think what we're seeing everywhere is that people don't put a lot credit in advertisements anymore; they don't put a lot of credit in political rhetoric; they don't put a lot of faith in what organizations and institutions say. You see that all over the place, and it's reflected in so many ways that people have declining faith in institutions generally. What they have faith in is what they're doing for their friends. Each person has more of an ability both to hear what their friends have to say and to shape what their friends hear and believe in. Every kind of organization is figuring out what that means for them, but it obviously means that caring about where people are is something that they have to do a lot more than they had to.

The thing that is important to note, though, is that people are getting pretty smart and pretty discerning to know when they are being condescended to or misled. This isn't really a marketing challenge. To me, this is more of a fundamental operating challenge: how you actually do right by all these people who are watching you and forming their opinions with more discernment, with more smartness, and with more visibility than they did ever before. There is no social strategy that will make a bunch of people love your brand, love your country, love your campaign if they feel like they've been manipulated or lied to, or overcharged, or given bad service. What smart businesses are doing is thinking about how they can actually just do better and do right by people. That is the best way to start a social strategy. It's very hard to just start with a lousy product and try wiggling your way out just with social.

What's your favorite digital tool, social media or digital in general? And why?

That's a great question. I would be unfaithful to my trusty phone if I did not say that it's my smartphone. I think the phone is just the thing that is changing people's lives the most. It's incredible, and I say this as a superuser of Twitter and a couple of other services. But we could all live without those services as new ones would pop out and provide more or less the same function. It's amazing, however, how the phone changes your life so fundamentally. I was talking to some friends the other day about how no one has to be lost anymore. Our kids are not going to know that feeling, the experience of being lost, ever. No one has to make plans anymore, because you can just text your friends and see what's up. It's a fundamental change, obviously.

You said: "The best thing we can do at least now with the technology we've got is try to get people talking to their friends. That's when you have to get into the sort of nitty-gritty of how these different [online and social] networks operate and the sort of language and vernacular of each of them and how you can actually be a part of it."[2] *While Twitter, Facebook, and other popular digital tools often seem an easy approach to communication and certainly a very popular one for government leaders, ambassadors, and diplomats, there's much more than that. Indeed, it takes resources and time to make any digital program and strategy work with your target audiences. What are the ingredients to success?*

You've said two: time and resources. I think people who don't live in the world of social communication have this idea that things just go viral and movements just happen. They think that is just the way things work on the Internet. The reality is like that sometimes, but very rarely. Most successful programs are done through making gain brick-by-brick and block-by-block in the same way that any other endeavor would. It is impossible to predict what is going to blow up, and it is very difficult to engineer that kind of outcome. The way most programs work, even highly successful ones, is that they grow slowly at first and then they try and get bigger. It takes money sometimes for acquisitions or to reach advertisements or the like. It takes investments in great content. It's impossible to get eyeballs on lousy content. It takes a lot of planning and work to grow a list, or grow a following, or grow an audience: one person at a time.

Where good programs tend to start is from this question of, "What do we actually have that is going to be interesting to people? What element of our message, or product, or identity as a brand, campaign, or country is inspiring to people, appeals to their hopes, is funny?" I think the Internet revolves around good content and revolves around content that is sharable, especially now that social media is so much more part of the Internet. There's a reason why you may read two articles, where one you might say, "This is pretty interesting" and you click out of it; and the other one you say, "Well that's pretty interesting, I want to share that to Facebook," or "I have got to tell all my friends about it." That is not an arbitrary decision you make. You're making a decision about how you want to communicate with your friends and how you want to present yourself to them.

The way every program I've run starts is by really thinking through: Who is our base? Who are the people who are already invested? Who is our target? Who are the people we want to go and get? What is it— starting from the base and building out—about us, our message, and our program that will make people feel hopeful, that makes people feel that they've just got to tell somebody about this? If you don't have anything like that, then you're in the position that you would have been ten years ago, except you would have operating on different platforms, just trying to advertise your way to new people. That might happen sometimes, but not as well.

You've said time and time again that people give too much credit to the strategy and not enough to the tactics. What do you mean by that?

People like to flatter themselves into thinking that there's a big idea that they can have and that is going to be their silver bullet to success. Again, that happens sometimes. Most of the time though, growth happens pretty slowly and gradually and sort of one person at a time, or one dollar at a time, or one whatever at a time. It's very important to have a strategy, it's very important to have great creative ideas along the way, but it's also very important to test and optimize while making sure you're doing the tactics right.

In the corporate world, there's a lot of companies that have sort of a big idea or message they're trying to get across. But then they've got a website that you can't sign up on. Now, maybe if they had a lousy idea but a website where you could sign up on, then they would be in a better place. Ideally, you would want a great idea and a website where you can sign up on. It's incredible how much I've seen: huge differences in results coming from tiny little changes to what kind of copier you're using or what a page looks like, what the experiences when you're trying to go, sign up, or donate, or volunteer. And you have to have a foot in the end. You know the bare-knuckle tactics of what kind of language gets people to do stuff, how simple can you make a page, how quickly does it load.

US President Barack Obama has changed the way world leaders address their audiences, both at home and abroad. Many have recalibrated their political campaigns to the their country's digital landscape with great success, others have focused on social media to reinforce their foreign policy agendas. In both cases, Obama has shown the world a new way to engage with the people. How would you define the word engagement in the digital era?

At a very fundamental level, people want to be treated with respect. For some people, sometimes that means they want to be given a chance to participate, or send a feedback, or volunteer, or get involved, or upload their video, or share their photo, or whatever.

A lot of the time, we tend to overthink what engagement means. So many people are doing their best to come up with ways to let people participate in programs and activities that most people actually don't want to participate in, or be engaged in. When you run these kinds of programs, you see that a fraction of the percentage of those people are engaging in that way. What most people want is just interesting stuff. They're not thinking about your brand or your campaign. They're thinking about their own lives. They're not thinking, "Boy, I really want to upload my photo to Coca Cola servers." They are thinking about their mom, their dad, their spouse and kids, and their job, and every so once in a while there is an interruption of something entertaining or delightful. If that interruption comes from a brand, then that's great. Every so often, they want to find out what's going on and dig a little deeper. They want to make sure there is an opportunity for them to do so and that they're not being stonewalled, that there's an inability to engage when they want to or inability to get information that they want.

I think it's funny that so many people are rushing toward this idea of big engagement, of a world where everybody is constantly involved in how our government works, how our campaigns work, and how brands work; a world where everyone is constantly given good feedback and sharing their stories. Rather, I think there's a small number of people who actually want to do that in a given situation, but what most people want most of the time is just to be happy and comfortable in their own lives; if that means watching a video that's good or having a comfort to know that their country has put whatever important data upon the website for them to search if they want to. But they don't want anything more than that; they just want to go back to their own lives.

What is one of the key ingredients when it comes to engagement, trust, reach, and influence in the digital world?

The ability to inspire is very important. There are ways in which social media makes people and conversations more substantive and there are ways in which they can get less substantive. I certainly think it has increased almost everyone in the world's ability to access conversations about policy and foreign affairs that they couldn't before. A friend of mine who works in a news organization said the traffic on international news stories has never been higher. I've always thought that's sort of interesting because people think the Internet dumbs down conversations, when, in fact, it's making people care and learn about complex and obtuse issues that were often difficult to follow when your only way of getting news was for half an hour at 6:30 on one of three stations on TV.

Also, it's important that social media puts a premium on humor, likability, instant satisfaction, and reward. That gives an advantage not to a politician, for example, who has a very elliptical, long way of speaking in scale, but more to a young, good-looking one, somebody good with snappy comebacks that can fit within a tweet. In this context, I also think that loyalty is very important. Brands in general—a company, but also a country, or an individual—have so much more of an ability to get stuff out of people who really care about them. As that's happening, they have less of an ability to get stuff out of everyone else, because advertising is so much less effective and because it's so much harder to get reach in the first place as the audience is so diffuse.

The ability to inspire is an aspect of developing loyalty as people are drawn to what they like, and don't have to pay attention to what they don't.

If I translate that into the diplomatic world, the ability to inspire fades as we often operate as bureaucracies rather than campaigns.

More than anything, what's going on is that people are having no more patience for empty speeches, for the usual PR-talk. They do not have to listen to that if it doesn't in some way relate to them or entertain them. It's really important to know that as the landscape changes, people's expectations change and people's responses change. The younger crowd in particular knows when it's being marketed to; knows when someone is trying to get something out of them. In those circumstances, it shuts them down right away.

If you're not going to be a charismatic celebrity—both for brands or countries—it's important to be on some human and authentic levels and try to communicate with people in a way that makes them feel comfortable—like they're talking to a friend. Your audience doesn't want to have a formal conversation, or a conversation that feels solicitous, where they feel we're trying to get something out of them.

Also, personality is not everything. Issues matter. While ambassadors some of the time might be perceived as bureaucrats, they are also representing issues that people care about; they're representing countries and the ideals and values of that country. Those countries have sports teams, landmarks, history, food, culture, music, and arts, and to the extent that they can find an element of connection with their audience, making them more personable.

When you use digital and social media platforms, you can run the risk of oversimplifying very complex theories. This is when digital tools can be tricky and even destroy your reputation online and offline. But this is an area in which innovation and tradition come together perfectly, harnessing the power of digital and the effectiveness of language and rhetoric. A perfect example is the tax policy debate during the Obama reelection campaign. Your solution was a hit, even beyond what you hoped, grabbing the atten-

tion of millions of voters. . . . Can you describe the idea behind the romneytaxplan.com[3] *project?*

Romneytaxplan.com was a site that we put out at a point in the campaign where we felt that Governor Mitt Romney[4] wasn't answering questions about his tax plan and our traditional communications strategy on the tax issue wasn't going anywhere. Your public, if you wind up in a situation where somebody is saying one thing and the opponent is saying another thing, is pretty much lost. At that point, you might end up with a tie, but if you're looking for a win, then you need to change your strategy. With romneytaxplan.com, we wanted to find a way to articulate the fact that Obama's opponent was not answering very important questions about his tax plan. We wanted to do that in a way that was going to resonate with people, as people dislike politicians when they bark back and forth at each other. Also, most of the public is not going to read policy white papers, and they're not going to look at a spreadsheet to understand the ins and outs of any tax policy reform. But there's got to be a way to take an issue that really does matter to people—I mean tax policy that affects you—and communicate it in a way that feels at a minimum human, relatable, and interesting. We wanted to find a way that people want to share and discuss with others. That's how romneytaxplan.com came about.

Romneytaxplan.com is a little website with only one button on the screen that, referring to Romney's tax plan, invites the user to "get the details." Well, when you try click on that button, it automatically moves away from your mouse as your mouse approaches it, virtually making it impossible to get details on Romney's tax policy—and in a way mimicking what we believed, the fact that Governor Romeny wasn't answering very important questions about his tax plan.

The website received more than a million Facebook likes and 75,000+ Twitter mentions within the first day from its publication. It was a huge success! Had we put out a white paper or a statement from the campaign manager—or anything of that nature—it might have been picked up in the news cycle, but it wouldn't have been the kind of success that compelled people to talk about it.

Obviously the romneytaxplan.com experience doesn't fit the foreign policy realm, but it shows how creativity and innovation

go a long way. What lessons did you learn from the Obama cam-
paign and how would you apply it to governments that are often
struggling to engage with their audiences?

There may not be a chance for most embassies and most countries to
have a piece of product like romneytaxplan.com. That was a very particular situation. On some level, however, everybody is dealing with something that people care about. If you're dealing with a nation, you're
dealing with all kinds of history and culture and music and sports and
arts, and there are ways to get people to care about it. Does that mean
that every embassy is going to have a microsite or video that gets a
million hits in a day? Probably not. That, however, isn't probably the
goal. Can they instead find a way that, either in their own country or the
country where they are stationed, connects them with their audiences
in a deeper more meaningful way? Can they find a way that lets them
engage around cultural commonalities? I'm sure they can, and if they
do in a way that's not about "We are the embassy of the United States
and we are trying to tell you this, please listen to us," then it will find
good success. It's about finding what an embassy could say that would
be interesting to your audience out there. Not with the goal of radically
transforming their lives but with the goal of entertaining them for a
couple of minutes and at the same time finding some kind of commonality that shows them how your organization can be part of their lives.

The goal is very achievable and even more so when you can be
funny, humorous, or even surprising and emotional. It's not an easy
thing, and I believe most embassies are not going to achieve massive
hits, where all of Twitter or Facebook are talking about a specific issue
at a time, something that you've locally created for your target audience. However, if you keep the goals a little narrower than that, ambi-
tiously but realistically about what they're trying to achieve, the result
might surprise you. Remember, you've got billions of people spending
an awful lot of time on the Internet.

NOTES

1. Fabio Rojas, "How Twitter Can Predict an Election," *Washington Post*,
last updated August 11, 2013, http://www.washingtonpost.com/opinions/how-

twitter-can-predict-an-election/2013/08/11/35ef885a-0108-11e3-96a8-d3b921c0924a_story.html.

2. Jon Ward, "Republican Party Path Back from 2012 Election Requires Shift in Culture, Not Just Tactics," *Huffington Post*, last updated January 11, 2013, http://www.huffingtonpost.com/2013/01/10/republican-party-election-2012_n_2443344.html.

3. The Democratic National Committee, "romneytaxplam.com," accessed June 23, 2014, http://www.romneytaxplan.com/.

4. Willard Mitt Romney was the Republican Party's nominee for president of the United States in the 2012 election. Before his presidential bid, he served as the seventieth governor of Massachusetts from 2003 to 2007.

7

PIONEERING TWITTER DIPLOMACY

A conversation with Arturo Sarukhan, Ambassador of Mexico to the United States (2007–2012)

You've had a long career in Mexico's Foreign Service, from being a young chief of staff to the Mexican ambassador in Washington to later representing your country in the US capital as ambassador from 2007 to 2012. You've been deputy assistant secretary for inter-American affairs, director of policy planning at the foreign ministry in Mexico City, and consul general in New York City. You also worked for the presidential campaign of Felipe Calderón as foreign policy advisor and international spokesperson and then became coordinator for foreign affairs in the Transition Team. There are many highlights of your long career, but one in particular certainly strikes the attention of many young diplomats as well as senior foreign officers: on October 19, 2009, you sent your first tweet, becoming the first foreign ambassador accredited to Washington, DC, to start using Twitter in an official capacity:[1] "Great to be the 1st Ambassador to the U.S. with a personal Twitter account; a good way to talk directly to America about Mexico!" How did you get to your decision to use Twitter as an official tool?

It was not an easy decision because there was an important division within my team as to whether I should tweet or not. Some felt that it was an unnecessary risk, particularly if you said something that either got interpreted the wrong way or that you later regretted; it could certainly and potentially create a problem, in particular due to the high profile of the bilateral relationship and the visibility of the embassy both in the United States and in Mexico.

I had been looking at how certain politicians and elected officials were using Twitter. I became convinced that—for an embassy of a country like Mexico in a country like the United States—it could become for starters a very important outreach tool to our diaspora community, especially if you are able to articulate something in relation to our fifty consulates in the United States. I also realized that it was a good way to circumvent the narrative that became encrusted in traditional media over what was going on in Mexico, in particular relating to the drug violence and the challenge of transnational organized crime.

At one point I told my staff I had made up my mind. For the first two to three weeks, we conducted a dry run, with tweets that weren't visible to the public. But then, we got the hang of it. We got the mechanics of what it implied, how much time it meant, how we would go about designing the tweets, what we would use the tweets for. We made a series of decisions in that direction. I would tweet nothing personal. Mine would be used solely as an official Twitter account. We felt at that moment that we really needed to turn it into a tool of engagement.

Our second decision was that we would validate the tweets amongst ourselves. Also, we would prepare a preapproved package of tweets, ahead of a special activity by our embassy or consulates—an exhibit, or a book launch, or a study. We would have everything ready, including links and images, to be published by my press team during the week. However, during the day, mostly at noon and in the evening, I carved out time so I could tweet myself. We would usually look at the news in the morning and think of what we had on our agenda before agreeing on specific tweets, or something to say after a meeting or public appearance.

When we slowly started this exercise, once we went public, it became almost natural after two to three months. We immediately saw the huge potential.

How did your government—as well as other ambassadors in Washington—react to your official profile on Twitter? Was it a stimulus for others to explore the potential of Twitter and start tweeting themselves?

I wouldn't say inspiration. I hope that those of us who became pioneers and trailblazers as ambassadors in using social media tools have proven that in this day and age you need to be on these platforms to communicate and get your positions out there. Of course there's also a certain degree of risk attached to it, but this is not a good century to be risk averse, especially for governments. There is an old political saying in Mexico, which in Spanish is "el que se muevo, no sale en la foto," or, "the person who moves does not appear in the photograph." It relates to politicians aspiring to be the next president—moving before he was given the go ahead by the incumbent president—meaning that he would not make it into the picture. In the same way, today, anyone who does not tweet does not appear in the photo. It is an indispensable tool. I would hope that, by the experiences and the road traversed by those who started doing some years back, we have made it more palatable and we have proven it works.

Everyone, except babies, hates change. And bureaucracies and foreign policy institutions are not the exception. They seem, however, even more opposed to change. It is often a change in cultural and operational habits within foreign ministries. Successfully using these tools entails a greater degree of autonomy for what an ambassador does and says because if you have to wait hours or days before you're approved to tweet, you are going to lose the opportunity, the impact, the relevance, and the timeliness. Foreign ministries have to let go and allow their ambassadors and embassies more independence in their communication responsibilities and tasks. Inevitably, there will be mistakes along the way—and the challenge to all of this will be to see how ministries react once there has been a mistake—but you cannot isolate yourself from the trends and instruments that will determine the future of public diplomacy and diplomatic engagement.

The basic hope is that those of us who have started early on in social media have proven that these are not only invaluable tools, but also that those embassies and ambassadors that don't tweet do so at their own risk, and have a huge problem, both in getting messages out as well as taking advantage of a fabulous window into open-source intelligence collection and analysis. Indeed, the amount of information—without having to plant a bug, to intercept a phone call, or to eavesdrop on any communication—that you get simply by following key feeds and players on Twitter is huge. Even when an embassy, an ambassador, or a foreign minister decides that they do not want to be putting out tweets, they have to be at least passively present on those digital platforms to be able to listen to the information that moves through social media.

Digital diplomacy, defined as the use of digital tools in foreign affairs to conduct public diplomacy and outreach, is, at the end of the day, diplomacy after all. It is an indispensable tool to succeed in our mission as ambassadors, in communicating our messages, changing the narrative, and correcting misperceptions, bad or wrong information, and yes, ultimately, for spinning.

That said, however, it is a huge mistake to see tools like Twitter and Facebook for more than what they are. They are tools. They don't substitute for traditional diplomatic work. They rather complement it. They will certainly allow us to be more effective, but they will not help in sugar coating or solving bad policies or the implementation of bad policies. You can have the best social media guru in your team, you can be on all online platforms, but if the policy that you are selling or that you are promoting is poor, badly thought out, or lacks vision, then your online activity is going to fail miserably. If the policies are sound, you will get much more punch out of them.

It is also important to understand that social media platforms should allow a country, and its foreign policy apparatus, to pursue three basic objectives, which are to listen, to react/respond, and to empower/engage. Those would be the three basic objectives that you pursue by using tools like Twitter and Facebook. As we move forward in engaging and understanding the intersection of digital tools and public policy and diplomacy, as governments, as foreign ministries, as elected officials, as state governors or mayors, we become more sophisticated in the use of online communications tools. Those should be used as opportunities for country branding, city branding, or state or province branding. They are there to enhance the soft power of how countries interact with one another and with global constituencies.

What is the difference between broadcasting and engaging? A lot of ambassadors that now use Twitter see the tool more as a way to putting out their messages rather than engaging with their audiences. Do you think it is because of fear of engaging or fear of risks?

A few key considerations. First, if you engage, it is much harder to cherry-pick and engage with some and not with others. That is inevitable. Second, a certain level of engagement opens you up to more scrutiny and to some opposing—and even negative—points of view and criticisms.

While some ambassadors prefer to use social media to broadcast a message, engagement is critically important. I discovered very early on, as I started tweeting solely in English, that Mexicans in Mexico were feeling left out of the conversation. My initial response was: "I'm the Mexican ambassador to the United States, and I communicate in the language of the country I am serving in." Then I realized that I needed to start tweeting in Spanish as well. I decided to publish most of my tweets in both languages. My decision translated into an expanded engagement on both sides of the border, because of the huge Latino population and Mexican-American diaspora living in the United States, but also because I could explain to Mexicans back home what we were doing and seeking in the bilateral relationship with the United States.

In an article titled "Twitter Isn't Spreading Democracy—Democracy Is Spreading Twitter" published in November 2013 by **The Atlantic**, [2] *author Kentaro Toyama,* [3] *a visiting scholar at the School of Information of the University of California at Berkeley, argues that "Silicon Valley feeds us a myth of technology trumping politics, but if anything, it's the other way around." He writes: "The reason why the Internet seems 'democratizing' in America is exactly because America is a democracy. We have free speech online because we have free speech offline, not the other way around. The fact that technology can be used either to buttress or erode democracy means that technology itself doesn't carry democratizing power—what it does instead is to amplify the underlying political forces already in play." Twitter and the like have gotten so much attention and are now becoming a new player in international affairs and in the democratic process, or so it appears.*

I do think that platforms like Twitter have become a very powerful force for societal costakeholdership of public policy. We have seen very powerful instances in which these platforms have been used to mobilize, to push for change. I still think of them as a lubricant in the democratic process; I think it adds heft to the ability of constituencies to take on issues and to engage with all stakeholders. If you look at some of the political manifestations that we are seeing around the world—whether it is the Tea Party or Occupy Wall Street in the United States, whether it's the students in Chile, whether it is the Indignados (the outraged) in Spain, the rising middle classes in Brazil, or the demonstrations in Israel in recent years to protest the high cost of living—every single one might have different triggers, but they all have one thing in common, and arise from one constant frustration. That commonality relates to the fact that the traditional political parties no longer seem to be an effective conveyor belt between public policy and citizens. That sense of costakeholdership between citizens on the one hand and political parties and public policy on the other is being broken in many places around the world. Here in the United States for instance, Occupy Wall Street and the Tea Party are two extremes on each end of that spectrum, and platforms like Twitter I think provide individuals, groups, nongovernmental organizations, and civil society a way to augment their points of view, their agendas and push for change. And it's happening in both open and closed societies; evidently, in the latter, at a more contained, limited, and controlled space, but it still occurs. This is why the key cleavage in the twenty-first century is between open and closed societies, and digital platforms and tools become a fundamental tool in taking in closed societies and regimes.

Digital platforms like Google and Facebook seem to dominate the web. Citing a recent study by the Oxford Internet Institute's Information Geographies,[4] Foreign Policy magazine writes in an October 2013 article: "Not only is Google the top site in 62 countries of the 120 countries tracked, but the researchers note that among the 50 countries that have Facebook listed as the most visited website, 36 of them have Google as the second most visited, and the remaining 14 countries list YouTube (currently owned by Google)."[5] As they're certainly bigger players than most governments, both in terms of reach and resources, what do you think is going to be the role of digital platforms like Google in the future of foreign policy?

There's no question that throughout the last ten years technology giants have acquired tremendous power. These new tech players have become power brokers and power players in their own right, for good and for bad. There may be issues where we agree with the positions and interests and agendas of these tech and digital behemoths. There may be issues in which we don't agree. They are true players, not only in the corporate arena, but also in shaping and impacting public policy. Back to the United States, look how these groups torpedoed the Stop Online Piracy Act (SOPA), the 2011 bill that was being crafted in the US Congress to expand capabilities in combatting online copyright infringement. The way these corporations mobilized and advocated for the defeat of this bill was a very powerful symbol of their maturity as political players.

What would be your advice to future generations of diplomats and ambassadors, considering that today's youths are not adapting to social media but rather they have grown up with it and they already know how to use those platforms very well?

First, I think that they have to understand the intersection of these tools and how these and the traditional craft of diplomacy need to be brought together. Again, you can be the savviest and most effective communicator—or user of these tools—but if you are lacking vision, the understanding of what the interests of the country are, the interests of the country you are serving in, how that fits into a global paradigm, a clear sense of the objectives you are pursuing, what are those goals, then all of that will come to naught. Second, they will have to embrace change.

NOTES

1. Arturo Sarukhan, Twitter post, November 12, 2009, 5:58 p.m., https://twitter.com/Arturo_Sarukhan/status/5662543976.

2. Kentaro Toyama, "Twitter Isn't Spreading Democracy—Democracy Is Spreading Twitter," *The Atlantic*, last updated November 11, 2013, 4:59 p.m., http://www.theatlantic.com/technology/archive/2013/11/twitter-isnt-spreading-democracy-democracy-is-spreading-twitter/281368/.

3. Kentaro Toyama is a researcher in the School of Information at the University of California, Berkeley, and a fellow of the Dalai Lama Center for

Ethics and Transformative Values at MIT. Until 2009, he was assistant managing director of Microsoft Research India, which he cofounded in 2005.

4. Mark Graham and Stefano de Sabbata, *Age of Internet Empires* (Oxford: Oxford Internet Institute's Information Geographies, 2013), http://geography.oii.ox.ac.uk/?page=age-of-internet-empires.

5. Catherine Traywick, "Passport Google Imperialism: Mapping the World's Most Popular Websites," *Foreign Policy*, last updated October 3, 2013, 1:50 p.m., http://blog.foreignpolicy.com/posts/2013/10/03/google_imperialism_mapping_the_world_s_most_popular_websites.

8

DIPLOMACY IN 140 CHARACTERS, OR LESS

A conversation with Matthias Lüfkens, Practice Leader Digital EMEA, and author of @Twiplomacy, Burson-Marsteller

"Twitter and social media in general have become part and parcel of any integrated government communications," said Jeremy Galbraith, CEO of Burson-Marsteller Europe, Middle East and Africa, releasing the 2013 Twiplomacy study.[1] *"While Twitter is certainly not the only channel of communication and will not replace face-to-face meetings, it allows for direct peer-to-peer interaction. I expect we will see an increasing number of corporations and CEOs also embracing the new tools that are connecting our world leaders," he said. What makes Twitter so appealing for world leaders, ministers, and ambassadors?*

Twitter is probably the easiest social media tool to master, thanks to its brevity and its intuitive, easy-to-use interface. It is also the most immediate and public way to communicate to a global audience. A tweet functions just like a newspaper headline. If it is well crafted, people will follow the link to read more and share it with their followers. The challenge is to write interesting, engaging, and concise tweets. Twitter has become a formidable communication tool, allowing world leaders to broadcast short, poignant messages to millions of followers. The most followed political users such as @BarackObama, the Pope @Pontifex, India's Prime Minister @NarendraModi, and Turkish President @RT_

Erdogan use Twitter as a one-way broadcasting channel. Hinting more engagement, Modi said in his inaugural message as Prime Minister:[2] "I am a firm believer in the power of technology and social media to communicate with people across the world. I hope this platform creates opportunities to listen, learn, and share each other's views." Within weeks of his election in May 2014, his Twitter account became one of the most followed among all world leaders.

Twitter is also very useful for public Q-and-A sessions, which might eventually replace traditional press conferences. In a 2013 Twitter Q-and-A session, then Swedish Foreign Minister Carl Bildt answered sixty-two questions in thirty minutes.[3] He could have never answered so many questions in a traditional media briefing. One added advantage is that you can see the questions in writing before answering them. Moreover you can dodge difficult or embarrassing questions, since nobody expects a leader to answer every single question on Twitter.

Twitter is also perfect for public diplomacy, and public exchanges between world leaders often make headlines in traditional media such as the Twitter exchange between the White House and Iranian counterpart Hassan Rouhani. If they followed each other, they could even engage in direct and private SMS-style communications.

Have governments, world leaders, and diplomats harnessed the full potential of social media?

While almost more than 80 percent of all government members of the United Nations have an official Twitter presence, many have not yet explored the full potential the social networks offers. Most are still in a learning phase and are slowly setting up digital teams and hiring community managers.

Before starting out on Twitter, a couple of key questions need to be addressed: Should world leaders have personal profiles or should they tweet on their organization's handle? Should their Twitter profile be "owned" by the organization or by their political party? Whom should they follow and make connections with? Should they tweet themselves—few actually do—or should it be a joint effort with their staff? One thing is clear: social media engagement is not free. It takes time, energy, and resources to manage social media channels.

Tools like Twitter and Facebook have changed foreign policy and diplomacy, democratizing the process and opening it up to new actors and players, from businesses to civil society organizations, from activists to regular citizens. Traditional diplomacy, however, has not disappeared and still represents the core of foreign policy. How do you think the profession will evolve and transform in the future for the new generations of diplomats and ambassadors?

Public communication on Twitter and other social media channels can reinforce traditional diplomacy. In the future, ambassadors will probably be hired on the strength of their digital network and the number of their Twitter followers and Facebook fans. Personal engagement in and listening to social media conversations will definitely enhance the diplomatic work as evidenced by the UK's digital star ambassador @HMATomFletcher, a self-proclaimed "Twiplomat."[4]

However, public communication on social networks can also jeopardize traditional diplomatic negotiations. "Please don't tweet this" will become the new mantra of secret diplomatic meetings. At the 5+1 talks in Geneva between Iran and the major Western powers about Teheran's nuclear program in October 2013, all sides agreed on a social media moratorium in order not to scupper the talks.[5]

Your 2014 Twiplomacy study shows that the governments of more than three-quarters (83 percent)[6] of the 193 member states of the United Nations have a presence on Twitter: almost half of the over 500 accounts analyzed are personal accounts of heads of state, heads of government, and ministers of foreign affairs, and around a third of them tweet themselves, but very few on a regular basis. How do you interpret those figures?

Social media and especially Twitter is a new tool which is not yet widely accepted by politicians and heads of government. As a new and younger generation comes to power, we will see more digitally savvy leaders who will personally dip into their Facebook feeds and update their Twitter timelines. Reading social media feeds will become as important as the daily newspaper reading. It remains to be seen whether they will do it personally or if their staff will prepare a summary of the best tweets and

Facebook posts for them. However, it takes time, which explains why most leaders today are not yet active personally.

Is a presence on social media making a leader more influential? How would you characterize influence in the age of Twitter?

World leaders who are active on Twitter are definitely more influential in the Twitter sphere. @BarackObama is the most followed world leader with over 50 million followers,[7] which is larger than the circulation of all US daily newspapers combined. When @BarackObama tweets, people listen, at least in the Twitterverse.

Alec Ross once said that social media "allows countries to punch above their weight." This is certainly the case for former Swedish Foreign Minister @CarlBildt who established Sweden as a digitally connected powerhouse. The governments of South Sudan and Kosovo have both understood that they too can have a powerful digital voice and a seat at the table through the strategic use of social media.

The study focuses on mutual relations on Twitter and specifically on the mutual connections that world leaders have made and nurtured with their peers. A quarter of world leaders and governments unilaterally follow President Barack Obama and the White House Twitter account, but @BarackObama and the @White-House have established mutual Twitter relations with very few. However, that does not mean that Obama and his administration are less projected internationally. How would you describe Obama's strategy on Twitter in terms of engaging the world? What does it mean to engage your audiences on social media?

The @BarackObama account is a campaign account, set up in 2007 for his election campaign. It focusses primarily on a home audience and is not engaging at all with other foreign dignitaries and rarely tweets about the president's foreign trips or foreign policy speeches. Interestingly for legal reasons the @WhiteHouse doesn't follow @BarackObama.

Since we released our second study in July 2013, the US State Department (@StateDept) has finally made Twitter contacts with its peers and is now mutually following twenty-one other foreign ministries. Even more surprising, the State Department has established direct

Twitter relations with the new Iranian leadership. The State Department is unilaterally following Foreign Minister @JZarif and President @HassanRouhani, despite both countries not having any direct diplomatic relations. I believe their Twitter connections are probably a first step to reestablishing normal diplomatic relations.

Former Swedish Foreign Minister Carl Bildt—@CarlBildt on Twitter—was certainly the best connected world leader, mutually following more than 40 peers. Indeed, his digital presence is quite strong, not only in terms of mutual connections with his peers, but also with audiences around the world. Bildt appears to be also very innovative in his use of social media, and back in August 2013 he took to Twitter to invite his then British colleague William Hague—@WilliamJHague—for a meeting in Stockholm, Sweden. Is Bildt's innovative approach the way to go to be successful on social media?

@CarlBildt, Sweden's former prime minister and former minister of foreign affairs is the most Twitter-savvy politician in Sweden, in Europe, and probably worldwide. Carl Bildt skillfully mixes his foreign policy statements with everyday personal thoughts. His tweets are often hard-hitting and tongue-in-cheek comments on international relations that make the evening news and make the headlines in tomorrow's newspapers. He is effectively leading the conversation through his personal use of social media.

Bildt's strategy couples with a recent push by the Swedish Ministry of Foreign Affairs to have all its embassies and ambassadors on both Twitter and Facebook. "We must be at the absolute cutting edge in digital diplomacy efforts," Bildt said in his address to the Swedish Riksdag in February 2013. Is Bildt showing us that foreign policy is becoming more personable and approachable?

Bildt had a special @fragaCarlBildt"ask-Carl-Bildt" Twitter account where he conducted regular Twitter interviews, making that account the third most conversational world leader account in 2013 with 85 percent being @replies. Bildt regularly engaged in Twitter conversations with journalists, ambassadors, or his peers, showing that foreign policy and policy making in general is becoming more personal, approachable, and definitely more open and public.

Twitter and other social media tools are a formidable way for governments to broadcast. But they're as good for listening . . . Are world leaders and government listening?

World leaders might not read every single @reply and rarely respond; however, their teams are monitoring social media conversations to capture public sentiment in real time. Getting direct feedback about policies and government decisions is one of the major advantages of social media engagement.

There are a handful of leaders, mainly in Africa, who use Twitter primarily to engage in conversations with their followers and their constituents. Rwandan President @PaulKagame is the most conversational world leader with 87 percent of his tweets being @replies to other Twitter users and he rarely shies away from a Twitter fight with his critics.[8]

Do you have any suggestions for Twitter in order to become an even better tool for diplomacy?

I think Twitter should address two issues. One problem is the archiving of official tweets from previous government administrations. The Vatican deleted the thirty-eight tweets sent under Pope Benedict XVI, archiving them on the Vatican website, while the @Number10gov account still has tweets sent under Gordon Brown's tenure, which now bear the effigy of Prime Minister David Cameron.

Another issue is the verification of official international government accounts. Twitter is still very US-centric, while 77 percent of its users are overseas, and while Twitter consistently verifies US government accounts, it should also consistently verify international public figures. Maybe Twitter could appoint a senior Twiplomat to handle international government relations.

NOTES

1. http://www.burson-marsteller.com/press-release/two-thirds-of-world-leaders-are-engaged-in-diplomatic-relations-on-twitter-the-latest-burson-marsteller-twiplomacy-study-finds/.

2. "As PM Too, Modi to Use Social Media to Communicate with People," *The New Indian Express*, last updated May 27, 2014. http://www.newindianexpress.com/nation/As-PM-Too-Modi-to-Use-Social-Media-to-Communicate-With-People/2014/05/27/article2247371.ece.

3. https://twitter.com/fragaCarlBildt/statuses/301679957908803584.

4. Ambassador Fletcher wrote the preface to this book.

5. https://twitter.com/JZarif/statuses/391092710506893312.

6. As of June 24, 2014.

7. As of December 1, 2014.

8. https://twitter.com/PaulKagame/statuses/359507690491351042.

9

FROM DAVOS TO GLOBAL VIRTUAL COMMUNITIES

A conversation with Adrian Monck, Managing Director, Head of Public Engagement, World Economic Forum

For over forty years, the World Economic Forum has committed to improving the state of the world partnering with businesses, governments, and civil society. It has been working on key challenges such as building sustained economic growth, mitigating global risks, promoting health for all, improving social welfare, and fostering environmental sustainability. As an international organization with a global reach, how has the World Economic Forum used technology and social media to reach its goals and overcome the challenges of the digital age?

For the forum, the communications revolution has enabled us to share more broadly what once could only be shared amongst a few. It has allowed us to communicate more of the institution's work, in areas few people might have anticipated—like gender equality. And it has allowed us to interact with critics, supporters, friends, and fellow travelers in ways that were previously impossible. Without it, I don't think the forum could have developed as far and as fast as it has.

Governments, businesses, and individuals across the globe are only beginning to understand the profound implications of living in a hyperconnected world. Technology is offering all stakeholders—within the forum and in the way we communicate with all partners—an opportunity to better understand concrete dynamics and contextualize the new challenges the world is facing, while putting them in the digital context. Every day, there are attempts to write new rules, or challenge existing ones, that relate to communication, privacy, and freedom of expression. The forum focuses on helping all stakeholders better understand the impact of their actions to date, and ultimately, work together to make progress. Technology and social media have become a key component of our strategy.

The forum believes social media can have a significant positive impact and be utilized as an effective tool to facilitate future discussion.

As a veritable actor in foreign policy and international affairs, how has the World Economic Forum and its leadership been relating to government audiences and world leaders? How has it been communicating with citizens around the world?

By giving a platform to anyone who wants to use it, social media has the potential to open and democratize societies. But social media can also create an illusion of community, diversity, power, and freedom. In addition, it is unclear where—if anywhere—the limits of communication lie. Social media may give disproportionate exposure to radicalized voices. We have examined the tension between identity and anonymity, as well as evaluated social media literacy.

Through these discussions, the emerging focus areas are threefold. First, time as an organizing principle on how people "consume" social media and use data should be explored. Second, the increase in visual content will produce a need for new measurement tools, which are currently lacking. Finally, the prevalence of data-generating media requires a credible system for safeguarding privacy and regulation. We also look at the concentration of social media companies, geographic differences in the use of social media, and misconceptions about the behavioral impact of social media.

Many of our global institutions were designed for the world of the mid-twentieth century and would not be as effective today in delivering information and global public goods if they were not changing in the wake of new technologies and new media. The way those institutions communicate has been adapting, matching the real division of power, the interconnectedness, as well as the complexity of the new economics of our world.

The Forum's annual meetings in Davos have driven innovative minds from all over the world, becoming the foremost creative force for engaging leaders in collaborative activities focused on shaping the global, regional, and industry agendas. If you're not one of the privileged few in attendance, you can still be part of the conversation through the web and social media. How have you been harnessing the power of tools like Twitter and Facebook?

When we started, we looked at the media as an interesting participant to what Davos was, and now we look at it as an engine for creating a global platform for talking about issues and nurturing a dialogue. We've enabled some media to get deeper in those stories, but we've also created our own platforms to distributing what we think are serious conversations on issues we care about. For example, when a report comes out, we follow through not just with the most traditional platforms, but also through our blogs and social media channels. Using tools that were not available at scale five years ago gives you your own media platform, which is per se a phenomenal shift in the media landscape. The key takeaway from what's going on in communications right now is that the more traditional way of PRing your message is complemented by your own ability to create your platform. It gives you a new role in the conversation, and a more direct way in shaping those global conversations.

When it comes to social media, different platforms offer different possibilities. On Facebook, the audience is more interactive, more conversational; on Twitter the audience is more engaged. Learning the possibilities of platforms, what works and what doesn't, is key. It is an iterative process.

Essentially, you are just following audiences you would like to talk to, and finding out where, how, and about what they will permit that interaction.

Also, every day, new players are starting to carve out space. Platforms that encourage image sharing are growing, reflecting the ever-growing interest in visual media, a trend underlined by the global boom in online video, video sharing, and platforms like Instagram and Vines.

When using those platforms, we cannot limit ourselves to a small cross-section of society. It's key to understand the developing themes in social media, and develop best practices in social media that can be used by the forum and all our stakeholders.

In an era more than ever defined by social media and real-time information, what is your advice to the future generation of communicators?

Dare not to be silent. Try not to be stupid.

More than any other organizations, the World Economic Forum has advocated for innovation as a priority for decision makers in both the public and private sectors. In the digital age—particularly in a world economy characterized but austerity and slow growth, if not contraction—as governments search for guidance and inspiration on scaling cost-effective solutions to social and economic problems, innovation has taken center stage. How would you describe the World Economic Forum's approach to innovation?

Innovations of all sorts were a key focus at the World Economic Forum Annual Meeting 2014 in Davos and a hot topic not only in technology, but almost all sectors and industries.

Indeed, while innovation is today dominated by technological advances and discoveries, such innovations are not simply technical and they certainly can create great anxiety in businesses and governments. This is a small price to pay, however, for the potential benefits.

Innovative ideas are per se disruptive. And disruptive ideas often fill niches or fulfil needs that are identified at the base of traditional power pyramids—among consumers living hand to mouth, or citizens who feel disenfranchised from existing spheres of influence. Through disruptive technologies, citizens are also able to organize themselves and ideas can percolate upwards. Ideas exist in emerging markets that have applications in other contexts.

But to truly take advantage of the changing landscape, business and government leaders can do more. Knowing that more disruption is on the way, they need to prepare for it and be vigilant against its risks, but also be bold and decisive in embracing the power of disruptive innovation. New approaches, business models, and partnerships are essential, and technology can be the enabler.

The new generations of leaders are key in implementing innovative agendas. In this perspective, the organization's Forum of Young Global Leaders represents a unique, multistakeholder community with more than seven hundred exceptional young leaders sharing a commitment to shaping the global future. The World Economic Forum has been running the program since 2006. What have been the challenges and the successes?

With any community, encouraging engagement is key. The Forum of Young Global Leaders community gives its members a peer network that challenges them to be better leaders in both their personal and professional lives. It is a support system that questions and constantly pushes its members to not only do more, but to be more too.

Refining the selection process, recognizing that not everyone will want to conform to a model, and also helping people when they have passed through the program en route to their next life stage or career role are all important. The key is to challenge them to turn their influence into impact and transform their success into significance through initiatives and innovations, both small and large.

The level of collaboration we have been able to produce is quite impressive, and one of the biggest successes of the program. Examples of large-scale collaboration among previous participants include: Deworm The World, which has helped forty million kids to succeed in school by treating parasitic worm infections; the Global Dignity Initiative, through which leaders in over fifty countries talk to high-school students about the human right to lead a dignified life; and Table For Two, which tackles obesity by encouraging healthy meals that subsidize school meals for malnourished children.

"The Internet helps all nations, no matter their political orientation," Rod Beckstrom writes in a World Economic Forum blog.[1] *He argues: "We may disagree on some aspects of its use, but most of us recognize the importance of keeping it working. Even those who hack and attack know that without the Internet, they couldn't achieve their broader political, social or economic*

goals." Indeed, the very nature of this new digital world has risks: cyber attacks, conflicts—ethnic, social, or economic in nature— and political tensions threaten our world. As we become more and more dependent from it, the web helps hold it together. So how do we strengthen and safeguard it?

We are not a lobbying or advocacy organization, and so we provide a platform for discussion amongst key stakeholders. One increasing concern is "digital protectionism," as the initial promise and "trust" in the neutrality of communications technology gives way to suspicion and security concerns.

In our 2014 Global Risks Report,[2] we identified "digital disintegration" as one of the three risks in focus. So far, cyberspace has proved resilient to attacks, but the underlying dynamic of the online world has always been that it is easier to attack than defend. The world may be only one disruptive technology away from attackers gaining a runaway advantage, meaning the Internet would cease to be a trusted medium for communication or commerce.

Two main twin trends demand new thinking about global governance of the Internet. First, the growth of the Internet of Things means that ever more devices are being connected online, touching many more parts of life and widening both the potential entry points for and impacts of disruption. Second, there is ever-deepening complexity of interactions among the many aspects of life that are dependent on connected devices, making those impacts potentially harder to predict.

Fresh thinking at all levels on how to preserve, protect, and govern the common good of a trusted cyberspace must be developed. Indeed, in today's hyperconnected world, a threat to the Internet increasingly means a threat to everything.

A critical element in advancing this discussion will be improving the collective ability to measure the economic impact of cyber risks, at all levels—within individual businesses, nationally and globally. Effective methods for measuring and pricing cyber risks may even lead to new market-based risk-management structures, which would help in understanding the systemic interdependencies in the multiple domains that now depend on cyberspace.

As the Internet keeps evolving and expanding, the world is focusing on mobile technologies making billions of people at reach. What are the opportunities at stake in terms of communicating with such a big audience?

Audiences are always local even when issues are global. You have to make your subject matter relevant and worthwhile to those audiences, be open to constructive criticism and true to your purpose. That is advice that would be recognized by writers from Thucydides to Ezra Klein.

NOTES

1. Rod Beckstrom, "Build a Safer Internet for a Safer World," *The World Economic Forum* (blog), last updated June 14, 2013, http://forumblog.org/2013/06/build-a-safer-internet-for-a-safer-world/.

2. The World Economic Forum, *Global Risks 2014 Report*, http://www.weforum.org/reports/global-risks-2014-report.

10

ENGAGING THE WORLD

A conversation with Stéphane Dujarric, Spokesperson of the Secretary-General of the United Nations, and Deborah Seward, Director of Strategic Communications, Department of Public Information, United Nations

At the 2014 World Summit on the Information Society (WSIS), more than 1,600 participants, including around one hundred representatives from governments and leaders from international organizations, from business, civil society, and academia met to discuss and set priorities for the post-2015 development agenda. "Information and communication technologies have long been recognized as key enablers for bridging the digital divide and achieving the three dimensions of sustainable development: economic growth, environmental balance and social inclusion," said Ban Ki-moon, secretary-general of the United Nations. "We must do everything in our power to increase access to ICTs and broadband connectivity across the world, including reaching people in remote areas, land-locked countries, small island developing states and the least developed countries. This will empower millions of people and enable us to meet our development goals in the post-2015 era," he continued. How has the digital age changed the way the UN looks at the most pressing issues around the world?

Deborah Seward: The digital age is offering us an unprecedented opportunity to reach billions of people at the same time, with the same message, in different languages, in the north, and in the south. Before we could only reach one audience at a time. This is an extraordinary opportunity for everybody to hear the same thing, on an equal footing, at the same time, from the source and with no distortions. At the United Nations, we're trying to make sure that our digital platforms, in addition to the more traditional ones, are used for a uniformed message so that the public can hear it, see it, or read it in many different ways but in real time. It's really important for us to reach all our audiences, no matter their time zone or location in the world, at the same time as people here in New York. It's also important to share information and reach those people who might not otherwise be able to know what it is that you're talking about. Although the UN runs its campaigns and runs its information on lots of different platforms, the purpose is really the same everywhere and that is to communicate the ideals and the work of the organization simultaneously in all our six official languages.

Stéphane Dujarric: The flip side of our broadcast capabilities through digital channels is the ability to listen, to hear, and to observe what happens and what is being said. That helps us stay more credible and, in a sense, stay more focused. However, when it comes to the UN's global accounts on the various social media platforms, it might be challenging to apply a two-way communication strategy. While those are the most impressive in numbers, there's a local component—and in different languages—in most of the platforms, where numbers are a bit easier to manage giving us the ability to really listen and understand what goes on in local and regional communities, even in rural areas.

A second important component is how technology is used for development and development communication. The UN has ground-breaking programs. Global Pulse is one of our flagship innovation initiatives centered on big data. It was established based on the recognition that digital data offers the opportunity to gain a better understanding of changes in human well-being, and to get real-time feedback on how well policy responses are working. It mirrors what technology giants like Google and Amazon have been able to do in terms of analyzing people's digital exhaust for commercial purposes—being able to tell customers what they want to buy before they even know it, based on your previous purchases. In the same way, Global Pulse is focused putting big data to work for sustainable development purposes. Global Pulse is working to determine what kinds of digital data sources and patterns can provide insights on what is happening in developing countries and in rural areas, and provide early warning of emerging vulnerabilities. New technologies allow for faster, more convenient, and more cost-effective ways of collecting and transmitting information. In Uganda, for example, a Global Pulse pilot analyzes data from public Facebook posts and responses collected through UNICEF's mobile-phone-based citizen-reporting system, that a quarter of a million Ugandan young people use, to monitor emerging topics and perceptions related to family planning and other health issues. This gives you the ability to intervene early if negative trends begin to emerge, and shape local health-service delivery. Programs like the one in Uganda are really leveraging the penetration of mobile technologies in developing countries and using it for development purposes. Years ago this type of real-time monitoring would not have been possible as we would have had to rely on reports from people on the ground, or on costly survey data collected locally—it could have then taken more than a year to collect and analyze data and sort out a plan of action to counteract a crisis. In Indonesia, for example, the UN is working with the government to analyze patterns of words related to food security that people are using on social media. The analyses can help provide early warning of community-level concerns about the rising price of food or other staple items. Analysis of habits and changing patterns on social media can help us monitor, or "take the pulse," of various development issues in real-time. We are using technologies that allow this kind of analysis to be done in privacy-protecting manner. The social media content is aggregated to reflect community or national level trends, not revealing any personal information.

On one side, a number of UN agencies, including UNICEF, are forging partnerships with technology and mobile companies to help put out messages around development issues. On the other side, other agencies like UNFPA and UN Women are collaborating with telecommunication companies on a number of programs: one, for example, helps mothers of newborn children ensure a healthy development of their children even in the most early stages of life when they go back to their villages, as professional midwives are able to keep in touch with the new mothers through mobile technologies. Those programs often require telco companies to either lower their rates or to offer pro-bono services. The UN is developing many innovative new programs, but clearly the role of technology companies is key.

The World Summit on the Information Society as well as all other summits and meetings organized under the UN umbrella show the growing role of civil society in the policy-making process. In the participatory age, technology and real-time communications have allowed civil society a bigger and better involvement in international fora like the UN. How has the UN embraced technology and social media to partner with civil society organizations in order to increase its reach and the success of its campaigns?

Dujarric: It is about using our civil society partners to amplify our message and to reach deeper into society. It is a critical partner for the UN because they have the local roots and knowledge that the UN may not always have. It's a partnership that leverages civil society's local reach and the UN's international experience to craft a better message and to understand what happens on the ground.

Seward: It is about enhancing our ability to share messages with civil society and for them to share our messages. It is also about better coordination that potentially expands our ability to reach locally and strengthens the partnership with those organizations that are working with the UN on any specific issue.

One of the most successful campaigns we ever did actually started locally in partnership with civil society. It started in Colombia. It started as a very simple idea: rolling up your pant leg and show people the impact and the effects of land mines in one of the mine-affected countries in the world—Colombia accounts for more than ten thousand recorded deaths and injuries from land mines since 1990. Partnering with local nongovernmental organizations in Colombia back in 2011, we were able to bring that issue to the public in Colombia. A year later, working with nongovernmental organizations, we were able to bring the land mines issue to people in more than seventy countries. Those are the kind of campaigns that might originate locally, with simple ideas, but in which technology can play a key role in amplifying the reach.

Dujarric: The campaign to ban land mines started as a civil society initiative before even social media platforms and digital technologies evolved. Technology, however, helped ramp up momentum, and increased the speed at which local and regional campaigns happened and spread out around the world.

The land mine campaign shows how technology has become a key component in the development agenda. We now see websites like Avaaz, a platform that helps organize citizens of all nations through online petitions. It shows in a way where there is noise saturation: the technology has empowered people. It has enabled them to have a voice and to organize campaigns, but the threshold to start a campaign is very low, anybody can do it. Sometimes I worry that the more important campaigns maybe get drowned out by the more trivial ones. Avaaz offers a great platform, but it offers it to just about anybody. That is a sort of gray area that we need to take into account.

The secretary-general has been championing the role of new technologies and innovation in the foreign policy arena since the beginning of his first mandate. In 2011, he became the first UN secretary-general to host a social media live event on Twitter, Facebook, Weibo, and other platforms (http://www.un.org/sg/askthesg/). The response was quite astounding, with almost six thousand questions received in all six official languages—Arabic, Chinese, English, French, Russian, and Spanish—as well as in Portuguese and Swahili. How has the UN evolved in its use of social media since then?

Seward: What's really important for us is that we are looking at social media not just in terms of straight communications, but in terms of substance. We want to have people who are working on social media who are very familiar with the subject matter, whether it's development, peace and security, or human rights. They are telling stories about their daily work, about what they do every day. It's not just communications, or people who are learning about a given subject. That helps you the voice to be authentic. Also, our goal is not having gigantic numbers. The goal is to be able to engage and to provide the information that people who support and want to work with the UN are looking for. As a result of that approach, the numbers have just continued to grow. For example, the Twitter account—which will soon approach three million followers—only three years ago had two hundred thousand followers. That is not because we're going out promoting and broadcasting, but because we are engaging and providing the information that is valuable to the people who want to know about the UN. To that extent, it's a very powerful way for us to communicate because it's about having the people who work for the UN write about the UN.

The way we get resources for our social media presence is something that's transforming the way that we do our work. We haven't received any additional resources that have been given to us by the member states. We haven't had an increase in budget. We had to really think ahead about where we can get the resources, what kind of resources they are, and what the purpose to use them is. Ultimately our goal is to enable and to help the leadership and the organization fulfill its mission. To that extent, we have taken resources—human resources, staffers for the most part—who have expressed an interest in social media. We also kept our focus on the content. It's also critical to think about how well we write our content: for us it's about storytelling. Everything that we do, the stories that we are telling, whether it's in 140 characters, or on Facebook, or through videos or podcasts, is about the story. Every aspect of the process is about bringing together the people and resources that we have at our disposal so that we can put out stories that are authentic and that portray the daily work of the UN. Content is now being produced on social media, so we have to constantly look about new ways of storytelling beyond broadcast television, radio, feature pieces. The way we are going to interact will keep evolving, and that's why we need to open ourselves and our minds up.

Dujarric: One of the things that social media has enabled us to realize is that there is a great thirst for information about the UN, about its work and the ideals of the UN charter. When you work within any large organization, you tend to be a bit more cynical that the general public. You don't always think that the people care about the work they do. On a more personal level, to know that people are actually interested in your work really helps you keep the focus and care about the priorities that you're given by the leadership. It helps knowing that people in China, for example, are very interested in UN peacekeeping and environmental issues. It helps knowing that people in Indonesia share the same values engrained in the UN charter. Social media and digital tools help us do our job better and at the same time meet that information hunger we see around the world, in ways that we've never been able to do before.

How would you define the secretary-general's relation with social media? Why has he decided not to open a Twitter profile or a Facebook page, following the very successful examples of some of the heads of the largest UN agency, including Helen Clark at UNDP, and international organizations like Christine Lagarde of the IMF?

Dujarric: We are very fortunate to have a secretary-general who's open to try new things and new ideas. We experimented with all sorts of different projects for him. Our first live social media event was very successful, but it was also a huge risk. It had never been done before on the same scale with any senior UN official. I think part of the success—with the first one and any subsequent live conversations—is linked to the secretary-general's authenticity and his willingness to take risks. People on social media feel that. Half of the battle is really to connect with your followers and to engage, to pay attention to them, to what they say. It's a fantastic frame of mind that the secretary-general has. The fact that he's a big risk-taker is in itself a big responsibility on our part, as we need to fully understand what we are planning for him and how it can affect the UN agenda and the relationships with member states and with our audiences worldwide.

The reason the secretary-general doesn't have personal social-media accounts loops back to him wanting to preserve his authenticity. Because of his daily agenda and frequent travels, he would not be able to spend the time he thinks is appropriate for him to be personal and engaging on social media. His personality would not fit a daily presence on Twitter or Facebook—and he would not be the same having his staff tweet on his behalf, even if that happens for many world leaders. The reason Helen Clark is so popular is because they know it's her. I worked at UNDP when Helen Clark started her Twitter profile. She has been very present since the very beginning. If you follow her on Twitter, it's clearly her, sometimes tweeting on a very personal level. She might go to a show or exhibit and tweet about it. It definitely brings a human face to the organization and its leader. For the secretary-general to have an account that is managed by someone else on his behalf would detract from the overall experience—his experience as the person who tweets and that of his followers worldwide. It would also bring inauthenticity to an account that would need authenticity in order to be engaging and meaningful. I think it's to his credit that he's not doing something that he wouldn't be able to dedicate himself fully. His LinkedIn profile, however, is a bit different as it does not require everyday interaction. It's about a policy debate, rather than daily engagement. For the secretary-general as an opinion leader, LinkedIn fits his personality better.

What's your experience of being the voice of the secretary-general online and offline? Do you have a different approach online as opposed to offline?

Dujarric: We have taken the decision from the very beginning not to use our spokesman Twitter account to engage in conversations with journalists who are not based at headquarters. We use it to disseminate information. That is because I have a responsibility toward the press corps that serves at headquarters—journalists and media outlets that are investing time and resources to be present in New York, at our briefings—to tell our side of the story. Our Twitter profile is a way to get the message out, but we continue to engage with journalists in a more traditional way. For what I've seen, that's what a lot of the large institutions are doing. I don't see many public conversations between the White House spokesman account and journalists around the world. We're still a little bit old school in that sense because we really want to make sure that our relationship with the media here in New York is well serviced.

As you mentioned, the UN main Twitter profile has reached almost three million followers. The Facebook page has a little over 1.1 million. The UN manages a total of eighteen Facebook pages, twenty-five Twitter profiles, two Tumblr blogs, two LinkedIn pages, including that of the secretary-general, and accounts on YouTube, Pinterest, Google+, Flickr, Instagram, Weibo, and other local platforms. With over 3.5 million total followers on all Twitter profiles and over one million likes on all Facebook accounts, the voice of the UN is heard all over the world. Everyone with a computer, a tablet, or a mobile phone—there are six billion mobile phones in the world, according to the International Telecommunication Union (ITU), almost six times higher than people with access to clean drinking water—and Internet connection can hear what the UN has to say and engage with the organization. What are the challenges and responsibilities of such a huge reach worldwide?

Seward: We are a multilateral organization and that presents challenges in itself. We don't interfere, intervene, or discuss issues at a local level unless the UN is involved. For example, if somebody contacts us on our social media accounts on election irregularities in their country, we would not necessarily be able to address any concern unless the UN was involved. On the other hand, some of the most interesting things come when people are writing to us about situations that we can use to inform them on the work of the UN. It helps us address questions about the working of peacekeeping operations, how they are created, and the role of the Security Council. What we found is that people, no matter where they're from, are very interested in knowing about the UN, about how the funds they contribute to the UN are used, what is the impact of those funds, whether or not a particular country contributes to peace operations. Also, social media can be used to explain complex issues. Not only issues related to sustainable development—which is per se not an easy topic for people to understand—but also other priorities for the UN, including electoral assistance, preventive diplomacy, and media-tion. The goal is to reach the public at large and all actors. They need information and they need to know how they can interact and with whom they can interact, and all of this has to happen in real time.

While social media allows you to reach out to new publics, you have to be very conscious of the need to not abandon traditional media. There are places in the world where there is no electricity. There are people in the world who have no phones. There are people who cannot read and cannot use social media.

I would look at this in terms of opportunities, but there are chal-lenges. One that is faced by everybody—not just by the United Na-tions—is about measuring the impact of what we are doing on social media. That is a huge challenge. Analytical tools are invaluable also at understanding what platforms we should use and where we still need to improve to increase our engagement. There are a lots of platforms out there, and you cannot be everywhere. We need to identify what plat-forms are best for a given message. We believe we have to make choices. There are organizations that are present on almost every social media platform, but the risk is that you end up doing none of them particularly well. We work very hard to make sure that we chose the best platforms for our messages and our leadership. What fits the people of the UN best; what fits our stories best.

The final thing we see as both a challenge and an opportunity is that as UN we have to take responsibility for the information that we put out there. It has to be balanced. It has to be impartial, and it has to be right. This is when you have to be particularly attentive, as we are a big organization that runs real-time programs. We take our time to make sure that what we try, we end up doing very well. You want to have a standard of excellence, but at the same time we want to try new ways and new platforms. We don't have a laboratory, and we don't have seed money. What we have is people who are passionate about their work and about the organization and its mission. There's a lot of collaboration and consultation to think about all the way around our ideas before we move forward, and so far we were able to manage the process well.

Dujarric: All of us who are involved in social media have made big mistakes at some point, sometimes very public mistakes. My first day as spokesman for Ban Ki-moon, I wanted to do something different, and I wound up making a huge mistake on Twitter on his behalf. The news cycle moves very quickly, and fortunately very few people picked it up. But I had to apologize to the secretary-general on my first day as his spokesperson. Thankfully, he was very gracious about it. Mistakes happen. It's like trapeze without a net. As managers we have the responsibility to have the right people dealing with social media channels, but we also have to make sure that we back them up when mistakes occur. It is a risk-taking endeavor, and mistakes are public and can possibly affect many people very quickly. Social media communicators and staffers need to have the right managers who are able to support them throughout the entire process, even when mistakes happen.

THE POWER OF THE HASHTAG

A conversation with Chris Messina, Godfather of the Hashtag

*The new chief digital officer at **The Metropolitan Museum of Art** in New York, Sree Sreenivasan, formerly at Columbia University's Graduate School of Journalism, defines what he calls the "dirty secret of social media" as follows:[1] "almost everyone will miss almost everything you do on social media."[2] While this is true about all forms of media, including journalism—social or not— tools like Twitter and Facebook can help direct attention in ways that were not possible before. How have hashtags changed social media and the way people interact with each other?*

First, that: *"everyone will miss almost everything you do on social me-dia"* isn't a dirty secret; it's self-evident to anyone who's *tried* to be heard in the sea of voices out there today. At the same time, this isn't new: if you scream your head off at an arena show (say, at a Nickelback concert), you're going to be equally drowned out (unless you happen to be on stage with the mic). Thus people who succeed on social media are hyperaware of context and the limitations of today's consumption tools; they rely on a number of channels to gain influence, and don't only try to say things that will resonate on social media—they take a broader view when it comes to spreading their views or ideas.

What's the history of the hashtag from your famous August 2007 tweet[3] "how do you feel about using # (pound) for groups. As in #barcamp [msg]?" to today?

I'd been thinking about the problem of creating more topical tweets and ad-hoc group formation for a little while. As it happened, there was a large BarCamp event happening in Palo Alto in August 2007 called BarCampBlock,[4] and I wanted a way for people to share their experiences and comments on Twitter. I posted that tweet to get feedback for a blog post[5] I'd been planning to write to introduce the concept of "tag channels" for Twitter, based on IRC and Jaiku. It was really very casual—just a kind of "Hey Twitter friends, what do you think about this?" I got a few positive (and negative!) responses, and incorporated them into my post.

On June 10, 2013, Hillary Clinton debuted on Twitter:[6] "Thanks for the inspiration @ASmith83 & @Sllambe—I'll take it from here . . . #tweetsfromhillary." She approached the micro-blogging platform with a dash of humor, as in her profile she describes herself as "hair icon, pantsuit aficionado, glass ceiling cracker" among other things. She appealed to a young and mostly tech-savvy audience by thanking Adam Smith and Stacy Lambe, the creators of the blog "Text from Hillary," for their inspiration. On top of that, her use of the hashtag #tweetsfromhillary opened not only a trending conversation on Twitter, but also a flow of speculations over her future. The tweet was retweeted almost 11,000 times and favorited more than 6,700 times. Can we say that her first hashtag emerged as the strategic key to a very powerful tweet?

That, or she was signaling her awareness and desire to conform to the norms of the network she was joining. There are plenty of politicians who join social media—Twitter or otherwise—because they think it's just another "channel to be on," but social media (as the "social" implies) is about two-way communication and conversations. Using a hashtag in her opening missive started a conversation that didn't necessarily end with her having the final word, and that's a big shift in the political discourse that points to *ongoing media conversations*, rather than the episodic "gotta get it right the first time" publishing paradigms of the past (like the newspaper). In this case, publishing is a fluid activity that evolves over time, and never truly ends.

When a former US secretary of state rumored to possibly run for the White House for the second time in 2016, possibly one of the most well-known politicians around the globe, uses a hashtag in her first tweet ever, it's safe to say that the very meaning of the hashtag has reached beyond social media into the political discourse, as well as the way leaders address their constituencies and their audiences, at home and abroad. What is the role of hashtags in today's politics?

Well, while Hillary (or her staffers) deserve credit for joining Twitter, since June 2013, she's only followed nine people, and has never favorited, replied, or retweeted anyone! There's still quite a ways to go before she—and other politicians (in particular)—develop public, open, discursive relationships with their social media audiences.

But, while she hasn't fully embraced the two-way, conversational nature of Twitter (most of her tweets appear to be mini blog posts or public acknowledgments of people she likes or wants to raise the visibility of), she has garnered almost 1.5 million followers—which is no simple feat. But what is she to do with it?

Ultimately, there is an opportunity here to set the example of what democratic speech looks like when everyone has a tiny Gutenberg press in their pockets (i.e., their phones!). Now that you really can hear from a much broader constituency (at least those with access to digital publishing tools—as basic as SMS), the possibility to become more responsive to local politics and needs is enormous, giving leaders a way to customize government to different constituent needs, much in the way that a network administrator gleans insights from a range of network users, and is able to plan capacity, access, and capabilities better. It's hard to do, and unfortunately there haven't been too many examples of success thus far (Facebook dabbled in being a "democratic company responsive to its users desires" at one point, but eventually decided to rely more on data than speech), but it's worth continuing to experiment in active listening via social media and other channels.

The art of the hashtag—just like Twitter and any social media tools—is a learning process. However, only few are going through it as most cabinet ministers, diplomats, and politicians tend to leave their social media duties to well-trained—and often young—teams of communicators and digital strategists. Even President Obama, who signs his tweets "BO," has posted personally very few tweets since the beginning of his first campaign and later as president. What are your thoughts on using social media personally vs delegating to your team?

I'm of two minds about this: historically I would have emphatically encouraged original content creation and participation—access and direct engagement, after all, are the promises of social media! But I'm also a pragmatist who recognizes the enormous growth of social media in the last several years, and the difficulty of responding thoughtfully to everyone that wants to talk to you. Social media, therefore, is just another source of signal for people in positions of power.

That said, what you put into social media—in terms of time, attention, and engagement—will often come back to you, sometimes magnified. If you create content that's interesting, valuable, and responsive to your audience—or actually demonstrates meaningful interaction with your constituents—you may find that they become useful defenders and advocates in contexts where you may otherwise be underrepresented.

As you say, "the art" is in understanding the medium and the native behaviors in order to participate successfully. And sometimes that means hiring people closer to these communities in order to do it well.

As we see more and more hashtags like #Egypt and #Syria, what do you think is now the role of hashtags in foreign policy?

There's still a need for tools to cut through the noise and make sense of what's going on when hashtag conversations erupt on the scene. Andy Carvin[7] has served as a kind of human information routing machine through many of these occasions—bringing levity and human insight where algorithms fail or can be gamed. Thus hashtags are simply a signaling mechanism—making it possible for more content to be associated with a certain topic, but do little to determine the relative value, relevance, or import of the content itself. So, you have more voices, but the age-old problem of providing editorial oversight, context-setting, or meaningful interpretation.

When it comes to foreign policy—hashtagged media (i.e., media that a user has tagged with some additional public, textual metadata) can be useful for getting a sense for what's happening *right now, on the ground*. It shouldn't necessarily dictate policy, but it should be used as a signal to *inform* it or guide it. It's unclear what the *absolute* power of tagged social media should be, only that it does exist now, is part of the landscape of public opinion, and can be useful for drawing from a wide range of perspectives *at a moment's notice*. Given that it's also pan-media, you don't need to restrict your investigation to Twitter—you can look at Facebook, Google+, Instagram, Vine, and any other network that supports text content.

Certainly it is just another source of information to lean on when making policy decisions, but the thing that's really incredible about it (in my view) is that you can always trace back to the source of something that's been published, and even compare and contrast different viewpoints that might have informed a certain decision. In this way, permalinks become part of the public record and provide a way to go back and examine the conversation when information hadn't completely diffused, to see how it evolved over time. You can look back to tweets or content that seemed significant at the time, but eventually proved to be minor in the scheme of things, with the inverse phenomena being likely as well.

Building on this point, another way to understand what I'm saying is to consider *nonhashtagged* content alongside contemporarily published *hashtagged* content. The latter is likely to be more accessible and dis-coverable with less effort, especially using unsophisticated search tools. So—if you want to be part of the public record and be counted in the history of some conversation that evolves through social media, the better you are at tagging and adding metadata and context to your content, the more visible your content will be, over time.

So—while there's clear reason to hashtag your content *in the mo-ment*, there's a latent benefit, which is that it becomes more valuable (and perhaps more relevant!) over time too!

*Hashtags for good vs hashtags for evil. Following the ban of Twit-
ter and YouTube in Turkey in the spring of 2014, many hashtags
started to manifest themselves on social media, including #Twit-
terBlockedinTurkey and #TurkeyBlocksYoutube. In the same period, during the Ukrainian crisis and Obama's trip to Europe for a
G7 meeting in March 2014, the US State Department launched
the #UnitedforUkraine hashtag together with many European
countries, generating a large volume of conversations on social
media. Is there such a thing as good or evil when we talk about
hashtags?*

Like most technologies, the hashtag itself is a neutral amplifier.
Wielded effectively, it can spark conversations or revolutions, or can be
used to mislead or obfuscate. Therefore, it's important to keep in mind
that social media is a reflection of the people who use it and the contexts in which they're found.

Broadly speaking, any technology that helps give a larger number of
people a voice efficiently and economically is a good thing; then, once
it's been adopted widely, the challenge is to hone its use to increase
social and cultural benefit. Hashtags are useful for targeting messages
and bringing together topical conversations. Whether the specific uses
are good or evil is a matter of perspective.

*Let me go back to Turkey's ban on social media—something that
citizens from many other countries are experiencing, including
Iran, China, and North Korea. In some of those countries, other
social media tools have evolved, like Sina Weibo in China, but the
use of hashtags is virtually the same. There's never been a ban on
hashtags. In some instances, hashtags have created an even better
conversation environment, and in some cases even veritable sub-
structures like Huati—which literally means topic—on Weibo, to
monitor the most popular hashtags and follow conversations
based on topic. What's your take?*

To understand this dynamic, you need to remember that the future has
arrived, it's just not evenly distributed yet. By that I mean that there are
people in positions of power with varying levels of technological sophis-
tication. In some cases, the availability of free social media represents

the same kind of threat that a free press does. In these contexts, the free press struggles to exist, and the same is often true of social media. When those in power are used to controlling how information flows, the hypersonic speed of information through social media means that unverifiable information can spread unchecked. When a population has not built up a sufficient skepticism of what they read, such information can lead to instability or overreaction.

It's worth pointing out that the use of hashtags is still relatively new, and requires a great deal of technical proficiency and awareness. First, you have to really use a computer—more likely a mobile device. Then you have to be aware of the Internet and how it works, and then you have to understand how people consume and use social media. You then need to have some sense for the difficulty of targeting content on social media, or of having your content be found by others, and then you have to understand that the simple use of the # symbol will create a clickable link in your content. That's a lot to understand, let alone do effectively. Many of us take this knowledge for granted, but as I said, the future is here, it's just not evenly distributed—and this knowledge gap also plays into why people fear social media, and why they act to shut it down, or censor it. Some know very well what's at stake, and want to maintain their control over how information is shared and spread. Others, in seeking to control what they don't understand, act out of fear and ignorance—attempting to take away the advantage that others may have over them.

This is why digital literacy is so important—and I believe we are still at the very beginning of informing the world of what technology is, what it can do, and how to use it for the best possible outcomes for humanity.

"We have massive global awareness of Twitter, and we need to bridge that gap between awareness of Twitter and deep engagement on the platform," said Twitter CEO Dick Costolo during the company's earning call in February 2014.[8] *Some have linked the comments to speculations that Twitter might reinvent core features, including hashtags. In March 2014, Twitter's head of news, Vivian Schiller, rejected rumors that Twitter is phasing out hashtags and @replies—rumors that originated from her speech at the Newspaper Association of America mediaXchange 2014 event in Denver—but didn't elaborate on what the company is working on,*

according to BuzzFeed tech editor Charlie Warzel and editor in chief Ben Smith.[9] *What do you think is the next evolution of the hashtag? Do you see it evolving in the future?*

This statement is worth unraveling.

First, I can believe that Twitter wants to make aspects of Twitter easier to use and more friendly. That you can tag people and brands on Facebook, for example, by using their real or proper name rather than a username is perfectly sensible. For example, I'm @chris on Instagram, and most of my notifications these days come from people incorrectly mentioning me when they mean to mention someone else. One might expect that "@mentioning" someone is an obvious and easy thing to do—alas, you'd be wrong once you get into the longtail of usernames.

Secondly, topicality of content goes beyond hashtags. Even without a hashtag, smart text and image-processing systems can guess at what some content is about—but it's not perfect, and an explicit signal like a hashtag can make the difference between a poor content experience and a quality one. Would Twitter move away from the hashtag? I don't see why it would. Will it continue to evolve its service to compete with Facebook and Google+? Absolutely. Twitter doesn't own the hashtag, and it has to be aware of this (even if it would like to).

NOTES

1. Sree Sreenivasan, "Social Media Talk @DISummit #disummit," Digital Innovators' Summit, https://docs.google.com/presentation/d/16ZL2_o19ZZ3i_s4A5sZELuBtKh5_b9TuFNVsFWyCIpE/present#slide=id.i0.

2. Sree Sreenivasan, Twitter post, June 8, 2013, 11:27 a.m., https://twitter.com/sree/status/343388813843910656.

3. Chris Messina, Twitter post, August 23, 2007, 3:25 p.m., https://twitter.com/chrismessina/status/223115412.

4. Tom Conrad, "BarCampBlock," *Tom Conrad* (blog), last updated August 19, 2007, http://tomconrad.net/2007/08/19/barcampblock/.

5. Chris Messina, "Groups for Twitter; or a Proposal for Twitter Tag Channels," *Factory City* (blog), last updated August 25, 2007, http://factoryjoe.com/blog/2007/08/25/groups-for-twitter-or-a-proposal-for-twitter-tag-channels/.

6. Hillary Clinton, Twitter post, June 10, 2013, 12:44 p.m., https://twitter.com/HillaryClinton/status/344132945122054144.

7. Andy Carvin is editor at First Look Media. He was previously a senior strategist at NPR's social media desk, where he led NPR's efforts to integrate social media into the newsroom. He pioneered NPR's use of Twitter and Facebook in its reporting, most notably during the Arab Spring, during which he used social media to become a virtually embedded reporter among revolutionary groups. Collaborating with his tens of thousands of Twitter followers, he broke news from across the region, debunked rumors, and authenticated footage. For this work, Carvin won a 2012 Knight Batten Award for journalism innovation and was named Best Journalist on Twitter during the 2012 Shorty Awards. He was also a finalist for the *TIME* 100 List of the one hundred most influential people in the world. He is also the author of *Distant Witness* (CUNY Journalism Press, 2013), a book about his experiences using social media to cover the Arab Spring.

8. Seeking Alpha, "Twitter Management Discusses Q4 2013 Results—Earnings Call Transcript," last updated February 6, 2014, 8:40 a.m., http://seekingalpha.com/article/1998991-twitter-management-discusses-q4-2013-results-earnings-call-transcript.

9. Charlie Warzel, "Twitter Hints That At-Replies and Hashtags Are About to Be Streamlined," *BuzzFeed*, last updated March 19, 2014, at 12:41 p.m., http://www.buzzfeed.com/charliewarzel/is-twitter-phasing-out-hashtags-and-at-replies.

12

CONTENT MATTERS

A conversation with Lance Ulanoff, Chief Correspondent and Editor-at-Large, Mashable

To view clips
from the conversation
with Lance Ulanoff
scan the QR code
or visit:
http://goo.gl/ESTxUt

In the digital age, content—whether original, curated, or person-alized—has multiple facets, multiple stakeholders, multiple plat-forms, multiple ways of being consumed and repurposed. Today, content needs to be real time and changes constantly, growing by the second, spreading virally from servers to mobile phones and social media platforms. How's the digital age reshaping the idea of news gathering, reporting, and offering a viable, sustainable product—after all, content is a product—to the public?

We don't have control anymore. The standard media outlets used to be the gatekeepers for all information. That has completely changed. The advent of Twitter in particular has turned everyone into a citizen jour-nalist; people on the ground who can tell you what is happening in real time. That has changed the game for traditional media, which first had to race and catch up and then had to adopt some of these same tech-niques that these everyday people were using on these platforms and that are free and available to anyone.

While anyone can build a following, some people really do because for whatever reason, even though they are not trained journalists, they are kind of trained "watchers." They get it, and they do not hesitate, there is no waiting. In effect, there is almost no reporting because they see something and then they say something—sometimes they do not know when they are reporting. The best example is the raid that killed Osama Bin Laden in May 2011, as on that very night, one of the witnesses, Abbottabad resident Sohaib Athar, live-tweeted[1] the entire operation, without even knowing what was going on. He sort of became part of the story.

We use to have our reporting done, write a story, and then publish it. We still do some of that, but as technology changes how we work, how and when we publish our news, when a piece of news breaks and something big happens, we have to tell our followers in real-time. We are in a position of having to very quickly verify all information and then get the word out, as quickly as possible. Only later we follow up on the story with a richer report. This process has created these sort of "tiers." It has not destroyed journalism, but it has certainly changed our approach to news. In a way, it has made the process more organic, more visceral, and certainly more real-time and exciting. To succeed in this new environment, you have to have a different set of skills to compete, and media companies have to really embrace digital tools in order to continue to be part of the next generation of content sharers. I don't see it as a negative thing, I see it as just a twenty-first-century version of what has been going on for the last few hundred years.

It's hard at times to establish exactly what's content and what's spam, garbage. We're inundated every day with tweets, Facebook posts, photos, videos, and blogs that for anybody to focus on what to read and what to discard is becoming almost impossible. Is the digital era the era of digital garbage or of digital excellence? In other words, is the risk of becoming spam forcing media outlets— as well as any other organization, including governments—to focus more on quality content and information?

I think the focus on quality is ongoing. Most media companies who have been in this business for any amount of time have always thought about quality, just in different forms. What they deliver and how it looks to people might have changed, but the goal of producing high-quality information really never goes away.

We have a very clear understanding of the amount of garbage that exists on digital platforms. Sometimes it comes from little startups, sometimes it comes from third-party entities, sometimes it comes from people who really have no business sharing news and information—and they are weeded out pretty quickly. It's a very self-correcting business because, while it is super easy to create false information, it is really hard to hide the fact that it is false. The whole community jumps on it and tears it apart. The self-correction comes into play because people don't want to go through that anymore, they don't want to be corrected. Rather, they want to get the information right. Not only do the media companies have a goal of quality, the platforms drive people to it one way or another. The people who are nonsensical or without values start to get ignored, while the people who create highly sharable and valuable news on a consistent basis tend to proliferate and succeed.

As a media company, how can you describe to a government what content is and how governments can really change the way they produce it so as to allow them to switch from broadcasting a message to engaging their audiences, whether their own citizens or audiences abroad?

More and more, even here in the United States, the government—including the White House and its various entities—has started to create content that is less about telling you something. It is more about showing you something or sharing something that you are so enchanted by that you are going to eventually share it. They try to play the same game as other people on these platforms. I think this is a significant development because, once you start to provide your audiences with information that they enjoy, that they share with their network of friends and followers, then they start to look at you as something more than just a government. They now look at you as a source of a wider variety of information. This is when a government gets the opportunity to start to deliver information that is maybe more valuable or more important.

In this environment, however, transparency is going to be key. The best social media accounts have a high level of transparency. You know who the people are, you know what their goals are, you know the kind of information they are going to share. While usually a government lacks that transparency, it is indeed what people want; people demand it. If a government can appear transparent in its social media, then the content it provides has the potential to do much better.

It is certainly more difficult for governments where there's strife going on as the audience will see them completely avoiding any level of transparency. Their social media accounts—if they even have any—will either act as if nothing is happening, or they will be shut down in order to deal with people the old-school way, offline and through propaganda. Rather, governments that want to have a great and deep relationship with their constituents are going to have social media accounts that touch people emotionally, that connects with them on the issues they really care about in a variety of ways, just like a good media outlet.

I think people understand the role of government. They understand that it's not just about telling people things, it's not just about municipal work or bureaucracy. It is about protecting your citizens. Obviously, given the nature of government, not everything is going to be transparent, but people get why. There is not much they can do about people like Edward Snowden. But that tension between the need for transparency and the need for secrecy is never going to go away. There are always going to be people digging, and there is always going to be government withholding. As a government is not truly a media organization, it will not be 100 percent transparent, so it has to find smart ways to put out a message that has the potential to engage people with issues they care about. When someone does come forward with some information that they consider damaging or controversial, that is when a government has to step forward in a number of ways, including social media.

Whether the quality of information is increasing or not, the quantity is growing exponentially. What's your advice for government officials who are struggling to use online media content and social media content to feel the sentiment of their audiences, in a way to listen to the world out there? How can they be helped navigate this immense sea of tweets and social content?

If you think of a government like a company, then the president is a CEO. The most successful companies on social media have learned that a big part of it is about customer service. When someone mentions your brand, or in this case your country, on social media you want to see what that person is saying. In the case of a government, there is going to be a lot of chatter, but you are going to be looking for the things that you can pick out that are going to be representative of your message. Only then you can start engaging directly and responding. If you can respond publicly, all the better because people will notice. If you see it that way, it's basically a customer service job, and you have to have people actively listening to what is happening on social media, using hashtags or keyword searches. There are a number of different ways to do it, but it has to be real-time. Social media cannot wait twenty-four to forty-eight hours. Your audience—whether you're a company or a government—expects it to happen faster.

Mashable founder Pete Cashmore[2] *once said, "Content is not a scarce resource; attention is a scarce resource."*[3] *Has technology made it harder for us to focus our attention or rather it has made it easier to concentrate and minimize our efforts?*

It has hurt attention. People are more distracted than ever. Even the way that people interact with websites and their phones, or feed on social media, has changed. We used to get people really spending a lot of time on websites. Now they spend just a few minutes on one page, then they dance around to something different as they are essentially getting all their information directly from feeds like Twitter or Facebook. Those platforms take the reader to a dozen different places; the reader is all over the place, but no true central place exists any longer. There are very few people now who stick to just one subject and just think about that and consume all of that at once. People are all over the map, and they are really not always paying attention.

When it comes to governments communicating with their citizens and audiences, technology seemed to have forced an adaptation process that at times focuses more on the tool, the medium, and not on the content. The attention is also what others are doing— similar, I think, to what happens in the advertising industry.

I think people are obsessed with these tools. They are obsessed with the way Facebook and Twitter work. When the platforms announce a change, people freak out. This happens over and over again: people freak out, then they start focusing on the content again, and then they forget.

What do you think makes Mashable so successful?

I think Mashable understands its readers. I think it is often served as a proxy for their interests, even their beliefs, their desires. We try to guide our readers across a pretty broad set of topics, often with a little bit of a digital core, starting with social media and technology. We really wrap all sorts of content around that: national and world news, entertainment, and business. These are what interests our readers.

Also, we have always tried to stay true to our nature. We are generally a positive publication. We are not looking to tear people down, but we are looking to be very real and honest about what we see out there and keep people on the cutting edge because they like to be.

Mashable reports on politics and foreign affairs, as well, and the digital side of it, the way governments harness technology. How would you rate governments in their use of technology?

It's a big world. I know everyone says "it's a small world," but there are a lot of countries out there, and there is great disparity. There are some countries that get it; some small countries that get it, some big countries that do not. It tends to be the places that need it the most where you see it the least.

It is hard to put a grade on it. I think that the places where social media and digital tools haven't really flourished will succumb to the pressure from other places and from society to give in. In China, for example, they developed their own kind of separate platforms. In a way—accidentally, I suppose—it keeps them all together in one place with less intermixing with other people around the world. In Iran, on the other hand, whether or not the government is trying to be more open with their foreign audiences, the situation is different as you have the executive who appears to be more open than before and the clerics on the opposite end of the path. It could all just be shut down tomorrow and back to the Dark Age as usual.

Again, I couldn't put a grade on them, but I would certainly say that we have a long way to go before the world's governments really truly gets this.

Let's talk about the numbers behind content. Mashable does it very well. What's the role of analytics in the production of content? A tool I particularly like is the Velocity graph, a way to show how quickly—not just how much—people are sharing an article online.

Numbers tell us a lot about reader interests. However, you have to be really careful because there are certain things that you know will always get good numbers. If you only write with that in mind, you basically feed the monster that already likes your content, and you lose your ability to teach about new things and inspire. We are always looking for that new angle, that new story, the thing that people are not already talking about. We talk a lot about being unique and having unique content. Sometimes you will put unique content out, and the numbers will not be great. But you know there is an important story there, so you continue on that path, and eventually others sort of pick up on it and it becomes a thing. We also try to balance it. Yes, we want traffic because traffic is important. Yes, we want high acceleration on popular articles; that is also very important. We know how to do that in a way that is sort of a reflex for us. However, creating the hard news, the deep, rich pieces that can become a thing unto themselves—an event—that is a real goal for us. Having a situation where somebody reads our reporting and thinks "I have not read that anywhere else," and they feel compelled to share it, that is our goal. And we are getting more and more of that.

NOTES

1. Sohaib Athar, Twitter post, May 1, 2011, 3:58 p.m., https://twitter.com/ReallyVirtual/status/64780730286358528. Sohaib Athar, Twitter post, May 1, 2011, 4:09 p.m., https://twitter.com/ReallyVirtual/status/64783440226168832.

Sohaib Athar, Twitter post, May 1, 2011, 4:44 p.m., https://twitter.com/ReallyVirtual/status/64792407144796160. Sohaib Athar, Twitter post, May 1, 2011, 4:48 p.m., https://twitter.com/ReallyVirtual/status/64793269908930560. Sohaib Athar, Twitter post, May 1, 2011, 5:02 p.m., https://twitter.com/ReallyVirtual/status/64796769418088448. Sohaib Athar, Twitter post, May 1, 2011, 5:10 p.m., https://twitter.com/ReallyVirtual/status/64798882332278785. Sohaib Athar, Twitter post, May 1, 2011, 5:16 p.m., https://twitter.com/ReallyVirtual/status/64800262354763776. Sohaib Athar, Twitter post, May 1, 2011, 11:24 p.m., https://twitter.com/ReallyVirtual/status/64892915167657984.

2. Pete Cashmore founded Mashable in Aberdeen, Scotland, in 2005 at age nineteen. In 2009, Cashmore was recognized in Inc.'s "30 Under 30," *Forbes'* "Top 25 Web Celebs," and *The Huffington Post*'s "Top 10 Game Changers 2009." In 2012, Cashmore made *TIME* magazine's list of the one hundred most influential people.

3. Joe Clarallo, "So What Do You Do, Pete Cashmore, Mashable Founder and CEO?" Mediabistro, last updated August 19, 2009, http://www.mediabistro.com/So-What-Do-You-Do-Pete-Cashmore-Mashable-Founder-and-CEO-a10600.html.

13

THE NUMBERS BEHIND SOCIAL MEDIA

A conversation with Vincenzo Cosenza,
Social Media Strategist, BlogMeter

Social media tools are a necessary step for companies, govern-
ments, and nongovernmental entities in order to better their rela-
tions with their audiences, to improve services and products, and
to establish and nurture a dialogue. However, sometimes it's hard
for companies—and even harder for governments—to understand
exactly how social media can improve the overall experience for
both the user and the provider. Your "World Map of Social Net-
works," updated twice a year since 2009, is a good start to reflect
on how social media have evolved during the years and what im-
pact they have around the globe. Can you describe your metho-
dology and how has the map changed over the past four years?

I've collected data from public sources like Alexa and Google Trends
for Websites. These services show web traffic information—aka visitors.
I scrape them every six months. Then I visualize them using a world
map[1] edited in Adobe Illustrator.

Now, it's not easy to understand how big social-media platforms are
as everyone uses a different metric to describe its presence and growth,
often confusing users, journalists, reporters, and analysts. Some of them
base their analytics on the number of registered users, others on active
monthly users, and the more transparent platforms on the number of
daily active users. In this environment, comparing data becomes more
difficult. I believe, the most relevant way to compare all players is by

monthly active users—what analysts call MAU—from which you can get a better understanding on how many people have interacted with a given platform during the course of thirty days. That includes users that have logged in through the platform—on desktop and mobiles/tablets—as well as those who have logged into the platform through third-party applications.

Now, if you look at my map (see figure 13.1), it clearly shows how Facebook has conquered the whole world but also its struggle to win China, Russia, and Iran. Obviously, there are political issues to be solved. In Iran and China, the social network is banned, and people get access via virtual private networks (VPNs), establishing a virtual and anonymous point-to-point connection through the use of dedicated connections, virtual tunneling protocols, or traffic encryptions. In those countries, for instance, the only way to enter the market is an official agreement with governments and/or through a partnership with local players (i.e., Baidu, the biggest Chinese search engine).

Google Ideas, Google's "think/do tank," has launched several new technologies designed to help people in repressive regimes to access the Internet. "There are billions of people around the world living in environments that severely restrict their free expression," Jared Cohen, director of Google Ideas, told TIME *magazine in an interview in October 2013.* [2] *"We want to empower them to have access to the same Internet that the rest of us experience. We talk about how we have a responsibility to our users. That also includes people in Iran, North Korea, Cuba, and Syria where the challenges are so serious." Do you think Google's new tools are going to have an impact in the social media environment in China, Russia, and Iran?*

Every new tool aimed to help people overcome any repression of freedom of expression is welcomed, but usually they have a little impact. Today, only a small fraction of the population is aware of how to use a VPN, for example, but in the future, as technical knowledge of those tools and how to harness them will grow, also thanks to initiatives like those spearheaded by Google Ideas. I believe it's a question of cultural change.

Figure 13.1.   Vincenzo Cosenza's World Map of Social Networks from 2009 to today.

Scan the QR code or visit http://goo.gl/K5iXCG to see the interactive map.

Already the Iranian government has shown greater social media openness in a recent Twitter conversation between Jack Dorsey and Iranian President Hassan Rouhani. The latter said,[3] "My efforts geared 2 ensure my ppl'll comfortably b able 2 access all info globally as is their #right." Did you observe any change through the data you collect?

No. Unfortunately for some governments social media are an on/off switch to use as they like.

Facebook, according to the data you collected, was the dominant social media tool in 2013 with around 1.15 billion monthly active users. More than 100 million users in six months. Africa and Latin America are the largest continents with 346 million users, Asia (339 million), Europe (272 million), United States and Canada (198 million users). Facebook's the dominant social network in 127 out of 137 countries analyzed, even winning South Korea— one of the key Asian markets—from QZone. Twitter, with around 200 million active users, represents only one-sixth of Facebook. However, it seems to be the social media of choice for many world leaders, including Barack Obama, who counts more than 36 million likes on Facebook and around the same number of followers on Twitter. Can you describe the difference among the two in terms of reach?

Facebook has more than 1.15 billion monthly active users. It's the social network for the masses, it's a closed, but comprehensive and simple-to-use, environment for general people—it's a symmetric network where you can play, chat, share your experiences with video and photos.

Twitter has 218 million monthly active users. It's more like a news network for people that have something to say—an asymmetric network. It requires more time to build an audience, and generally it's perceived like difficult to understand. That's why many people join and then leave it: 100 million daily active users. User engagement is the real issue there.

Twitter will never be as big as Facebook, but it could be a useful and profitable niche social medium. If you take a look at the latest figures from the quarterly financial report, you will see an 8 percent decrease in timeline views/users.[4] It means that there's a lot of people whom it's not engaged. They log-in only sometimes; they read some tweet, but they are not really tied to the platform. To address this issue, they are trying to redesign the whole user experience, with the new design released in the spring of 2014.

In the meantime, they have to prove that they can be profitable. They have to convince businesses that their ads are effective. To do this, they have bought an ad platform called MoPub[5] that serves ads outside Twitter. So businesses can buy ads and reach Twitter users plus one billion mobile app users.

What makes it harder to engage on Twitter?

It's harder because basically news is less engaging than friends; because the platform is not designed to offer continuous stimulus to people. For example, visual notifications based on interests, alerts based on following, activities, and so on.

One of the most common questions when it comes to social media is about return on investment (or ROI as it's known among experts). Can you describe what social media ROI is and why it's so important to measure your presence and influence?

Given the standard formula—ROI = ($ Gain − $ Cost) ÷ $ Cost—it's important to understand that you can't measure the true ROI of social media for the same reason you can't measure the true ROI of mass media. What you can measure instead is the ROI of a specific action (i.e., a social campaign) on a specific place (like Facebook or Twitter). For example, you can measure the return on investment of shifting 10 percent of your customer service resources from a traditional call center to Facebook—what often is referred as social caring.

Although there is no silver bullet formula, without measuring, without analytics, you're lost. Measurement should focus on the relationship between the activity and the outcome. But the goal is always a business goal, not a social goal/metric (like the number of followers and fans). The right measurement framework starts with a business goal that you can measure with a business metric and subsequently a social metric.

Measuring social media happens in two different stages: the intelligence stage is when you gather analytics before you start the verification stage, after your social media or PR campaign, or after a particular event. In both cases, there are three main phases: relations analyses to locate and understand the networks of people following a certain account, a certain discussion, conversation, or theme (it's key at this stage to understand what strong or weak links can be created); conversations analyses to understand what topics are developing around a given product or brand; interactions analyses to measure the potential and the ability of a company or brand—or country, if we talk about governments—to enter new relations and nurture old conversations. Also, if in the Internet of forums, web pages, and blogs it was sufficient to analyze conversations, in that of social media, relations do not only appear as comments. Likes, shares, retweets, retumblrs, pins and repins, check-ins are all elements (often weak) that need to be taken into consideration to fully understand how healthy your brand is or how successful your campaigns are.

Measuring ROI for governments is certainly more complicated than for businesses and advertisers. Governments don't sell products but rather offer services to citizens. What would be your advice to governments to measure ROI as well as understand basic social media metrics?

Governments need a measurement culture. But their business objectives are good services for citizens. They can use social media in various ways: to drive citizens to use public services; to quickly respond to their questions; to engage them in useful conversations, even in time of crisis. All these goals are measurable if you adopt the right mind-set. My advice is obvious but often underestimated: start listening to citizens before you engage them.

Sometimes listening is hard. We're bombarded every day with information from various sources, including governments and social media. How can analytics help us focus our attention and better listen to our audiences?

Technology has given people a sort of sixth sense: we can now obtain data that helps us foresee future behaviors—both our own and of others. Companies use that sea of data to grow their business. Governments could do the same to understand the dynamics of bureaucracy and change them to better the services for our citizens. Citizens as well have a role, as in a data society citizens can have an impact on consumption, health, services.

When it comes to listening, both governments and citizens need to play a role. It's certainly not easy. In the past, listening and analytics tools were very basic. They offered simple statistics. Now there's a new breed of tools that are designed to offer better insights on what is important. They can offer a real-time view on what's trending, sentiment analysis, social competitive benchmarking. They let you discover who the most influential people to engage with are, or what are the pieces of content that might work best for your campaign.

Hopefully, in the future, extracting information from existing data sets will help decision makers to determine patterns and predict future outcomes and trends. But we're still not at that stage, yet.

NOTES

1. http://vincos.it/world-map-of-social-networks/.

2. Sam Gustin, "Google Unveils Tools to Access Web from Repressive Countries," *TIME*, last updated October 21, 2013, http://business.time.com/2013/10/21/google-digital-rebels/.

3. Jack Dorsey, Twitter post, October 1, 2013, 11:00 a.m., https://twitter.com/jack/status/385056531269427201. Hassan Rouhani, Twitter post, October 1, 2013, 4:24 p.m., https://twitter.com/HassanRouhani/status/385138174822850560.

4. Twitter, "Twitter Reports First Quarter 2014 Results," last updated April 29, 2014,https://investor.twitterinc.com/releasedetail.cfm?releaseid=843245.

5. Anthony Ha, Kim-Mai Cutler, and Ingrid Lunden, "Twitter Buys MoPub for $350M to Up the Ante in Mobile Advertising," last updated September 9, 2013,http://techcrunch.com/2013/09/09/twitter-said-to-acquire-mopub/.

II

The True Nature of Innovation

14

THE POWER OF IDEAS

A conversation with Lara Stein, Founder and former Director, TEDx and TED Prize

TED's Chris Anderson says the rise of web video is driving a worldwide phenomenon he calls Crowd Accelerated Innovation— a self-fueling cycle of learning that could be as significant as the invention of print.[1] In other words, the Internet is accelerating cycles of improvement through videos mostly, some going viral. It all starts with a crowd: the bigger the crowd, the bigger the impact and certainly the number of innovators in it. How would you describe these new ecosystems where innovation becomes viral and what do you think is the role of TED and TEDx in nurturing it?

Ideas are not born within you. They are found around you.

The whole concept behind the TEDx community of TED is the idea that the best ideas—those that can fuel innovation—come from within communities, and often start from very simple ideas. TEDx helped TED expand to a global community of nine thousand events in 1,200 cities taking place in 133 countries. Before TEDx, it wasn't really possible to hear some of these interesting ideas. What the web, videos, and social media have made possible is that today everybody has the opportunity to broadcast their ideas, with the potential for them to become viral. Inside the TEDx ecosystem of local communities, amazing innovative ideas find a platform to grow naturally and sustainably, having an effect at many levels: with the local community nurtured by a TEDx event; with a larger audience when videos of TEDx talks go online on the TEDx YouTube channel and are shared on social media; reaching a viral potential if they land on TED.com, the online platform of TED. Indeed, the most exciting part of the process is the impact those ideas are having on a very local level in the same environment where they originated from and that TEDx only helped nurture. Those kinds of stories are the most difficult to track as it's more challenging to really capture what the cause and effect are of each and every TEDx talk, especially when it's a very local and small-scale event.

The examples of how local simple ideas become viral are numerous. At the 2012 TEDxRiodelaPlata in Argentina, Jorge Ernesto Odon, a car mechanic, showed how he came up with an idea for a new way to deliver babies after watching how you can take a loose cork out of an empty wine bottle without breaking the bottle and using just a plastic bag.[2] With a very humble background, Odon was completely unknown before his TEDx talk. His invention had very little impact, if any. Today, his invention has been tested in some one hundred deliveries in Argentina and will now be taken to Africa, Asia, and Europe with the endorsement of the World Health Organization (WHO). In her address to the Sixty-fifth World Health Assembly in Geneva, Switzerland, Dr. Margaret Chan, director-general of the WHO, said about what is now called the Odon device: "[It] offers a low-cost simplified way to deliver babies, and protect mothers, when labour is prolonged. It promises to transfer life-saving capacity to rural health posts, which almost never have the facilities and staff to perform a C-section. If approved, the Odon device will be the first simple new tool for assisted delivery since forceps and vacuum extractors were introduced centuries ago."[3] Thanks also to his appearance at TEDx, his story has now been covered across the world by media like the *New York Times*,[4] the BBC,[5] and many more that wrote to us after watching his video at TEDx.

TEDxMogadishu is another clear example. Before its launch in 2012, Somalia was largely off limits to the media. The only stories coming out of the country were about the Al-Shabaab militant group[6] and the widespread violence. TEDxMogadishu opened the door to untold stories and unsung heroes: the chef who returned from London to open restaurants in Mogadishu; the young Somalian girl who returned from Canada to work with victims of gender-based violence and rehabilitate child soldiers; the first bank opening in Somalia; the first dry cleaners;

and the first flower shop. The discussion changed from violence to progress.

This kind of grassroots change has an effect not only locally, but also nationally, with both citizens and governments able to see the potential of what these local events are creating.

Sometimes nurturing innovation—and the millions of innovators around the world—is not enough. Sustainability is key. How can we ensure the sustainability of innovation?

I think there is always innovation. The biggest challenge is where those innovations get seen or heard. We live in a time, now more than ever in the past, where we have the technology to allow for those innovations to be seen and heard, to grow and spread. On the sustainability front, I think within local communities there does have to be an ecosystem of support. The brilliance of what the world enables, though, is that if these ideas get out beyond their local community, the sustainability will come from outside the community. What we do see with TEDx is a lot of collaboration. An idea gets presented at a TEDx event somewhere in the world and other TEDx organizers from other TEDx communities just happen to be at that event. Through their collaboration, the idea expands beyond borders.

Kakenya Ntaiya refused to accept the continued oppression of women in her Maasai village—so she built a school, the Kakenya Center for Excellence,[7] that's shifting gender expectations in her community. When Ntaiya spoke at 2012 TEDxMidAtlantic in Washington, DC, her talk went up on the TED.com platform.[8] The video went viral with over two million views, making her work with girls' education known to the public and to mainstream media. After her TEDx talk, Ntaiya was selected as a CNN Hero for 2013,[9] nurturing even further the sustainability of her work and allowing her to open more schools and reach more girls.

Often innovation is synonymous with technology. TED and TEDx prove that technology can be part of innovation, but the real necessary ingredients are ideas. "Ideas worth spreading," is TED's motto. What is the real power of ideas outside of technology?

Ideas fuel progress; with bad ideas there is no progress. The challenge is that these ideas have to have support in order to nurture. Then you can find ways for them to be exposed outside of their local ecosystem so that they get additional support. If they're good ideas, they can be leveraged in other communities that face the same challenges. Today, that is very possible. It's a question of whether the existing structure is willing to give those ideas a chance. That's what TED and TEDx do so well: they allow these ideas to have exposure that they might not necessarily have had otherwise.

In societies where innovation is encouraged, it becomes a fundamental right that happens anyway. In societies where basic human needs aren't being met, it's much harder to find a space for those ideas to flourish. What we've seen with the TEDx program is that in the developed world the role that TEDx plays is just to give a platform to ideas. However, there are many other platforms out there in the developed world that allow great ideas to bubble up, and environments, politicians, and policies to support these ideas. In communities where there isn't that kind of support, where basic human rights aren't being met, where there's a lack of basic amenities, the issues are much more difficult and the circumstances are more challenging. In those cases, what TEDx has done is to create the space where ideas can flourish organically, because it's nonpolitical, nonpartisan, and nonreligious. In many cases, like in the Middle East, where this space, this kind of dialogue, and these kinds of ideas don't tend to be prevalent, TEDx has enabled the creation of a safe space to allow these ideas to grow. In many cases, the regimes have been allowing TEDx events to happen precisely because the platform is nonpolitical, nonpartisan, and nonreligious. They have this confidence that the event will stay focused on innovation and ideas, not on political ideologies, revolutionary movements, or a Western approach. In this kind of environment, innovation and ideas are safe. Our approach has worked very well in many areas of the world, and there have been cases where it has worked exceptionally well. There have been communities, however, where it has been more challenging to keep an event just focused on the ideas and not politicize the ideas in any way. But for the most part, TEDx has enabled this safe space that allows ideas to flourish.

When you think about governments and bureaucracies, how can we find a safe space to nurture ideas and challenge ourselves, our officials, our political representatives, so to find ways to implement new ideas and organically learn from failures—rather than preventing failures and error to happen?

There are governments, and then there are governments.

In the Western world, it's difficult to find a safe space where you can nurture ideas. The innovative process and the nurturing of an innovative culture has to be nurtured from first grade. An innovative person, an innovative leader has to be nurtured from a very early age. I think a lot of educational systems beat it out of kids. Especially the more traditional, colonial educational systems are very structured. They are very much about conforming rather than innovating. For starters, government has to look at the education process, because if they really want to inspire innovators and nurture ideas, it's all going to start at school. It's all going to start with the whole way of thinking about how you learn and whether you're given flexibility within that learning process to become an innovator, to think about life creatively. The only way you can become an innovator is to be able to think about challenges from a lot of different perspectives and in a very creative way. I don't think a lot of Western education systems are inspiring that to the degree they could be. So if you go through the first twelve years of our educational process and change it to a point where you're actually growing innovators, then by the time you get to college, you've developed the kind of personalities that want to innovate and can do those things outside of the box. They're able to take challenges, think about them from different angles, and find sustainable solutions. They really become creative leaders. You also bring in different voices. The only way in life to find solutions to a problem is to be able to look at the problem from nontraditional angles and step outside of conformity. To many—and governments in particular—that represents a scary, threatening process. If you nurture innovative thinking and ideas from a very young age, then it eventually becomes part of the culture of government as well. Our political and bureaucratic leaders have to be willing to accept that innovation is going to happen, and they have to step outside this completely safe comfort zone into a place where they're willing to allow individuals to take risks, and embrace failures.

In early 2013 TEDx also landed in Iran, with TEDxTehran. Ideas are certainly worth spreading in countries like Iran where repression is a constant and freedoms are not enjoyed by all, rather by only few. In a country where the Internet is not free, where online videos are blocked by the regime, what can be the role of a nonpolitical platform like TEDx in planting ideas and helping them spread? What are the challenges?

One of the most interesting parts of TEDx is the cross-cultural exchange of ideas. Tehran is only one of many. The real possibility for TEDx is the idea that not only can you learn from people outside your normal traditional walks of life, your bubbles, and your existence, but you can also learn from people on the other side of the world, as technology has enabled so many TEDx events to be live streamed.

For example, early on we had an event in the West Bank, TEDxRamallah. For a whole variety of reasons, it ended up happening in Bethlehem. The talks were live streamed to around twenty countries in total, enabling people across the world to see the reality of what was happening in Ramallah. It happened to be the one time probably that the TEDx platform wasn't successful at keeping it nonpolitical, but I don't know if you can be in that part of the world and expect to stay nonpolitical. In addition, it was one place where it was very hard to create a safe environment, and the whole confluence of events that led up to it made the emotions of the speakers very high by the time they got to the event. For instance, Pulitzer Prize winner Alice Walker[10] was in attendance,[11] but it took her nine hours to get across the bridge into the venue. Indeed, a lot of pent-up emotions and, while we were able to create a very safe space, it wasn't nonpolitical.

We've had events very early on in Pakistan and Iraq. A volunteer at TEDxAmsterdam ended up using the TEDx platform to go back to his home country of Iraq—a country his family fled from—to host a TEDx event. He now lives there. He had to fight very hard to actually host the event, and he took the government on at so many different levels to get it to actually happen. He has many stories. For example, it's a tradition in Iraq, before any event, to play the national anthem; certain people have to be dressed in a certain way, and they have to be standing up. He was able to have young kids on stage, drummers and percussionists, dressed in jeans, to play the anthem in a nontraditional manner. It was a battle with the current regime. But it was his way of saying, "Fine, I'll play the anthem. I'll give you what you want, but you have to meet me halfway on this and let me do it in a nontraditional way."

There have been many instances where the TEDx platform has been able to host events in very challenging environments, including Afghanistan. In early 2014, we tried to have one in Damascus, Syria. It was going to be called TEDxUmmayadSquare—the domain name still exists but with no content. The organizer was accused of being a pro-Assad supporter, and an online campaign was mounted to stop the event from happening. There was a lot of social media targeting him. A Facebook page was launched to stop the event, and the hashtag #StopTEDxUmmayad followed.[12] In environments like that, by virtue of the fact that in order to host an event you have to get permission to actually host it, you could say that the regime was endorsing it and therefore had some influence over it. In this case, to my knowledge, they had no real input in this event, but because the environment was so politicized, just the fact that they were given permission was perceived as being a political bid.

What happened in Syria has happened in several other places. In Sudan for example, the 2013 edition of TEDxKhartoum happened when the situation in the country was getting worse. The government was clamping down. They felt the event was some kind of a threat to them. They went after the local organizers. They said that they didn't have the right certificate to hold the event and the right credentials, even though they indeed obtained all clearances in advance. Sudanese authorities showed up the day of the event, several speeches and talks into it. They pulled the power. It was a very emotional, difficult moment.

One place we haven't been able to pull off a TEDx event is North Korea.

There just has to be a champion within the local community. In Tehran, for instance, the event was really spearheaded by an American expat, an aide worker, in conjunction with a local physician. After the first TEDxTeheran, the organizer had to go back to the United States for personal reasons, but we tried to get his Iranian coorganizer to participate to a TEDGlobal[13] event so that he could have the TED experience and go back to hold a second Teheran event. Unfortunately, his visa to TEDGlobal was denied.

We have a very solid infrastructure within TEDx, and partnerships, both at local and international levels, are key. Our strategic partner is the Bill and Melinda Gates Foundation. They've supported me and TEDx since 2010, with the mission of launching TEDxChange,[14] and to bring TED programs to communities that might not otherwise have access. As part of their grant, we get to give scholarships to fifteen people to participate to TED conferences. That enables us to handpick key people in some of these more challenging regions of the world, or in areas where we want to strengthen the TEDx community. It enables us to cherry-pick people, invite them to the conference, and allow them to have the full TED experience, ready to go back home and locally implement the learnings from the conference in an effort to grow their local community, or to even host a TEDx event, a much stronger and better informed event.

What's most extraordinary about what TEDx has evolved into is that it's less about the talks, and it's more about the fact that this global community has now connected with one another. There's this ecosystem of TEDx organizers around the world that are very close to one another. They all are innovators and entrepreneurs, and they now all support each other—when we landed in Iraq with TEDxBaghdad, about ten TEDx organizers flew to the country to help. The platform has created this really global web of very passionate people that want to see this world changed for the better. They are very focused on doing it from a grassroots perspective.

The real power in the TEDx platform is the connections between the local organizers and their teams of volunteers. I think in the long term, it is really going to create this web of interconnectivity of powerful people who really have a similar DNA. I've said this a lot, and I really believe it: I think a lot of these people have more in common with each other than their next-door neighbors. They have a common DNA, they have a common way of looking at this world that is truly unique.

Going back to the challenges and the rewards in countries where ideas don't spread free, I think if politicians respect the TEDx platform, understand it for what it is, and give it the space to flourish, it could really become a powerful thing for these communities. They have to do it in a way that is very much hands-off, though. That's the biggest challenge, but in many cases we were able to be successful. Politicians tend to want to influence things, but the power of TEDx is not about politicians influencing it. It's about giving the organizers the space to allow these TEDx events to thrive, giving them space to set their own agenda, invite their own speakers, and allowing it to flourish. That's a very hard space for policy makers to live with because they are no longer in control. There's no possibility for them to control what's said and what's thought, and in some environments that's far more challenging.

Another big challenge is the absence of links between organizers and funding of a TEDx event. But that represents also one of the biggest successes of the platform. The way TEDx events are structured is that they are self-organized, so they've got to find their own funding; they've got to find their own venue; they've got to find their own speakers. Finding the ideas and the speakers is the easy part; finding the funding is very difficult—and finding funding that doesn't come with strings attached is even more difficult. One of the core problems of TED is that a funder can't speak on the TED stage, so there's a wall between fundraising and editorial. In a lot of environments, that is not something that comes naturally or that is not something that is acceptable. If you look at most conferences that happen in most parts of the world, somebody who funds is allowed to step on the stage and speak. A lot of what has been challenging, especially in third world countries or in the Middle Eastern regions, is training organizers to understand why that line is so important, why it's important for people who fund an event not to have an influence over the editorial side of it. It would be great if every local community organization and government could respect that and give these events some support, and then just stand back and allow them to flourish on the grassroots level, with a very independent voice. That's an environment where people feel free to express these ideas.

What's your favorite TEDx talk of all time, if any?

I don't really have a favorite. With thousands of TEDx talks and thousands of TEDx events, to single one out would really be unfair. We've had an event on a floating motel in the middle of the Amazon rainforest to talk about sustainability. We've had a series of TEDx events in shanty communities around Kenya, starting from Kibera, the largest squatter city in Africa and home to nearly a million Kenyans. We've had a TEDx event at the Sydney Opera House. We have TEDxYouth events where students are empowered to give their own TED talks or where schools are able to bring interesting voices into their local communities. They all have very different functions.

There are also TEDx events in corporations. For example, Samsung created a whole new corporate culture thanks to some fairly young guy fairly low down in the ranks, who was allowed to host a TEDx event within the corporation. It really was a change agent inside Samsung. Before, Samsung was very siloed, compartmentalized. TEDx was for the company a very organic way to allow people to come together across these silos. The same has happened in multiple corporations.

The presenting part of the TEDx structure has a series of rules, but those rules are flexible enough and are shifting. With the feedback from the community, those rules constantly evolve, but they're also successful enough to allow the format to go to any kind of environment. They can be localized in that environment, and create this very authentic event or platform for that local community. I think that is really what has made it successful—that it's authentic and based on structures that allow it.

What would be your advice to somebody who wants to organize a TEDx event or is going to be a speaker at a TEDx event?

There are great stories in your community. The most important part is finding those great voices. Most people who make it to the TED stage have an interesting background and have done a series of interesting things. We tell speakers that standing on the TED stage isn't about reading your resume. Really think about your body of work and focus on one or two things that are really innovative or really authentic, that can change your community in some way, big or small. Have a unique perspective on something that has already been presented or that exists but really try to find that unique angle—that's what will make your talk really interesting. And that's what TED is really all about, to find a new way of looking at an old idea or to find some way of tackling a problem with a new perspective.

The only way you're going to be successful in life is to be passionate about your ideas. Anyone who gets to the point of standing on the TED stage has gone through this long, hard road being passionate about something, eventually getting it to a point where the idea takes shape and flourishes. But it's also about failures. Most TED speakers have failed many, many times in their lives. We need to learn to embrace failure as part of the journey.

NOTES

1. Chris Anderson, "How Web Video Powers Global Innovation," TED.com, last updated July 2010, https://www.ted.com/talks/chris_anderson_how_web_video_powers_global_innovation.

2. TEDxRiodelaPlata, "Jorge Odón: Del taller mecánico a la sala de partos," last updated August 18, 2012, http://www.tedxriodelaplata.org/videos/del-taller-mec%C3%A1nico-sala-partos.

3. Margaret Chan, "Best Days for Public Health Are Ahead of Us, says WHO Director-General," World Health Organization (WHO), last updated May 21, 2012, http://www.who.int/dg/speeches/2012/wha_20120521/en/.

4. Donald McNeil, "Car Mechanic Dreams Up a Tool to Ease Births," *New York Times*, last updated November 13, 2013, http://www.nytimes.com/2013/11/14/health/new-tool-to-ease-difficult-births-a-plastic-bag.html.

5. Vibeke Venema, "Odon Childbirth Device: Car Mechanic Uncorks a Revolution—Vibeke Venema," *BBC News*, last updated December 3, 2013, 7:32 a.m., http://www.bbc.co.uk/news/magazine-25137800.

6. Harakat al-Shabaab al-Mujahideen (HSM), more commonly known as al-Shabaab, meaning "The Youth" or "The Youngsters," is a jihadist group based in Somalia. In 2012, it joined the militant Islamist organization al-Qaeda as a cell.

7. The Kakenya Center for Excellence (KCE) is a nonprofit organization focused on serving the most vulnerable and underprivileged girls in Kenya. It seeks to empower and motivate young girls through education to become agents of change and to break the cycle of destructive cultural practices in Kenya such as female genital mutilation and early forced marriage.

8. Kakenya Ntaiya, "A Girl Who Demanded School," TED.com, last updated October 2012, https://www.ted.com/talks/kakenya_ntaiya_a_girl_who_demanded_school.

9. CNN. "CNN Heroes: Everyday People Changing the World," Last accessed June 24, 2014, http://www.cnn.com/SPECIALS/cnn.heroes/2013.heroes/kakenya.ntaiya.html.

10. Alice Malsenior Walker is an American author and activist. She wrote the critically acclaimed novel *The Color Purple* (Harcourt, 1982) for which she won the National Book Award and the Pulitzer Prize for Fiction.

11. Alice Walker, "TEDxRamallah—Alice Walker آليس ووكر—How I Learned to Grow a Global Heart," TED.com, last updated July 6, 2011, http://tedxtalks.ted.com/video/TEDxRamallah-Alice-Walker-How-I;search%3Atag%3A%22palestine%22.

12. Stop TEDx Ummayad 2014, Facebook page, accessed June 24, 2014,https://www.facebook.com/pages/Stop-TEDx-Ummayad-2014/518126811616756.

13. TEDGlobal is an annual five-day conference that celebrates human ingenuity by exploring ideas, innovation, and creativity from all around the world. The 2014 conference was held in Copacabana, Rio de Janeiro, Brazil.

14. The Bill and Melinda Gates Foundation partnered with TEDx to raise awareness around global health and development through TEDxChange, and to develop programs to help bring new information and ideas to underdeveloped communities. As a part of the partnership, the foundation also offers scholarships to selected TEDx organizers to experience an official TED Conference. TEDxChange Scholarships covers the cost of preselected TEDx organizers from across the globe to attend official TED Conferences.

15

THE INNOVATION LAB

A conversation with Joi Ito, Director of the Media Lab,
The Massachusetts Institute of Technology

To view clips
from the conversation
with Joi Ito
scan the QR code
or visit:
http://goo.gl/wMwvWj

A 1984 memo[1] signed by architect Nicholas Negroponte describes MIT's Media Lab—founded by Negroponte and former MIT President Jerome Wiesner the following year—as "designed to be a place where people of dramatically different backgrounds can simultaneously use and invent new media, and where the computer itself is seen as a medium—part of a communications network of people and machines—not just an object in front of which one sits." The same year, Steve Jobs and Apple launched the very first mass-market personal computer featuring a graphical user interface and mouse. Negroponte wanted the Media Lab to be an institution to foster "antidisciplinary" thinking. What is the Media Lab today, almost thirty years after its founding?

The personal computer was just coming out. The Internet wasn't here in its current form. We were still struggling to empower the individual as the primary mission—with things like user-interface, man-machine interface, and displays. In a sense, consumer electronics was one of the key areas of impact, followed by the proliferation of the Internet, new and improved devices, and of course networks. What happens when you change from man-machine to networks is that it becomes less about the individual and more about the society, the community. It goes from objects to systems—and while we still have to understand the objects, we now need to think about the system much more.

When you think about the Media Lab, we have always been very applied—we like to build things, we like to deploy things, we like to have real-world impact. When you think about the individual, the impact can be helping with inventing the Kindle or working on personal computers, but in networks the application becomes a little bit more abstract: it's the future of civic action, or it could be analyzing big data, or thinking about how psychology and behavior work in groups. Indeed, that one thing that has changed is a shift toward networks.

At the beginning, the Media Lab itself was almost like a container. It had a very open inside where everyone shared, but it wasn't well networked with the outside world. Rather, it was its own special place. What I'm trying to do now, as we go into the world of the Internet, where everyone's connected, is to make the Media Lab itself become a platform and become part of the network, rather than just a container. It is about transforming its methods.

Lastly, we have moved from just electronics. We're now working in synthetic biology and in thinking about the brain and about health. We've always had learning as a core, but now we're thinking about it more broadly. What we call "media"—which is plural for "medium"— has gone from just software and hardware to biology, and economics, and music, and beyond. We've always had a music thread, but it's just becoming more diverse.

How would you define innovation and what are the most important ingredients to foster innovative ideas that can help the world and world governments move forward?

Everyone has his or her own definition of innovation.

I would suggest that innovation is new ideas and new technologies that have a positive impact on the future. It's a sort of technological progress. Also, there's incremental innovation and disruptive innovation and all different kinds of innovation. The Media Lab tends to be quite good at innovating in those spaces that are antidisciplinary—between disciplines—places where it's not just doing more of the same thing but something that no one else is or will do.

One of the things that we think about a lot is innovation on the edges—for instance, when we hire a faculty member and students, we look for people that no one else will bet on. If you can get funding somewhere else, we'd rather you did it there. But, if what you want to do can't be done anywhere else, we would like you here.

The other thing is we do is undirected research. We don't like to say, "Make this bottle lighter" or "Make this pen sharper." We like it when somebody comes and doesn't know the question yet. We help them with an answer for a question they didn't know to ask. It has to be somewhat surprising. We use the words "impact," "uniqueness," and "magic;" so it has to be unique, it has to be impactful, but it has to be somewhat magical, which is something that's both surprising and exciting.

When you think about innovation in the context of governments and other traditional institutions, a lot of what they do is measure, plan, and strategize. However, if you create a strategy, a plan, and measurements, you are very unlikely to come up with something innovative outside of what you can already imagine. What we like to do is get out of the measurements and try to empower people, so they try things without us telling them what we're looking for. Only after something surprising happens, we think about how do we measure it, and how do we understand it.

I often say "practice over theory." Instead of trying to come up with a complete theory first, you can have your hypotheses, and tests, and different ways to get there. In some cases for innovation, you have to allow people the freedom to go outside of the standard measured tracks. Not only in the government environment, but in many other organizations, even in R and D (Research and Development) and research, there are all these deep measurements. There's an obsession with measurements and analytics. I think some of the most interesting things that ever happen are things that wouldn't have happened if we were designing to meet measurement requirements.

Do you think that governments are scared about going outside of already established platforms and trying to be innovative?

I think that a lot of it has to do with accountability, rewards, and careers. There's an inherent risk in trying something that isn't measured. There are successful government-innovation programs, like for instance the Small Business Innovation Research[2] (SBIR) packet system. They push people to take risks, and they fund them for their risks. They have milestones, but they are fairly flexible in allowing the entrepreneur to try new things or change course. It's not easy though. You have to be intentional, and you have to have an idea.

Part of the process is to sort of admit that you don't understand everything. Japan, for instance, is very bad at this—bureaucrats like to think that they understand everything, and whether it's culture or technology, they like to plan it and give it to people they trust. In this environment, it's very difficult to innovate. There's an inherent leaning against innovation, but I think that with leadership we can do it.

When we talk about innovation, we often talk about technology. But if you go to the core of innovation, innovation is about ideas and the power of ideas. How do you define technology as associated with innovation? As a tool that facilitates innovation? Can innovation become real for governments without technology?

There's an interesting quadrant[3] that Rich Gold[4] once drew. It depicts a scientist, an engineer, an artist, and a designer (see figure 15.1).

Figure 15.1.   The four hats of creativity and innovation: drawing by Rich Gold [Gold, Rich. foreword by John Maeda., The Plenitude: Creativity, Innovation, and Making Stuff, figure: Artist, Designer, Scientist, Engineer, © 2007 Massachusetts Institute of Technology, by permission of The MIT Press].

A scientist is looking for scholarly and theoretical truth in science. An engineer is somebody who is looking at the constraints of the real world and trying to create a technical solution that has some kind of utility. The scientist inspires the engineer. The scientist isn't really thinking about the real world, but there's a relationship there. Similarly with artists, artists are often trying to pose questions and make people think about the world. A designer is really trying to look at the world, observe it, and come up with a solution to the problems he/she sees. Designers and engineers are very similar. A designer is kind of an engineer of ideas and an engineer of aesthetics, and an engineer is kind of a designer of technology.

If you think of those four quadrants, the best people at the Media Lab have all four. They can move between those, or they can do them at the same time. I think that it's all very connected because a great engineer is also a great designer and the best designers also understand technology. I don't think you can separate them. The greatest artists are very much like scientists: they tend to work together quite well. It's kind of an ecosystem.

You defined yourself as a "serendipity person." You described the Media Lab as aiming "to capture serendipity." What's "serendipity" in innovation?

In short, serendipity is luck. Luck, however, is something that you only get if you're paying attention to what's going on around you. If you're very focused, you will only see what you're looking for. There's a very famous study on luck where researchers invite people who think they're unlucky and people who think they're lucky to do perform a test. In it, they give them a newspaper and ask them to count the photos in the newspaper. As they're counting, they see a big headline in the newspaper they've been given that says, "There are 43 pictures in the newspaper, tell the examiner." Then there's another headline that says, "You win $250 if you tell the examiner you saw this." All the lucky people see the headlines and go to the examiner and say, "OK, give me $250 and there are 43 pictures." The unlucky people are only looking for the pictures though, so they don't see the headlines. They go to the examiners last because they're sitting there counting all of the pictures. Similarly, if you're driving a car and you're looking at the road, you may not see all the stuff going on around you.

Now, what's important for serendipity is that you need to give yourself some peripheral vision. You have to have some skill of pattern recognition, and you have to have a little bit of space. If somebody comes to us at the Media Lab and they see something exciting, they say, "Oh, this is really exciting, but you know that's really not my job." Then that's not serendipity. But, if you say, "You know, this may connect with something here" or, "I'd like to do that," that requires an inquisitive mind. It requires permission. It requires what we call creative confidence—the confidence to be able to say, "Hey, I'm creative, I'm going to come up with an idea."

Serendipity is something that you can generate. In order to do that, there is a culture, a physical design of the space, the way you do scheduling, and how you fund things. For example, after we made a sensor[5] for cellist Yo-Yo Ma's bow,[6] magicians Penn and Teller[7] wanted the same sensor for a magic show. And eventually an engineer from NEC came to us and said, "We can use that to protect child seats from airbags." That was serendipity. It wouldn't have happened if the engineer hadn't said, "Wait, this is for a magic show, but this sensor could also work here." That to me is the kind of interesting serendipity that happens at the Media Lab. But you have to allow it to happen.

You said, "Failure is another word for discovery."[8] But often failure is also seen as the byproduct of bad risk management, even if failure is, after all, part of the innovative process. What is your advice to governments that might reject innovative ideas because they're too risky to explore?

I think there are different kinds of risk. First of all, you shouldn't take unnecessary risk. However, a key element about failure is that if you fail, you actually get a fact. Let's say I tell you that an object is hot and you say, "OK fine." You don't know for sure, as you believe that is the truth. Though, if you touch the object and it's hot, you'll now remember it. And now you have a fact—you know that object's hot.

Sometimes you have studies that cost millions of dollars to come up with a theory that something may not work. Sometimes you spend more money on the study than on what would have been the cost of failure.

For example, I had a company that cost six hundred thousand dollars to fund. Well, a Japanese company spent three million dollars on a feasibility study to decide whether to spend six hundred thousand dollars to fund that other company. When the cost of risk management exceeds the cost of the risk, that's a different kind of failure because you could have actually learned from it. In fact, if they had funded that company, then if it was successful, it would have been great. If it was unsuccessful, they could have gotten the same data for a mere six hundred thousand dollars instead of three million dollars. The problem is that the cost of trying things has gone up, while the cost of failure has gone down. You don't have to wait three years to try a new product. You can do it in a week. Now it often makes more sense just to try it, rather than to have big meetings about whether you should try it or not.

At the Media Lab, it's a permissionless system: none of the students, none of the faculty have to ask permission to try anything. They just try it because we can build everything here. If it works, it works. They just tell me if it worked or if it failed. Asking for permission would slow down the ability of people to just keep working on a project. Right now we spend very little time discussing whether we should do anything. We spend most of our time just doing stuff. We also spend a lot of time trying to learn from what we did, success or failure. I believe that's a better model.

Just like academia, the foreign policy community has been trying to reinvent itself. Social media has been a key ingredient in harnessing the diplomatic community with new tools. Now that we're trying to look beyond social media, innovation has become the mot du jour for foreign ministers and ambassadors around the world, often taking examples from entrepreneurs and startups. You've been an entrepreneur, you spent years as a venture capitalist, and you work every day with innovators from different sectors of activity. Do you think the foreign policy community is well equipped to use business strategies and entrepreneurial thinking to find solutions to today's new challenges?

A lot of it is about working together. Code for America,[9] for example, is doing very well—although more on the municipal side—by bringing together the software and developers communities with local governments and citizens. Working on some projects together can be a very good way to inspire and learn from each other. It certainly happens much easier in cities and smaller agencies as there are fewer layers of abstraction. Bigger government entities have a harder time because the people are—and feel—so far away from the system, and because politics become a little bit more abstract as well. A lot of citizens want to be more involved in government, amplifying the importance of the idea of civic action.

Innovations in software have a tremendous amount of lessons that a government can learn from. I believe the function of the chief innovation officer, chief information officer, or chief technology officer inside of government can become more amplified.

In the public sphere, traditional media, government, and citizens are three groups that should come together, rather than remain as separate entities. I think that's where we're going in the future. It would be interesting to look at a large country like the United States and choose a smaller unit like a city. With a smaller country, like Finland or Singapore, you can do it at the national level. You can try to do trials or conduct online tests, like James Fishkin's[10] deliberative polling. I think those trials can be very beneficial. I do think, however, it's important to make sure that the software infrastructure is there. Facebook, Twitter, and other social media tools can be useful, but it's key to really try to experiment with writing new code to make conversions between policy making and law making with citizen participation. I believe it's also important to bring in Internet entrepreneurs who understand distribution and engagement, because one of the problems—in Iceland for instance—is just to get enough participation. There is actually a design science to engagement, and incorporating some of those people in the design of a system would be extremely helpful.

You said, "The Internet, the DNA and the philosophy of the Internet is all about freedom to connect, freedom to hack, and freedom to innovate."[11] But that freedom is not shared all around the world, especially in places like China and Iran, making it more difficult for some to truly understand the world and thus bring innovative solutions to new challenges. Do you think governments are working hard enough to make Internet freedom a reality? What do you think they should do?

On one side, Rebecca MacKinnon of the nonprofit Global Voices, Yahoo!, Google, and some of the Internet service providers are working together to try to protect freedoms and accountability to the free speech and human rights organizations. The NSA incident has even pushed them harder to try to set a level of responsibility for their users. On the other side, there are international forums, like Internet Corporation for Assigned Names and Numbers (ICANN),[12] where people can come together and talk about issues and challenges.

We need to be very strategic because countries like Russia and China are coming together—but even the United States as some of the Americans were on the same side—trying to get rid of certain types of freedoms. The Chinese and the Russians want to go after dissidents while the Americans want to go after terrorists. If we want to protect the Internet ecosystem, it's mostly going to require a lot of civic action in cooperation with industry. Because of the NSA scandal, we have a little bit of momentum but we need to take some thoughtful time to think about the architecture. My argument is often that the Internet boom could not have happened if it wasn't open. In countries that are more closed, you're really stifling your economy by not allowing open innovation: your cost is going to be higher than what you're preventing. Sometimes the closing of the Internet is not just for political reasons, as it can also be to prevent a telephone company from competition, for example. I often say that's short-term revenue at the expense of long-term growth. And that is a policy decision.

Do you think that the expansion of cellular networks around the world is helping innovation and Internet freedom?

It's certainly better than nothing, but telephone companies in general tend to be old, large, and very close to government. They're not necessarily the policy innovators. They would rather have control. They're not really open Internet people. We're building an Internet on top of an infrastructure that has a closed DNA, and we have to start thinking about how. Companies are starting to feel the pressure and are experimenting with open models. Innovators and disruptors are going to try to push that layer and make it open, but it's tough.

With mobile, you have the spectrum, and it's still controlled by politics and governments. The relationship between spectrums and telephone companies on one side, and disruptors and innovators on the other side is just taking a little bit longer to play out.

Now, does an innovator need to be a disruptor?

Not necessarily. As there is incremental innovation, you can have incremental innovation in infrastructure and in policy. Incremental innovation is still innovation and represents an important step toward the right direction. It's not necessarily what we do at the Media Lab, but incremental innovation is certainly underestimated.

NOTES

1. David Rowan, "Open University: Joi Ito Plans a Radical Reinvention of MIT's Media Lab," *Wired UK*, last updated November 15, 2012, http://www.wired.co.uk/magazine/archive/2012/11/features/open-university.

2. The Small Business Innovation Research is a highly competitive program that encourages domestic small businesses to engage in Federal Research/Research and Development (R/R and D) that has the potential for commercialization. Through a competitive awards-based program, SBIR enables small businesses to explore their technological potential and provides the incentive to profit from its commercialization. By including qualified small businesses in the nation's R and D arena, high-tech innovation is stimulated, and the United States gains entrepreneurial spirit as it meets its specific research and development needs.

3. See Rich Gold's book *The Plenitude: Creativity, Innovation, and Making Stuff* (Cambridge, MA: The MIT Press, 2007).

4. Rich Gold (1950–2003) was an artist, composer, designer, inventor, lecturer, and writer. Equally at home in the worlds of avant-garde art, academia, and business, he worked at various times for Sega, Mattel, and Xerox PARC.

5. A technology that uses smart computers to augment virtuosity.

6. Yo-Yo Ma is a French and American cellist. He was a child prodigy and was performing by age five. He completed a bachelor's degree from Harvard University in 1976. He has played as a soloist with many major orchestras. His seventy-five albums have received fifteen Grammy Gold Awards.

7. Penn and Teller is a duo of American illusionists and entertainers who have performed together since the late 1970s, noted for their ongoing act that

combines elements of comedy with magic. The duo is composed of Penn Jilette and Raymond Joseph Teller. The duo, having been featured in numerous stage and television shows, currently headlines a show in Las Vegas.

8. David Rowan, "Open University: Joi Ito Plans a Radical Reinvention of MIT's Media Lab," *Wired UK*, last updated November 15, 2012, http://www.wired.co.uk/magazine/archive/2012/11/features/open-university.

9. Code for America is a US nonprofit working toward helping citizens and governments harness technology to solve community problems. It encourages and empowers residents to take an active role in their community; it facilitates collaboration between government staff and fosters forward-thinking approaches to solving city problems; it supports civic-minded entrepreneurs and startups.

10. James S. Fishkin holds the Janet M. Peck Chair in International Communication at Stanford University where he is professor of communication and professor of political science. He is also director of Stanford's Center for Deliberative Democracy and chair of the Department of Communication. Fishkin is best known for developing deliberative polling—a practice of public consultation that employs random samples of the citizenry to explore how opinions would change if they were more informed. Professor Fishkin and his collaborators have conducted Deliberative Polls in the United States, Britain, Australia, Denmark, Bulgaria, China, Greece, and other countries.

11. Joi Ito, "The Internet, Innovation and Learning," *Joi Ito* (blog), last updated December 5, 2011, 9:56 p.m., http://joi.ito.com/weblog/2011/12/05/the-internet-in.html.

12. As per its bylaws, the Internet Corporation for Assigned Names and Numbers (ICANN) is a "nonprofit organization based in California (United States) aimed to coordinate, at the overall level, the global Internet's systems of unique identifiers, and to ensure the stable and secure operation of the Internet's unique identifier systems. It coordinates the allocation and assignment of the three sets of unique identifiers for the Internet: (a) domain names (forming a system referred to as 'DNS'); (b) Internet protocol ('IP') addresses and autonomous systems ('AS') numbers; and (c) protocol port and parameter numbers." ICANN bylaws are available here: https://www.icann.org/resources/pages/bylaws-2012-02-25-en

16

INNOVATION

Buzzword or Reality?

A conversation with Alexander B. Howard, Fellow (2013–2014), Tow Center for Digital Journalism, Columbia University's Graduate School of Journalism and Research Fellow (2013), Networked Transparency Policy Project Ash Center, John F. Kennedy School of Government, Harvard University

To view clips
from the conversation
with Alex Howard
scan the QR code
or visit:
http://goo.gl/U9Zzgf

Every year since 1985, the Ash Center for Democratic Govern-ance and Innovation at Harvard University's John F. Kennedy School of Government awards the Innovations in American Government prize,[1] the nation's preeminent program devoted to recognizing and promoting excellence and creativity in the public sector. These government initiatives represent the dedicated ef-forts of city, state, federal, and tribal governments and address a host of policy issues including foreign policy, crime prevention, economic development, environmental and community revitaliza-tion, employment, education, and health care. When it comes to innovation in government, however, understanding exactly what it means might be challenging. Can you define innovation? Does innovation only come down to technology and technological advances?

Innovation in government—or elsewhere—is not just about technology. Technology can enable it and empower people to be more innovative.

If you are creating connections between offices, departments, agencies, there's an opportunity for people to not only share ideas but to find and use some of the better tools for rating ideas or voting ideas up and down. One of the interesting things that have happened because of so-called "connection technologies," including collaborative or social software—is that a large group of people can share what they're working on and what they're thinking. Over time, you can get a sense of who is actually knowledgeable about a given topic and who other people think is knowledgeable and influential about a topic. That, with social networks, is really a powerful thing. To me, innovation is really about finding better ways to do things.

True innovation is actually hard to come by. Simply launching a new mobile app—something that has become very popular in the last few years, and not surprisingly so, as mobile devices and tablets have exploded—may not in of itself be innovative. For example, if your app is simply a PDF version of the magazine that you've been publishing for years, is that innovative or is it just delivering the same content on new platforms?

I think when it comes to city and state government, some of the most interesting pressures and outcomes have very much surfaced in a time of austerity, at the same time that there has been increasing interest in improved services online. Lower or flat budgets are often one of the main drivers for innovation, as governments need to deliver more but not spend more.

The possibility of being innovative rests upon leadership, upon someone who says, "We're going to be doing this differently," even though you might be coming up against fairly powerful bureaucracies or powerful processes, regulations, and rules. It's quite easy for big organizations, whether they're huge businesses or government institutions, to say "no" and stop a process. "Risk avoidance" versus risk-management strategies are quite common.

At this point, however, the way citizens and residents have been empowered and connected to the confluence of mobile phones, pervasive Internet, videos, and social networks have changed the dynamic. Governments have to figure out how to address political and economic concerns. They have to find ways to provide services where people are, when they are needed, and respond to what people need from our government, or risk public upset. That will inevitably force many institutions to become more innovative.

You talked about leadership. Since innovation is often attached to technology—or people usually think of innovation as something related to technology—do you think the leader of the future or even current leaders need to be technology-savvy or is that not a relevant requirement?

I don't think innovation is intrinsically dependent upon technology. One of the interesting stories that I came across recently was about a US State Department office in New York City being much more efficient than most departments of that city's administration. Customer service was better, time processing was better, and a significant part of that was because of an investment in people. The person in charge had thought about how things were flowing and how people were queuing. That person looked at who was assigned to different stations, thought about how people were actually engaging with what was provided to them, and optimized it. That is not about technology: it's about understanding the process, management, and culture, which are huge factors.

The two issues that have been pointed out the most to me by people who work in the trenches in Washington and state and local government are human resources and procurement. Those were the two issues that were holding up being innovative, because you couldn't get or obtain the people that you needed and they couldn't use or access powerful technology or new, small firms that were available.

I don't think at this point that it's possible to be a political leader and not be savvy at a basic level about technology, and thus be credible to young people. There's already a predisposition for some young people to view older generations as less savvy, or digitally illiterate in terms of understanding what consumers are experiencing on an everyday basis. Former President George W. Bush was famously mocked in the press regarding consumer scanners at the grocery store. It was inaccurate to say he didn't understand supermarket scanners, but the perception that he was out of touch is what spiraled and became a political liability.

If you are a leader, it's important to have connection with the people you are leading, in particular in countries that are committed to a democratic leadership. There's a reason, for instance, why a lot of members of Congress or heads of government like to be photographed with technology visionaries and technology company founders: it's because they nurture that idea of dynamism. They want to be associated with intelligence and a "world-changer" mentality—"We're going to create something that ups an industry or enables something to happen that didn't before and also, in some cases, that creates jobs."

It is important for leaders to understand technology. It goes to an even deeper level with respect to the decisions that a leader makes about how a country uses technology, or the laws that a country makes to govern technology and its use, especially due to information flowing across borders and across firewalls.

Obviously, since the summer of 2013, after Edward Snowden disclosed classified NSA documents to several media outlets, that discourse has been dominated by digital surveillance, collecting intelligence, and the many issues surrounding that debate. We're talking about immensely complex issues here. In many ways, we are all, as a society, trying to understand what has been done on our behalf. Understanding this is important, in particular its ramifications: understanding who is doing what, why, how, what's legal or what's not. These are all very important questions, and if your elected representatives don't understand them or demonstrate that they have exercised oversight, then that actually creates real issues in a representative democracy.

Modern democracies need to have both an informed public and informed representatives who understand both the issues and how we can use technology to respond to those issues. The latter needs to understand the potential for the technology to be used or abused in oversight, and what it means. There are simple misunderstandings or misuses of technology, such as a US senator not knowing where the settings tab is on the iPhone. I saw that here, where a senator clearly had no direct experience with the device that millions upon millions of people have been using. A situation like that doesn't bring confidence in the ability of that senator to make laws that are effective now. We always hope that people have a staffer, a trusted right-hand or left-hand, who understands the technology, who understands the regulations, who understands the policy and understands the potential, but that's only a hope.

Today, there are a lot of different technologies out there that hold the potential to be incredibly influential and abused if they are not carefully guided. Unfortunately, humans, being humans, will adapt the tools for good and bad. This is why the leaders of the moment need to have a basic grounding. Increasingly, when it comes to how leaders campaign and how they govern, understanding these tools and using them well is and will continue to be a strategic differentiator across cities, states, governments, and countries. That is not just a matter of tactics, but strategic thinking as well. Those leaders who do that better will be able to lead better.

Government innovation and civic innovation: both are aimed at improving the lives of citizens within a community or the function of society. Any thoughts?

Innovation has become a buzzword.

Everybody wants to slap the word "innovative" or "innovation" on what they are doing. You can go out to Silicon Valley and everything is innovative. Everything is disruptive. There's a huge list of words that have been adopted and overused, and thus innovation becomes something to be skeptical about today.

There are some people who think that government can't be innovative. I say that's not true, and that there are a lot of examples to prove it. No matter what institution they're employed by or within, people can be innovative. There *are* constraints in government that don't exist in other places, because of the rules and regulations that govern how governments hire employees, elected leaders, or how political appointees work. Those constraints, those choices—we mentioned earlier procurement and human resources—also have a real effect on how innovative a government can be, but the potential is certainly there.

By way of contrast, the discussion about "civic innovation" has become much more dynamic over the last five years. It has a loaded meaning as it refers to civic—and thus to citizens—and when applied to a given city, state, or country, a lot of people there may not be citizens but may be contributing to the tax base, live within cities, consume services, and be very much part of a given local society, even if they don't vote.

Civic innovation rests at the intersection between society and government. As such, it contains some useful categories and taxonomies for different approaches whether it's distributing intelligence, using mobile devices, data, and so on.

Indeed, the Ash awards prove how governments—city and regional in particular—have been able to initiate and sustain innovative programs that encourage a generation of smart solutions to existing and seemingly intractable public policy problems. How can governments be innovative and use the power of ideas to better their services and at the same time foster internal and external communication, public-private partnerships, and security?

As I said before, governments have the ability within themselves to be innovative, even without the involvement of the private sector. I think that's possible. I think that it has depended upon the culture of management. Rethinking how processes work, thinking through different approaches to address challenges, which then may be enabled by technology, or catalyzed by technology.

There's no question, however, that the private sector plays an enormous role in terms of developing tools and services we use. It makes sense in many different places for governments to keep working with private sector institutions to accomplish the policy goals that a given government has, from working with hospitals or insurers to dealing with the data broker industry.

That's something that's happening right now, in many sectors, from technology, telecom, and networking companies, to cloud storage, and certainly startups as well. These are all players that are relevant to helping the government's delivery of the services or the political changes that people are asking for and often demanding.

For whatever reasons, if a government is limited in terms of its capacity to deliver that change, the question is philosophically an ideological one: which services, functions, or actions are the ones that government can only do itself and which ones can the private sector subcontract from the government? Also which products or services can or should only be done by the private sector? There are immense political battles about who does what and to what extent, especially when it comes to being innovative and experimenting with technology.

The option about whether to enter a partnership or not has to be analyzed from different perspectives. Is it long or short term? Would it serve the best interest of the people that are being governed? Can it be delivered more quickly and effectively for a smaller cost? In what context and by whom? It truly is context-dependent in many ways, but there are, I think, many places where those kinds of partnerships are relevant to the policy goals that agencies, cities, and governors have. "Public–private partnerships" have themselves descended into near-bureaucratic doublespeak: what does public/private really mean? Does it mean you are paying a private company to accomplish the actions of government? Does it mean contractors working in the military in a diplomatic context? Does it mean they are helping with the census? Does it mean they are helping to run call centers for the new insurance? How does that function? Does it make sense in terms of the function of government? Does it make sense in terms of delivery, of the need?

Former US Secretary of State Hillary Clinton described how nurturing innovation is key in a speech to the Clinton Global Initiative in September 2012: "We must think and act innovatively and be willing to change ourselves to keep pace with the change around us, and at the same time, we must stay true to our values. Otherwise, we will lose our way."[2] In government environments, how important is to nurture a culture of innovation?

It's hugely important. One of the things that I've seen be effective in and outside the public sector, especially in big organizations, is when managers ask people, "How do you make things work better? What are your ideas?" and then show initiative by addressing challenges by experimenting with applying those ideas. What works is then expanded. Sharing challenges and ideas to address them are actions that are rewarded and valued. This is very much a cultural decision. It's very much a cultural fit, in terms of how you start up an agency or transition to a new administration. Leaders have to demonstrate that they have a healthy respect for the institutional knowledge of a place and want to tap into it.

There are endless stories of people who come in with big ideas and then run up against the beast of bureaucracy. Often that reality is grounded into the culture that may exist there, for decades upon decades. In many cases, the people who are the most effective are the ones who understand the culture and work to change it, and work within it. They are leaders in the sense that they make people feel that they are heard, address their concerns, understand their constraints, and create incentive structures for people to be able to do their best work, often by insulating them against risk. In many different contexts, particularly in government, the goal of a manager is not to get fired or not to make the decision that exposed you to scandal, that created the appearance of corruption or fraud, or actual corruption or fraud or led to something not going well.

The challenge here is that being innovative often means failing, learning and experimenting, trying different things. The only way that you can do that is if you don't have to do everything right, every time. There *are* some kinds of failures that are very difficult to tolerate, and that in fact, governments can't experiment with; protecting a sitting president from assassination is a good example. You can't experiment with different kinds of manufacturers for a car or helicopter if there is only one contractor whom you can trust to build and dispatch it.

In terms of making the best version of a website, application, or rule making, however, you can beta test that in terms of thinking through the most effective way to guide someone through a complicated bureaucratic process. You could test and experiment with different versions. There are many different places where processes and systems can be improved and optimized through experiments that don't necessarily lead to catastrophic failures and or cause the downfall of an administration. Available options often have to do with the culture of the environment or a leader who enables experimentation, even if it sometimes means failure.

Increasingly, we're working in networked environments today. That means we have to think it through whether classic top-down, hierarchical control structures will continue to work in this new norm. If we're all connected and we all can see what's happening at the same time, how does that shift the way that someone must manage and lead? Or shift the way that you share knowledge? How does it shift the way that you listen? How does it shift the way that you deploy products or services? These are all the right questions to be asking now, but in many cases, I think, if the culture of a place doesn't welcome those kinds of approaches, the organization isn't going to get very far, nor will people be rewarded for asking them. We'll see initiatives succeed and fail in years to come based upon the ability of places to adapt.

Is the foreign policy community—in the United States and elsewhere—embracing innovation?

Sometimes grudgingly, but yes.

Often innovation in foreign policy is associated with the use of social media. Certainly, Twitter and Facebook have had a role in transforming diplomacy in a more innovative industry, but innovation goes beyond 140 characters and to the very essence of democracy and democratic governance. What does it mean to be innovative in foreign policy?

I'll take that in a couple of directions.

First, limiting it to social media would be, I think, grossly small. To just look in that context is to consider the matter in a far too narrowly defined way. There's not really a question that the use of social media has become widespread over the last decade. Now, we're so much into a more visual universe of services and platforms. It's a new, expanding world.

Social media platforms have all, without a question, shifted how people are communicating, where they discover new information, and how we can see groups of people self-organize and observe the dynamics of social interactions around given topics, movements, or revolutions.

The challenge is that, in many cases, the current slate of social media platforms are better for campaigns than governing. There is the talk about the difference between governing via tweet versus a wiki. In the latter model, you have something that's more collaborative, more permanent, and substantiated, with the ability to have many versions and have discussions over a given topic. There's an obvious limitation to

Twitter, as we are talking about that, because of the characters and asynchrony of communication, along with the perceived ephemerality of the interactions. Even though the service itself has become much more interactive, with much more media, cards, and the ability to embed tweets or media within tweets, even if a tweet has become much more than just a text message, it's still a limited service. I enjoy using it a lot, but there's a legitimate question around whether someone has used it innovatively or not.

This is where the existing questions of models of communication and culture come into play. If you look at how people and governments, including the diplomatic corps, are using social media, you may observe that they have simply applied a broadcast mentality to it: "I'm going to talk, and you are going to listen." To do so is to misunderstand social media, because it's a profoundly two-way medium. One of the most useful things for a leader to do is to ask a question and see what people say, and then to demonstrate that he or she is actually listening.

Every couple of months, there seems to be a study that comes out about diplomatic uses of social media that looks at who has the most followers and how much they are updating, and so on. I always wonder, "How are they actually doing there? How many of these world leaders are on these services themselves? How many of them actually understand how they work, what the etiquette or the style is? What are the social dynamics and why do some messages resonate? How many understand the impact of demonstrating those things?"

Diplomats lose the trust of the public when people learn that they have not done things or gone places when they make it seem like they have done so, including social media. That's a breach of trust. I thought it was surprising to many observers when President Obama, years ago, said that he wasn't tweeting personally on his @barackobama Twitter profile. This was the campaign that did it, and now it's the Organizing for America team—but it's not actually him. The only time that it is him is when he signs it '^BO', like at the @whitehouse. I recall a real furor when he told Jay Leno this on *The Tonight Show*.[3] People became aware that @barackobama wasn't President Obama personally. Someone who watches this carefully might mock people who say, "Come on, you didn't think it was really him, you know, have some sense and skepticism," but in reality there was a huge reaction.

Limiting the discussion on innovation and diplomacy to social media is far too much of a constraint because of the importance and relevance of other forms of media besides social media, from radio to television to newspapers. That being said, giving people the ability to advocate for change or document what's happening around them is very important. Simple things like understanding the price of the common commodity can have a huge social impact.

There are some people in foreign policy who think that using technology to connect across geographical distances will create huge shifts in terms of the ability of governments to conduct certain kinds of policy. Although this is not necessarily a fresh insight, it is an important one. On the other side of this lies the concern of critics who note that social media, as well as other forms of connective technologies, exposes people living under autocratic governments to surveillance, tracking, and retribution from those governments. We've seen that play out in China, Russia, and the Middle East.

Ultimately, whether you work for the public or private sector, it comes down to transparency and accountability, as consumers and citizens look for more information about what they're eating, buying, breathing, and drinking as well as increasingly how they are being governed. What do transparency and accountability really mean in the digital era?

It seems like transparency has become something that everyone likes to talk about but not always follow through upon personally. "Transparency" has become a panacea in both government and business, though I'm not sure it's entirely sincere. Sometimes being "transparent" shows that things aren't working very well and that there's fraud, corruption, or incompetence, which might discourage trust. In an ideal world, that might create virtuous feedback; you might think that discontent will lead to political change, which will lead to improvement. That scenario can only happen if other conditions are met.

There are organs, like the media, that document issues with fraud and corruption to hold people accountable in government, and then there are political agencies within the institutions that may or may not act to reform in response to those issues. The former might help in terms of the international community holding accountable a government that is gassing its people or stealing all of the revenues from their natural resources. That kind of transparency is still relevant, even if there isn't a political agency within a given people's hands or a functioning press within a country. You can look at different places around the world where that might be the case. The issues around rare earth and extraction industries are particularly relevant in that context, but if there is transparency around a given action by government—that the government shares—it might not be complete disclosure. It may be what people have colloquially referred to as "openwashing," meaning, "We're being open but not fully open" or, "We're disclosing what we want to disclose, not the complete picture." Technology is relevant there in terms of increasing the capacity of the people to go and look at what is being said and say, "Well, what you said is not actually the case."

There is still an ongoing debate about what's happening in Syria, mostly about the use of chemical weapons as portrayed by a variety of different online videos from different sources that went online in 2013. The current analysis shows that all of those videos could not have been faked and released simultaneously, so therefore this happened. There's clearly a difference of opinion about why there was sarin gas released there, who did it, and under what conditions.

The popularity of people sharing what they "see" through the eyes of social media has helped to expose a wide variety of inappropriate behavior on infrastructural and leadership levels. At the Ash Center, I'm looking, to some extent, to see whether those systems are actually effective or not, or are leading to improve outcomes for citizens. Data is part of that without a question. Data is created by phones, by sensors, by people writing reviews of things, even medical claims. Such claims create data that show pricing because of the charges that doctors in hospitals have put back. When such Medicare data gets released and moves into the system, it will add more transparency to what people are actually charging for given procedures. Centers for Medicare and Medicaid Services (CMS) and the Department of Health and Human Services are actually trying to release some of that data to create more understanding of the dynamism for health care pricing, adding public transparency to the actions of a given group of people who have a lot of power in that field.

My sense is that the capacity for institutions to adjust to these shifts has to increase or else their legitimacy and efficacy will be significantly eroded by the currents of history, washing away at their roots. That brings us back to effective governance. People care about development; it's one thing to want reforms, but there are many things that make it happen.

Having a democratic society needs to come first in terms of this discussion around innovation and technology. My sense is that one of the biggest challenges is that the focus on technology will inevitably have great potential to empower elites within societies who are digitally illiterate and literate. If you can't read, then how will you participate in social media? If you can't connect to the Internet, you can't comment on a given proposal or rule or regulation, and if you don't have broadband, you can't watch a debate that is only streamed online. One of the great challenges for people in this space is to ensure that there is greater equality of access to the wealth of digital resources and to education, in order to make the most of them.

NOTES

1. The Innovations in American Government Awards highlights exemplary models of government innovation and advances efforts to address the nation's most pressing public concerns. Since its inception in 1985, the program has received over twenty-seven thousand applications and recognized nearly five hundred government initiatives since it was established in 1985 with funding from the Ford Foundation.

2. United States Department of State, *Remarks at the Clinton Global Initiative*, accessed December 20, 2013, http://m.state.gov/md198094.htm.

3. President Obama first admitted he was not using Twitter himself on November 16, 2009, at the Museum of Science and Technology in Shanghai, China, during a Town Hall meeting with Future Chinese Leaders. Answering a question from the public, he said: "Well, first of all, let me say that I have never used Twitter. I noticed that young people—they're very busy with all these electronics. My thumbs are too clumsy to type in things on the phone. But I am a big believer in technology and I'm a big believer in openness when it comes to the flow of information."

17

TRAINING MINDS AND IDEAS

A conversation with Nick Martin, Founder and CEO, TechChange

To view clips
from the conversation
with Nick Martin
scan the QR code
or visit:
http://goo.gl/fZ18C2

What's innovation and how can it help us chart a better future?

Innovation is about disruption. It is about looking across sectors.

At TechChange, we primarily work and operate in the education technology sector, so for us innovation is about disrupting models of how we currently do things—like workshops and classroom teaching. We have one foot in the education sector and one foot in the international development sector. We do a lot of work with governments, where the typical model is often to put a trainer on a plane and fly him/her to a country to do a workshop. Obviously, that can be very costly and inefficient, especially in an era where budget cuts are a real and tangible frustration for many folks trying to implement projects. For us, innovation came in the form of taking a need, which was building skills and capacities of people around the world in topics like health, education, finance, and others, and keeping them current in the latest technologies. The key is delivering it in a way that is cost effective and efficient while harnessing the power of technology. Everything we do is about creating a very powerful, innovative, and creative online learning experience so that international development practitioners—some of whom are working in formal government positions and some of whom are working in nonprofit sectors, academia, private sectors, and so on—to allow them all to collaborate more effectively.

When you define innovation as disruption, the word disruption usually denotes a negative connotation. A government can be fearful of disruption. How would you help government officials— for instance, those in the aid sector that you have been working with—understand that disruption is not necessarily about failure, but it's in itself a learning process?

That is a huge question, and for us, building failure into the process of program design is really a key aspect of what we do. We talk a lot about lean startup methodology and iterative design: trying something quickly, getting it to market or to your users quickly, and then evolving it and iterating it over time so that you have lots of user input that shapes the product. What we often see is that government, by its design and nature, is a very low-risk environment, where there is no interest in taking risk, or even considering it as part of the process.

Part of that is getting into the nuance of "these are taxpayer dollars at work" and no one likes taxpayer dollars to go toward things that seem to be failing. On the other side of that, it's the fact that often we have such high expectations, many times irrational and unreasonable when it comes to success, whether it is a development project or some other government agency trying to implement a project. In these situations, there is limited room for creativity and innovation.

TechChange has focused on identifying pockets of government and individuals that are pushing for an innovative process—sometimes they even have the title of innovation officer or something similar. Those people are trying to be what we call "intrapreneurs," someone inside an organization who is trying to approach problems from an entrepreneurial lens. These intrapreneurs are working very strategically across their organization to bring stakeholders together to create an environment that fosters innovation by welcoming experimentation and failure within constraints. It is a matter of finding people that are able to take risks and are not just interested in doing business as usual.

You called it low risk. Others might call it high-risk management. Governments spend millions of dollars just to manage risk and to avoid failure. How do you think a government can overcome that high-risk-management process so that they can see the successful final result instead of seeing just the failures that might happen along the way?

Let me give you an example. The United States Agency for International Development (USAID)[1] has recently launched a program called the Development Innovation Ventures (DIV). DIV operates like a venture capital fund where they give grants from one hundred thousand to one million US dollars to organizations that have proven to have a scalable technology that they can implement in a variety of countries. The goal is to evaluate these technologies and operationalize them in an atmosphere that doesn't create the kind of reporting infrastructure and criteria that are typically associated with aid grants. The program focuses on finding the right amount of money and then creating the right process to attract folks who are at the forefront of this innovation.

USAID is just getting off the ground with its ventures and certainly there are already many challenges. As governments are adjusting and are starting to act like venture capitalists, there are several lessons that can be learned from a Silicon Valley approach. In fact, if you look at Silicon Valley, people who fail at their first companies are often the first people hired to run their second company. So, we need to try to understand and implement a culture where failure is encouraged and supported. People are always learning along a trajectory from past mistakes, which we are starting to see evidence of more and more. Even the World Bank is trying to figure this out too, as well as other large institutions that are now developing so-called innovation hubs to pilot projects and think about new approaches.

When you are a company, you always think about returns on investments. When you are a government, working in the aid environment or in civic participation, you think about social returns on investment. What do you think are social returns on investment when you are a government and not for profit, especially in dealing and using technology?

We go from a traditional corporate mind-set where the metric of success is the money earned and the company's profit margins to what we call a "triple bottom line," where there can be many ways to measure success and impact. This is something that every sector is struggling with. If you look at the health sector, are we saying that the number of kids with vaccines is our metric of success? Are we saying it's the numbers of kids not getting sick? Or are we saying it's about the quality of living for folks who have access to those vaccines? How far do we go along this path and how do we then create structures to evaluate whether or not these interventions work? Have these innovations actually had success? These are big questions, and I would say that we are still in the process of figuring it out.

When we talk about behavior change—when we get somebody to take a pill because they participate in an SMS program; that they would not have otherwise taken that pill—we can trace a line from point A to point B and say, "This intervention made a difference for this group of people. We start to see some tangible things." Certainly, this approach depends on the field, and in some areas it gets very difficult. If you think about education, that is a means to so many other things. How are we evaluating that more kids have access to a classroom where they can learn because of educational technology or one laptop per child? Is there a way to say that access to the Internet is actually making these kids more prepared for their lives down the road? I think we start to get unclear about how we gauge that impact. I don't know if there are any easy answers to those questions, but I do know that we are making headway in that sense.

It is dangerous to just say that a project is successful or not successful from the social space, based purely on money. However, it is also dangerous to forget about the money spent or budgeted for a particular project. We see a lot of startups in the social sector that are working with governments through government funding. They are awarded the pilot project, they implement it, and they get a big grant from the government. But then the pilot can fall apart when the government changes its priorities. In that sense, there is still a lot of growing up that this industry needs to do to figure out how to navigate these challenges and better partner with the public sector.

You said: "New and emerging technology is giving millennials, social entrepreneurs and bureaucrats the opportunity to become invaluable intrapreneurs and generate new and sustaining value for their companies."[2] What's the role of new technologies, especially when governments often times see and think of new technology as just social media?

We look at social media as one piece of that puzzle. I believe Twitter and Facebook are really a part of a broader category of citizen engagement. How do you create new mediums for citizens and constituencies to engage with your policies, with your programs as a government? It is not just about social media, it is about an ecosystem of engagement. In some countries, for instance, it takes the form of being able to use a phone to call into a radio show and having government officials come onto that radio show. Twitter and Facebook make sense for some contexts but not for others.

A big part of what technology represents lies in the many opportunities that mobiles and smartphones create. In a world where around 96 percent of people have access to phones, even in some of the most remote areas of the African continent, there is a lot of interest and excitement around what the phone can do. Part of our job at Tech-Change is to mediate that excitement and to be able to distinguish between hype and real, tangible possibilities; to be able to identify the skills you need as an entrepreneur, as a government official, an academic; to be able to make sense of this evolving landscape.

Certainly, we are excited about what technology, including social media, can do.

When I think of technology, I usually think about open platforms and open source. And today, those technologies are becoming key for the development and aid sectors. What do you think is the future of open technology given the increasing role of tech giants like Google and Facebook?

We are definitely big fans of open source and open platforms. The biggest challenge around open source is the sustainability of these platforms. A number of different players around the world, including developers and governments, have now been working with open technologies—I think about Ushahidi,[3] for example—to map crisis response even in some of the most remote areas of the world, thanks to open-source mapping tools. Governments have been embracing these tools, but we still see challenges, as some of these technologies are billed as "do it yourself" while in fact they are not. Companies are getting better at making these tools more intuitive and more user-friendly, but we are still not at a point where open-source tools are for anyone to use. That represents a big issue: if you need a programmer to make it work, you then have to weigh the cost of the programmer against a proprietary solution that is maintained and seen as sustainable by an organization. On the other side, it is about data and who owns data as it is moved. There has certainly been some conversation around this in the United States lately.

Millennials and new generations: why are they key to the innovation process? They have grown up with social media and open-source technologies. For once, they don't need to adapt to those, and they feel comfortable using them.

There is no question that millennials who have grown up as digital natives have an important role to play. We see this in our courses represented fairly ubiquitously. They can mediate technology in a way that older generations generally cannot. Of course, there are all kinds of exceptions to that. But there is a responsibility that comes with that, and part of it is appreciating and understanding that years and years of development experience is not irrelevant because somebody does not know how to use Twitter. The question then is, "How do you bridge this source of wisdom that we have got from people who have done development work for many years—who may not be as digitally savvy—with people who are growing up with these skills?" It has made for an awkward time as organizations are trying to find that balance. I think it is also incumbent on the older generations who may be less familiar with technology to do things like take courses and to actually make an effort to be able to have the right conversations.

When it comes to government and foreign policy, some leaders seem detached from technology. But I do believe the gap between generations is reducing. I think there are plenty of people in leadership positions that "get" technology and its potential. They understand it's part of our present and future and, as such, it needs to be embraced. We need to understand how to realign and be adaptive to maximize our impact as a government agency or governmental organization. We need to embrace the notion that learning is a lifelong process. I often give the example of my father, who had an incredible government career as deputy secretary at the Department of Energy after graduating from the University of Pennsylvania and the Massachusetts Institute of Technology. Now, he is going back to community college to learn French. He is using tools like Blackboard and is taking online classes as well. Also, he has taken several courses with us at TechChange. It is that kind of willingness to always be learning that will really distinguish true leaders. We need to see more of that.

"So as leaders, you have a choice," writes Colonel Eric G. Kail,[4] *an active duty Army Officer and former director for military leadership at West Point, in the* **Harvard Business Review**. *"You can make assumptions about the next generation or you can invest in them the way that others have invested in you." He continued: "The central position to what I'm suggesting is that we lead millennials forward and not drag them back to what we believe to be the 'good old ways' of developing people. Seasoned leaders don't need to turn their backs on decades of experience, but they also don't need to subject emerging generations to the same techniques of learning and development that made sense 10 or 20 years ago." Do you agree?*

How do you respect that wisdom but also be able to be adaptive? People are passionate; they do want to make a difference, and they want to learn from those who have had this experience. I do think it is a balancing act. Training becomes the key in that notion of lifelong learning. Millennials don't have the wisdom of a thirty-year career; we just don't. There is no replacement for that.

It is about understanding and being able help older generations be able to tell their stories in a way that is meaningful, memorable, and relevant to younger generations. That is partly what we try to do at TechChange. When we build a course, it is a combination of compounding that wisdom of the ages and development with the latest technologies. It is about how to make a difference harnessing experiences and technology. It is about finding the right technology for the right context. It's about understanding the challenges as well the potential for technology to tackle them. It is about the conversation between tradition and innovation. You need all the parts represented to have that kind of critical discourse.

In this context, it's also very important to understand the role of technology, not just its end-users or whether the users are millennials or older generations. There are in fact a number of ways we approach technology. In the field we say technology is only 10 percent of any development solution. That means that about 90 percent of it is thinking about strategy and design, as well as how the community will embrace it or how it will be rolled out in a way that all stakeholders can benefit from it. It's also important to understand that technology in itself is not good or bad; rather, it is just a magnifier of human intent. In a development project, if you are headed in the wrong direction already, technology will help you get there faster. So, for us the real innovation happens when we start to design technology projects from their core with the communities we are going to serve. That is happening in a number of contexts, in a number of countries. Solutions aren't just being shipped in from overseas and saying, for example, "Alright, now you have your new way to collect water, congratulations!" It does not necessarily work like that, as applications and technologies need to be adapted to a specific context.

Technology, in our case, is just a medium to facilitate the conversation around the challenges we are facing; to bring people together around a learning objective and around learning goals. We do this without necessarily a clear outcome, but with a way that takes into consideration the incredible amount of collective wisdom and experience already built in a course through its participants.

What's your advice to the future generations of leaders?

Creating a collaborative, innovative space is really powerful. It is about understanding your community, your partners, and your stakeholders. I think that a tolerance for risk is also important: it is okay to fail as long as we are constantly learning from that experience. I do think leaders can encourage that space for failure and build programs within big government agencies to better support an innovative culture. Leadership can be about creating a culture where it is safe to fail, particularly because in any innovative process, the problems that you start with are not the problems that you end with. We are seeing this approach more and more, but it is coming slowly.

NOTES

1. USAID is the lead US government agency that works to end extreme global poverty and enable resilient, democratic societies to realize their potential. US foreign assistance has always had the two-fold purpose of furthering America's interests while improving lives in the developing world. USAID carries out US foreign policy by promoting broad-scale human progress at the same time it expands stable, free societies, creates markets and trade partners for the United States, and fosters good will abroad.

2. Joe Agoada, "Entrepreneurs in Institutions: Why Intrapreneurs Are So Valuable to International Development," *TechChange* (blog), last updated June 14, 2013, http://techchange.org/2013/06/14/entrepreneurs-in-institutions-why-intrapreneurs-are-so-valuable-to-international-development/.

3. Ushahidi is a global organization that empowers people to make a serious impact with open-source technologies and cross-sector partnerships by building open-source technologies, fostering innovation, and nurturing entrepreneurial ecosystem in emerging markets. Ushahidi, which means "testimony" in Swahili, was a website that was initially developed to map reports of violence in Kenya after the postelection fallout at the beginning of 2008. Since then, it has grown into a global nonprofit technology company headquartered in Kenya. Ushahidi is responsible for founding the iHub, a technology hub in Nairobi that has helped build the technology community in East Africa, growing to over fourteen thousand members, and has incubated 150 tech startups that have created over a thousand jobs.

4. Eric G. Kail, "Don't Make Assumptions About the Next Generation; Invest in It," *Harvard Business Review* (blog), last updated January 25, 2013, 1 p.m., http://blogs.hbr.org/2013/01/dont-make-assumptions-about-the-next-generation-invest-in-it/.

18

INNOVATIVE IDEAS FOR
NEW CHALLENGES

A conversation with Alain Brian Bergant, Secretary
General, Bled Strategic Forum, Ministry of Foreign Affairs
of the Republic of Slovenia, and Timotej Šooš, Director of
the Young Bled Strategic Forum and Digital Diplomacy
Coordinator, Ministry of Foreign Affairs of the Republic
of Slovenia

*Over the past eight years, the Bled Strategic Forum (BSF) has
grown into a successful platform for high-level strategic dialogue
among leaders from the private and public sectors on key issues
facing Europe and the world in the twenty-first century. From the
state of the world economy and the challenges facing Europe to
the changing nature of power in the digital age, the forum has
become an important platform for the international community to
discuss ideas and new strategies. How has the forum evolved during the years and how do you see the future ahead?*

Alain Brian Bergant: Back in 2006, when we were organizing the first
forum, we could not have predicted either its long-term success or the
direction it would take. Today, it is clear that the Bled Strategic Forum
reflects the dynamics of Slovenian foreign policy. Over the past seven
years, it has grown from a regional conference into an important annual
gathering—a successful platform addressing globally relevant topics
and attracting prominent intellectuals from politics, business, and academia from all over the world. And with maturity and relevance, it has

also gained a clear vision, seeking to make commitments to implement new strategies designed to confront the most pressing issues of today's Europe and the world.

As the world is changing rapidly in the wake of globalization and global interconnectivity, the emergence of new global players is adding an extra layer of complexity to the foreign policy agendas of government, as well as to the world economy. How is Europe facing this new reality?

Bergant: Europe is designed to constantly change itself to respond to the challenges it is facing, internally and globally. Therefore Europe, and the EU in particular, has the capacity to adapt to the new realities and situations. The most serious challenge, which brought about the latest most significant change of Europe, is probably the economic and financial crisis in the Eurozone.

In 2008, the financial crisis came from the outside, but has had an immense impact on Europe internally. It has become a crisis of confidence in the European model, as the financial crisis mutated into first an economic and then a social and political crisis.

The EU has taken very tough measures to tackle the crisis. The solution to the economic difficulties is one of the key factors that will change the EU's international profile and has, on the other and, the capacity to influence world affairs. The EU is designed to use its collective weight to shape international affairs in order to promote Europe's interests. The unanimous stands of EU member states on specific points of great interest are bringing the EU further and make it stronger.

How has the Bled Strategic Forum been relating to the new global players?

Bergant: BSF has, during the years with its topics "From the Caspian Region, Middle East to the Politics of Economic Crisis, from the European Union 2020 to the Global Outlook for the Next Decade, from energy and climate change to the Power of the Future," covered all major global challenges we faced. Prominent panelists, politicians, businessmen, and other high-level guests and media representatives from the region and beyond (BRICS,[1] the United States, Canada, etc.), as well as highest representatives from the international organizations (UN, OECD,[2] OSCE,[3] etc.) have shown that BSF plays an important role among the international conferences and forums in the region and has the right connections with the new global players.

Despite the various approaches, it is clear that the future EU will be more integrated and based on three unions—banking, economic, and political. All three, from the emergence of the bitcoin to issues related to cyber security and big data, have been affected by the digital revolution. Is the digital age making the European banking, economic, and political union easier to achieve, or are they rather complicating the process?

Bergant: At first glance, it is difficult to read both processes together. Creation of an enhanced economic and monetary union is a long-term process, depending on the will of European political masters. It is true that if the financial crisis had not occurred, the deeper integration of the economic and monetary union would not have even started. On the other hand, it seems the digital revolution is happening by inertia, regardless of the national borders, let alone of the political will.

But they do link at a certain point. Let's take an example. Bitcoin, a virtual currency, might at this point of time rather appear as an obstacle to the euro. The EU is fighting hard to fend off attacks against the single currency, or at least this was the case immediately after the crisis broke out in 2008. Preserving the single area currency is at the center of creating a banking and economic union.

Consequently, the EU is far from accepting the idea of the competing currencies. But that does not mean that member states are not being more active in this regard, but within their national competences. This phenomenon is interesting, since we value a digital currency as being nongovernmental. Germany has already recognized bitcoin as a financial instrument, not as a foreign currency. It could be used for tax and trading purposes. We have also been witnessing the activities of the Cypriots investing their money into the digital currency.

Although we still have to see the history to unravel proving real success of the virtual currency, the trading in bitcoin seemed to be increasing. Therefore this issue will probably be tackled at some point at the European or global level, not least because some regulatory framework should be drawn up. Offering a dispersed business model, without regard to the established central bank systems, the digital currency poses a threat to the established currencies.

Europe was also discussed at the first self-standing Young Bled Strategic Forum (YBSF) in 2013, bringing together aspiring young leaders, thinkers, and entrepreneurs from all over the world. In particular, the 2014 European election was the first in which social media tools played a significant role. What are the challenges ahead and how is social media changing European politics?

Timotej Šooš: While social media gives an additional channel of participation to everyone, it especially provides a very easy way for the younger generation of Europeans to get involved in the democratic processes. The negative consequences of the crisis have pushed European youth into a quite apathetic stage, but social media gives them a new opportunity to raise their voices and take a more active role.

Technology and social media have certainly been key components of technology per se—and new innovative ideas have been the real driving power behind the changing foreign policy agendas of many governments. Digital diplomacy, entrepreneurship and tech camps, and economic diplomacy are all products of innovative ideas. How is innovation reshaping our world?

Šooš: Innovation is—as it has always been—a step forward, also in diplomacy. While traditional tools in diplomacy are still very relevant, new technologies serve as a tool to make the field of diplomacy broader and even more interdisciplinary. A communication between two foreign ministers is not more effective (and not necessarily quicker) because it is done via Twitter. It is just done more publicly and allows everyone to observe and take part in it (influencing the FP agendas).

Making up names such as economic diplomacy, digital diplomacy, green diplomacy . . . might not be the best thing actually. All of this is simply just "diplomacy" done by using different tools and engaging different kinds of audiences. In the end, each country has one general goal: to engage and to influence (may it be business, politics, democracy, or human development).

However, innovation (including technology) enables governments to achieve this main goal and other more specific goals much quicker, and in a more effective and efficient manner. While social media tools are a public face of digital diplomacy, there is much more than just that. Innovation, for example, has enabled more effective internal communication in national diplomatic networks, including the analysis of the information and consequently the developments of strategies. Moreover, a decade ago, it was impossible to imagine that a country would replace an embassy with a website, which recently became a reality in many cases (due to financial and security reasons).

Innovation is where governments and the private sector can work together with the new generations of leaders to build a true platform for growth. The Bled Strategic Forum and its YBSF are a good example of how tradition and innovation can coexist, how old and new generations of leaders can collaborate on common issues. . . . In this regard, what has been the Bled experience?

Šooš: So far, we are very satisfied with the coexisting of both events. We believe that placing a young person in a panel at the Bled Strategic Forum just for the sake of doing it would not necessarily make any difference. For this reason we decided to develop a new product—Young BSF—in order to provide young leaders with an environment where they can discuss, brainstorm, and share their ideas. We aim to bring relevant topics to that table (pertaining to the whole society, not just the youth) and to invite main stakeholders to that table as well. With this first step we are inviting the "older generation" to the "young generation's" table. In the future we plan to do vice versa as well. By doing this, we will provide opportunity for both generations to discuss among themselves and to share their views with each other. At the same time, this allows members of each generation to do things "their way." In 2013, for example, we organized bilateral meetings between Young BSF participants by using the online tool Jublia Match,[4] which is a product developed by a Swedish–Singaporean startup. At the same time, about several people were necessary to set up bilateral meetings among Bled Strategic Forum participants in a traditional way.

Actually, multisector cooperation itself could be seen as innovation as well. While everybody agrees that societies have to firth the crisis by all sectors working together, it rarely occurs that leaders from different corners of the society would sit at the same table, listen to each other, and bring the discussions to a common denominator.

This is why we organize also a third event—Business BSF—where both generations meet to discuss the collaboration of governments and businesses in order to achieve common goals. With providing these different kinds of events, Bled Strategic Forum is a very good meeting place for different types of stakeholders, and I believe that is one of its comparative advantages.

The generational divide was at the center of the debate at the YBSF in Lubjana, dedicated this year to "The Clash of Gs." The young delegates discussed how, over the past twenty years, the clash of civilizations has been transformed into a clash of groups, geopolitical powers and, most recently, generations. Can you elaborate on that?

Šooš: In 2013, we came up with a list of very interesting and timely points about ourselves and societies we live in. This is what we agreed upon:

1. Youth in the EU: The promise for the future or a lost generation?

    a. The EU has to promote economic growth and social cohesion through creativity. The EU framework should be redefined with due consideration for the European tradition with a view to creating a new social model with new services and products. The alternative should be creativity-based and respect the human capital, which is the EU's main asset.

    b. EU citizens have to stop dwelling on the past. All EU citizens, including the youth, governmental policy makers, and EU officials, have to find new paths forward. How can we conceive and cocreate something new while pushing forward? Often faced with the platitude that the youth is the future, we have to realize that the youth is in fact the present, and act accordingly.

c. The EU integration process lacks democratic and transparent decision making. EU citizens have to take specific steps in demanding democratic and transparent EU processes at all levels. A new system must be defined in which governments, the European and the national parliaments, the European Commission and other institutions, including those in candidate countries, are accountable and obliged to respect and abide by the same standards. The educational system should enable rather than disable. The youth are hemmed in by the educational system rather than encouraged by it. How could the system be modified to stimulate potential and include the development of informal skills and hobbies?

d. High morality = better society = more opportunities (jobs). Morality and ethics should underpin and change the way we live. Translating words into actions means implementing change in a way that improves our society. How can better societies create opportunities for young people in the EU and what is an individual's role in this process?

e. The youth has to be open to physical and mental mobility. Mobility provides fresh ideas and new opportunities. It also creates an attractive environment for people and business. While the EU should redefine and promote its four freedoms to make itself more open, perhaps in a different way, young EU citizens should tap into its networking potential to truly embrace mobility as an integral part of the EU.

f. What is equality of opportunity? Can the Youth Opportunities Initiative or other EU mechanisms respond to the needs of all the young people who are unable to fulfil their potential? What kind of partnerships between the EU and individual member states should be devised to guarantee equal opportunities and how can the youth in the EU become a relevant player in this progress?

2. Digital revolution: DIY politics

   a. Good causes get lost online. The Internet is flooded
      with information, and meaningful data are often hard to
      access. Keeping abreast of the relevant causes is diffi-
      cult. For an individual, it has become virtually impos-
      sible to get the message across.

   b. Are our real and digital lives one and the same? How
      can a person effectively put forward demands online? A
      surge of online activism has been recorded, generally
      facilitating and consolidating political change, but its
      true impact remains questionable. In comparison to en-
      gagement in real life, online participation is effortless.
      How large is the gap between the human and the digi-
      tal, and how can online contacts affect real lives?

   c. We lack uniform digital ethics. No uniform framework
      to guide our online behavior has been set up yet. In the
      comfort of anonymity of online discussions, ethics, in-
      tegrity, and honesty are often left behind. The purpose
      of democracy is to form a community in which opinions
      can be shared in an organized fashion. In the face of
      hate-speech proliferation and the unlimited freedom of
      expression, a digital ethics regulatory framework should
      be considered.

   d. Has the Internet created a generation gap? Online par-
      ticipation requires an understanding of the Internet and
      its tools. A digital divide exists in terms of Internet ac-
      cess and command of its main functions. How can digi-
      tal inequality be overcome, and what kind of digital em-
      powerment mechanisms are necessary for the Internet
      to become a mediator and facilitator of the democratic
      processes rather than a wedge between the genera-
      tions?

   e. Can politics truly happen online? Political parties have
      been successful in getting their messages across; howev-
      er, the question remains whether they use the new digi-
      tal tools for communication or promotional purposes
      only. Do political parties, often seemingly unaware of

the limits and the influence of the digital progress, listen to the online clamor, act accordingly, and use online participation to improve their political agenda? Do online participation and activism leave an imprint on the real world and can we ever hope to make a considerable impact in this way?

3. Doing Business: New tools and new rules

    a. Funding change during a crisis. Depending on whether the creativity, pilot projects, and different R and D activities are being funded by corporations or from their own pockets, innovators might look at their business differently; in the second case, they might be motivated to work harder and more relentlessly. With the evolution of new nonstandard business models, it has become essential to educate about other possible sources of funding. What are the alternative models of securing financial resources?

    b. Innovation-oriented education is the key. A bridge should be built between formal and informal education to serve as a generator of ideas. Education can open doors only when combined with practice and development of skills, and incorporating individual interests. Learning should be stimulating rather than restrictive. Practical education, such as internships, is effective education.

    c. Are we savvy risk takers? We are afraid to take risks and experience the unknown. We fear failure, which is in fact instrumental in learning, growth, and development. How can we learn from failure and cope with it?

    d. Governments have to reduce red tape. Bureaucracy stifles progress and innovation, and is often the greatest obstacle to entrepreneurship. What can governments do to reduce red tape and costs for businesses?

    e. Is social entrepreneurship the start of a virtuous cycle? The crisis has changed the way people think and the way of doing business. Social entrepreneurship is socially responsible—it is people- and communities-oriented, eventually empowering employees, the entrepreneur, and the society. Its innovative solutions and bold decisions overcome social obstacles and enable sustainable development. Can social entrepreneurship be the savior of the current situation?

f. Holidays and coffee breaks won't solve the crisis. The youth has to understand its responsibility and should not be afraid to take action or seize the opportunities. Idleness has become an obstacle to development, and young people should face their fears and work harder to achieve their goals. How can the society encourage the youth to take bolder actions and become more proactive in finding opportunities on their own, thereby fulfilling their potential?

g. Today's youth will be tomorrow's leaders, more connected than ever and more digital than ever. What are going to be the issues they will have to confront? Timotej: As the demographics are changing globally, the tensions between generations have the potential to grow in the years to come. Tomorrow's leaders will have to find a suitable way to connect these diverse generations, and digital dimension (tools, processes) might be an obstacle they will face. Why? Because the young generation will be connected digitally (elections, administrative procedures, banking, etc.) while the older generation might not want to fully adopt these new ways of "doing business." Solving this issue—connecting online and offline generations—will be one of the challenges the future leaders will have to deal with.

What would be your advice to future leaders? And what advice would you give to current leaders?

Bergant: There are many new things that future leaders have constantly to learn. Investment in education remains a priority. Therefore we should invest in, work with, and thereby provide them maximal support as we strongly believe in the next generation of leaders. The best way to learn is to learn from the current leaders, especially older and experienced people. So they can gain mutual trust, and exchange best practices and experience.

Current leaders should give them constant feedback and encourage them to use new ideas and solutions in their own minds. But one of the most important skills future leaders have to develop is definitely the ability to listen. They should be always prepared and open for fresh ideas, as well as different opinions or positions. They should think positively and use all the help they need.

As leaders are readers, they should read a lot, have a clear vision, and be an encourager. The fear of failing should be eliminated; instead they should feel more willing to take risks. Each and every moment is right to start and develop something new. Young leaders should be patient and teachable, be responsible, and be prepared to work hard to achieve the things they want. Self-respect should drive them to self-confidence and respect to others.

Last but not least, young leaders should have an early voice, a seat at the table of influence, and feel to be part of the team. Teamwork is important. All this will stretch and make them to become a better leader.

NOTES

1. BRICS is the acronym for five major emerging economies: Brazil, Russia, India, China, and South Africa.

2. The Organisation for Economic Co-operation and Development (OECD) is an international economic organization founded in 1961. It's aim is to promote policies that will improve the economic and social well-being of people around the world. It currently counts thirty-four member countries.

3. The Organization for Security and Co-operation in Europe (OSCE) is the world's largest security-oriented intergovernmental organization. It addresses a wide range of security-related concerns, including arms control, confidence- and security-building measures, human rights, national minorities, democratization, policing strategies, counter-terrorism, and economic and environmental activities. It currently comprises fifty-seven participating states.

4. Jublia Match is a private networking system for B2B Conferences. Jublia brings networking software that analyzes the event networking potential in conferences and exhibitions and saves operational business matching costs.

19

INNOVATION FOR DEVELOPMENT

A conversation with Aleem Walji, Director, Innovation Labs, The World Bank

To view clips
from the conversation
with Aleem Walji
scan the QR code
or visit:
http://goo.gl/A3W1SX

Throughout your career, you have seen all facets of development—from projects in the field to Google.org where you focus on governance, access to information, and improving public services delivery. What are the main differences that you see in how the public and private sectors deal with development issues and technology?

The major difference that I've observed between the public and private sectors has to do with speed and the willingness to make mistakes and learn fast. I think in the private sector, especially if you're a small enterprise, you expect to reinvent yourself or your business model or your approach constantly. A business plan is not necessarily mapped anywhere. It's a starting point. I read the book *Rework* a couple years ago and there was the sense that you just have to "do."' Meetings are killers; overplanning is not helpful. You just move fast, and you learn as you go along. You never get it right the first time, you adjust and you course-correct if you're successful. What ends up being successful is version eighteen, and it's sort of what you intended to do. In the public sector there's just not a culture that allows that—you have to go through detailed and often cumbersome processes, you have to deal with things like procurement, which just take longer. So, you tend to overplan. I went through a process this morning that I know is going to end up looking very different when we roll it out.

There's a certain discipline and rigor that's associated with spending public resources (large amounts of money), but it just means that you can't move very fast and you don't have as many iterations.

In terms of using technology, I think the public sector is still trying to get a sense of what technology is out there. Often, by the time you integrate it and use it, you're two generations behind.

Now, you're constantly learning about technology from what your kids do at home. In the past, the best computers, the best photocopiers and fax machines were in the office and you'd go home and tell your kids about it. Now, you tell your colleagues what your kids are doing at home. Things have sort of inverted.

In the private sector, you either innovate or die. A lot of that has to do with how quickly you adapt to new information and technology. Competition compels you to move, and move fast.

In terms of innovation, both in the private sector and in the public sphere, I always say technology is an enabler. It's not the solution. If we get too caught up in technology as the answer, we sort of tailor our questions to the answer. Having said that, I think that ideas are important, but innovative ideas are not enough. Lots of people have ideas. Very few people are able to do the hard work and have the discipline to execute and measure results. We have to be really disciplined about the experiments where we test our ideas.

There's a very interesting body of work by Vijay Govindarajan[1] and Chris Trimble[2] from Dartmouth who talk about the other side of innovation. The metaphor is that most climbers who climb very large mountains die or get hurt when they are going down the mountain and not up. Coming up with an idea is analogous to climbing a mountain—feeling really good, being excited—but then the hard work of execution, when you have to implement an idea in an organization, is like going down the mountain. That's where you most often trip up and get hurt. A lot of folks, myself included, think of themselves as "ideas" people. However, unless you have a team around you that can slow you down and say, "Well, how are we going to do this? What's the execution plan?" you can get lost in ideas.

Joi Ito of the MIT MediaLab actually sees innovation as a multi-faceted process where creative people—architects, poets, authors—not just technology developers, coders, and project managers, should be part of the process.

I could not agree more. I think diversity trumps singular intelligence every time. The book *The Difference: How the Power of Diversity Creates Better Groups, Firms, Schools, and Societies*[3] by Scott Page[4] talks about how when you put teams together with different backgrounds—as hard as it is for those folks to work together and respect each other—if you can come up with a way to work together, then they do far better than "uni-intelligent" teams. If you put a group of economists—and they may be the best economists in the world—versus a team that's made up of an anthropologist, an economist, an architect, and a poet, my sense is that the latter team will come up with more creative, more interesting, more innovative, and hopefully more impactful ideas and outcomes. The ability to integrate different kinds of intelligence, different kinds of perspectives, is really how innovation happens. I think the challenge for any group like ours is how do you attract enough diversity in the team to allow that to happen but at the same time have enough shared vocabulary that you can speak to your colleagues? That's the challenge.

But the notion of innovation is not just about people and team, it's also about constraints. The more problems you have, the more opportunities you have to innovate. In Kenya, for example, you saw the emergence of a very powerful mobile payment platform that probably wouldn't have emerged in California, because in the United States we have so many other ways to pay—credit cards, cash, transfers, Western Union, and all the rest of it. Having said that, we're now looking at ways to adapt "frugal innovations" to low-income segments of the United States. So, what is it about that context that allows those kinds of innovations to emerge? I think what you might call "frugal innovation" is likely to happen in places where there's a greater resource constraint. The kinds of innovations that we care about at the World Bank are much less likely to be found in the United States, and much more likely to be found in the contexts in which the problems exist.

I'll go back to the definition of innovation. If you consider that innovation often entails disruption and failures, how does a large bureaucracy like the World Bank or any government push an innovation agenda? How do they make it part of the ecosystem considering that disruption is usually not a part of any government process and failures are usually things we try to stay far from rather than taking them into consideration?

It's really hard is the short answer. I've now been here for over four years. The f-word is just not something that you say. In fact, just yesterday somebody said to me, "Failure is for other people." We just can't use that word. And don't talk about experimentation or failure because you'll sort of be talked out of a lot of different rooms and contexts. The money we lend to developing countries is public money, and therefore there is apprehension about how we talk about it. Yet, I still feel like that's what we need to do. We need to create the space to do that. But, how you talk about it, how you create the space is nontrivial.

The very first thing that you have to create is a culture led from the very top that does not penalize learning from mistakes. The fact of the matter is that most of us learn more from mistakes than from successes; and we fail much more often than we succeed. If we hide that failure, we lose the opportunity to learn, not just by ourselves but as a community. World Bank President Jim Yong Kim[5] is trying very hard; when he talks, he uses the term "science of delivery," to refer to an approach that is really data driven, that is evidence based, that allows us to test our assumptions and course-correct as we go along. Many of our best people do that anyway, but to call it learning from a failure is another step that a lot of folks do not embrace.

The question is how do you create a culture of continuous learning? I think that's the trick. We used to call ourselves the "Knowledge Bank" and now the "Solutions Bank," but what's at the heart of that is continuous and constant learning. I think if you can create a culture of learning, then there's a recognition that learning happens even when you don't succeed. What we've tried to do is to create a space that's more experimental; this notion of a lab, where you can bring people and ideas and resources to do things that couldn't happen elsewhere in the institution—that's an experiment in itself. The challenge with that is how to not become an island where what you're doing may be interesting but has very little relevance to the rest of the institution; yet, at the same time, create a space to do what you can't in the rest of the institution. We're constantly negotiating how closely we're affiliated with the mother ship. We want to be the tugboat that sort of pulls the ship, but if we're not tethered, then we're on our own and we're not relevant.

Bureaucracy is often seen as a negative factor in the innovation process. Going back to the MediaLab at MIT, is it safe to say that the World Bank would probably never hire somebody like Joi Ito, famously without a college degree,[6] *even though he's known as one of the biggest innovators, at least here in the United States? How do you see that changing—if it's changing at all—and how is it going to change? For instance, if we want to bring a team that is diverse, is the way we interpret learning and education a problem?*

It is a problem.

In an organization that is large and bureaucratic, you have to create systems and filters; what happens is that a lot of stuff gets lost in the filters. We're very blessed in that we have very good people from all over the world. I don't think we're wanting for talent, but diversity is not just about the countries you come from. We may all look very different, but in some senses the way we think may be very similar. The diversity of thought comes from bringing genuinely different experiences to the table. I think if you have experiences without a certain type of qualification, institutions like ours are very hard to break into. I think where we have been able to surface those sorts of people is through the work that we do in the field. The Development Marketplace is a program that we do in India, Egypt, and in a number of different countries where we look for the innovations and delivery models that are helping to solve key development challenges in those countries. We're not concerned with who the leader is or what degree they have; we're interested in the delivery model and what's working. In those sorts of contexts, we meet all kinds of remarkable people with or without prestigious degrees. But really great ideas, especially disruptive innovations, are not only invisible where they surface, but offensive when visible. That's the challenge for the World Bank and many "established" organizations.

I believe innovation is also about modeling your approaches and bringing in new partners in a way that nurtures new innovative approaches to old problems. In today's world, organizations like the World Bank and the government can find a plethora of new partners as the role of nonstate actors, networks, and less traditional players is expanding. What's the approach of the World Bank?

There's an increasing recognition that the problems that we deal with today are not complicated, but rather they're complex. Complicated problems generally have a technical answer. If you're building a bridge, there may be certain conditions that are different for a bridge from Panama to Uruguay to Turkey. It's a technical challenge, likely with a technical answer. The algorithmic approach to problem solving is helpful in building infrastructure—bridges, roads, highways, and so on. Increasingly, the World Bank is taking on much more diffuse, multivariant problems that are much more like calculus than they are like addition or subtraction; problems where you have lots of moving parts, and you have complexity. No matter how good the technical solution is, unless you understand the underlying politics, unless you understand the conditions on the ground—which may vary from one context to another—you're not going to fix the problem. It's like playing 3-D chess.

But how do you take an expert-driven culture and draw on that expertise, but also figure out how to adapt and adopt local innovations happening in the countries? More and more, I think there's recognition, and it's in our strategy, that we can't solve these problems ourselves. If we're going to eliminate absolute poverty and boost the prosperity of the poorest 40 percent of the world's population, no one technical answer will do that. No one institution will do that.

We have to be able to draw upon the best ideas, innovations, and things in the world, and then figure out our unique contribution. We talk about our convening power, we talk about our access to finance, we talk about our technical assistance, access to knowledge, and we talk about our ability to influence governments. These are the things that we can do, but we must draw upon the best thinking anywhere to solve the world's hardest problems.

What do you think the role of social entrepreneurs and social startups is in this context? They're emerging partners for not just the World Bank, but also many governments, including the United States. Can you give us a few examples of projects you work on with social entrepreneurs and startups?

The Development Marketplace that I mentioned earlier is precisely designed to surface, understand, and adapt innovations and put them in front of our government clients and the private sector as a way to scale up development solutions.

In India, for example, over the past three years we've surfaced dozens of innovations from the private sector—some not for profit, some for profit. We look at ways to scale them up through the private sector working with the International Finance Corporation (IFC)[7] and other investors. It is a really powerful model worth investing in for the organic growth of an enterprise. We're also seeing innovations by the not-for-profit sector that the government could or should be doing. These organizations that are not for profit are far more efficient and effective in some cases than the public sector. For example, Water Life in India is a private sector provider of clean water. It has come up with a business model to provide clean water to the urban and rural poor at a very low cost. So, we look at ways in which they can partner with the government to expand Water Life's model. While they're operationally viable, the capital expenses to set up these "water kiosks" all over the country is such that they need upfront soft capital to expand. We're looking at ways in four low-income states in India where the government can become a partner and help this model expand more quickly. That's an example of how public–private partnerships can help social enterprises go to scale.

Now, let's look at mobile payments in East Africa. One of the reasons why M-Pesa[8] took off in Kenya was because the Ministry of Finance decided not to regulate it early on. They decided this is not a product that earns interest, and so it's not a product that needs to be regulated in the same way as a bank. Therefore, the government let experimentation happen. I think by allowing that space for experimentation early on, the idea was able to take off, correct itself, innovate, grow, and so on. But then it got to a point where people were holding large amounts of currency with no financial guarantees. People were at risk of losing their "virtual deposits." That's when the government stepped in to protect consumers without killing the innovation. I think one has to take an approach like that where you allow something enough space to organically grow, but then you watch to make sure that the very purpose of the innovation is not compromised. It's a delicate balance.

In both developed countries and in the developing world, more and more people are now looking at the private sector to access public goods and not governments or the public sector. Do you think this is a failure or a positive process that we're now going through?

I think it's the recognition of a need. The expectation that governments are going to be able to meet the needs of all of their citizens in all cases is just not right. There are instances both in remote areas where you have government failure and a fragile state, postconflict, and so on where the public sector is simply not able to meet the needs of all citizens, or where there are existing models, but they're inefficient, ineffective, and so on. This happens in democracies just as much as in other settings. So the question there is: what is the ecosystem? And what is the role of civil society institutions that help to buttress and meet gaps where government is not able to succeed? Our learning suggests that the private sector is both a partner and a nascent opportunity. It's an opportunity for delivery; it's an opportunity to recognize innovation; it's an opportunity to create space where private enterprise can expand; and it's an opportunity for them to dialogue with the government in ways that can be mutually beneficial and good for the poor, rather than saying, "the public sector is bad, there are opportunities to complement public sectors with private sector solutions."

Technology also creates dichotomies. For instance, according to a 2013 UN report,[9] *6 billion of the world's 7 billion people have mobile phones, but only 4.5 billion have a toilet and even fewer have access to clean water. But that increasing number of cell phones also creates opportunities. What's your take on that?*

The emergence of mobile as a platform makes a number of things possible, anywhere from mobile payments to gathering citizen feedback, to ways to analyze blood samples on your phone. I mean there are all kinds of interesting opportunities that should be harnessed. But, there are also really difficult problems in the world where there's no quick fix. Sanitation is a good example—2.5 billion people in the world don't have access to toilets and clean drinking water. The mobile phone is not going to fix that. The Gates Foundation has this toilet grand challenge. I think that if the assumption—and I saw this recently in a description around big data and technology—is that everybody has access to the same technology, then there's a real risk of overpromising what technology alone can do. The example was about fixing potholes in Boston through the use of accelerometers on smartphones. You don't even have to do much. There's an app on your phone, and as you bump up and down, it records where the potholes are. The claim is you don't need anybody to go out and inspect potholes because we know exactly where they are through smartphones. Well, you know where the potholes are amongst people who have smartphones with accelerometers, right? So, you could be very precise in certain parts of Boston or New York or London. But what about places where people don't have smartphones? One has to be very careful as to what we can infer through the proliferation of certain platforms and who is included and excluded. There has to be a recognition that connectivity does not necessarily mean greater connection. There are many instances where a subset of the population is online, but a whole other group is not. That creates certain divides, and I think one has to be very mindful of that.

Going back to your experience at Google, what do you think is the role of technology giants today like Google, Facebook, Twitter, and so on, as well as large technology companies in the broadband and mobile markets in the developing world?

They can play a big role in bringing infrastructure and connectivity to more people. If you look at what folks at Google have done—whether it's the "loon project" or low orbiting satellites—what they do really well is take technology platforms and make them available to lots of people. They have their own reasons to do that—building a large user base allows them to have more potential customers, ads to serve, and so on. But, that still can be a win-win. Many of us use Gmail accounts; we're served ads all the time. We ignore almost all of them, but we can still have access to many useful tools. I think what they often do well is recognize opportunity where others don't. They get ahead of the curve and invest in certain markets. That can create an enabling infrastructure for others to build upon; small local firms benefit from infrastructure investments like a SEACOM[10] in East Africa. Broadband has created all kinds of enterprises that build upon access to the Internet. I don't know if you've seen the work on hybrid value chains. It argues that a company like Dannon yogurt can work with local nongovernmental organizations (NGOs) interested in nutritional enhancement. If you just add a few nutrients to a product that's eaten by a lot of folks and use existing platforms to distribute, you can have a huge impact on health. So, where can large companies act as a distribution platform for something that a small NGO or small entity, no matter how good the work, couldn't do at scale?

What do you think the role of those large technology companies is in the government and the international organization arena? If you look at their lobbying infrastructure, it's huge.

One has to be very careful. This is where the World Forum for Ethics in Business[11] is important, and that is why we are part of it. There are clearly conflicts of interest in many areas, especially in the extractives industry and mining. It's very important that transparency emerges in those situations. I always say you can't change what you can't see. A lot of our work at the World Bank Institute has been around open government, open contracts, open aid, open data, and so on. There's a sense that the public can hold you accountable, global organizations can hold you accountable, only if they see what you're doing. While there will always be conflicts of interest in many industries, openness and transparency can be one powerful way to manage risk.

What do you think are still some of the biggest challenges for innovation and development?

Imagination. An ability to recognize what's happening. I'm very inspired by the notion of positive deviance, which says that in the same environment in which most things don't work, there are a couple of things that do. For organizations like ourselves, it's less about creating innovation and more about spotting them. It's more about recognizing what's happening and what can we do to help the success of indigenous innovations. How do we bring our attention, our resources—what I call the spotlight and the megaphone of the World Bank—to help them grow? If we think that we're going to sit in Washington, or London, or Rome and come up with the answers, then we are our own worst enemy.

NOTES

1. Vijay Govindarajan, known as VG, is the Coxe Distinguished Professor at the Tuck School at Dartmouth College. VG is an expert on strategy and innovation. He was the first professor in residence and chief innovation consultant at General Electric. He is the author of *New York Times* and *Wall Street Journal* best seller, *Reverse Innovation* (Cambridge, MA: Harvard Business Review Press, 2012) with Chris Trimble. In the latest Thinkers 50 Rankings, VG is rated #1 Indian Management Thinker.

2. Chris Trimble is adjunct associate professor of business administration at the Tuck School at Dartmouth College. Trimble has dedicated the past ten years to studying a single challenge that vexes even the best-managed corporations: how to execute an innovation initiative. Most recently, he published "How GE Is Disrupting Itself" in the October 2009 *Harvard Business Review*, with Jeff Immelt and Vijay Govindarajan.

3. Scott E. Page, *The Difference: How the Power of Diversity Creates Better Groups, Firms, Schools, and Societies* (Princeton NJ: Princeton University Press, 2008).

4. Scott E. Page is the Leonid Hurwicz collegiate professor of complex systems, political science, and economics at the University of Michigan, where he also directs the Center for the Study of Complex Systems. In 2011, he was elected to the American Academy of Arts and Sciences. His research focuses on the myriad roles that diversity plays in complex systems.

5. Jim Yong Kim, MD, PhD, became the twelfth president of the World Bank Group on July 1, 2012. He is chairman of the bank's Board of Executive Directors and president of a group of five interrelated organizations: Interna-

tional Bank for Reconstruction and Development (IBRD); International Development Association (IDA); International Finance Corporation (IFC); Multilateral Investment Guarantee Agency (MIGA); and International Centre for Settlement of Investment Disputes (ICSID). A physician and anthropologist, Dr. Kim has dedicated himself to international development for more than two decades, helping to improve the lives of underserved populations worldwide. Dr. Kim comes to the bank after serving as president of Dartmouth College, a preeminent center of higher education that consistently ranks among the top academic institutions in the United States. Dr. Kim is a cofounder of Partners In Health (PIH) and a former director of the HIV/AIDS Department at the World Health Organization (WHO).

6. In May 2013, the New School awarded Joi Ito an honorary Doctor of Letters (DLitt) degree, along with Nate Silver, Caterina Fake, and Kahlil Gibran Muhammad. In a March 2013 blog post titled "Ito to Finally Get a Degree," Joi Ito writes: "Last year, MIT asked me to walk with the faculty during commencement, but I didn't have an academic robe. MIT offered to let me wear an MIT robe, but I felt it would be 'grammatically incorrect' for me to wear a robe posing as a college graduate so I opted not to attend the official commencement. This year, I'll be able to walk with the faculty proudly wearing my gown from The New School." Joi Ito, "Ito to Finally Get a Degree," *Joi Ito* (blog), last updated March 18, 2013, 4:17 p.m., http://joi.ito.com/weblog/2013/03/18/ito-to-finally.html.

7. The IFC, a member of the World Bank Group, is the largest global development institution focused exclusively on the private sector in developing countries. Established in 1956, IFC is owned by 184 member countries, a group that collectively determines our policies. Our work in more than a one hundred developing countries allows companies and financial institutions in emerging markets to create jobs, generate tax revenues, improve corporate governance and environmental performance, and contribute to their local communities. IFC's vision is that people should have the opportunity to escape poverty and improve their lives.

8. M-Pesa—M for mobile, pesa is Swahili for money—is a mobile-phone-based money transfer and microfinancing service, launched in 2007 for Safaricom and Vodacom, the largest mobile network operators in Kenya and Tanzania. It has since expanded to Afghanistan, South Africa, India, and in 2014 to Eastern Europe. M-Pesa allows users with a national ID card or passport to deposit, withdraw, and transfer money easily with a mobile device.

9. "Deputy UN Chief Calls for Urgent Action to Tackle Global Sanitation Crisis," *UN News Center*, last updated March 21, 2013, http://www.un.org/apps/news/story.asp?NewsID=44452.

10. SEACOM's network consists of multiple subsea cable systems that connect Africa to Europe, Asia, and the Middle East. Investments in terrestrial connectivity provides services into key interconnection points in landlocked centers and countries across Africa. SEACOM's network enables truly pan-African connectivity solutions that give carriers, network operators, and service providers the ability to expand and grow their operations across Africa and beyond.

11. The World Forum for Ethics and Business is a registered public interest foundation ("fondation d'utilité publique"–N° 822.216.342) based in Belgium. The mandate of the forum includes all manners of pursuing and establishing the indispensable ethical foundations of business in a globalized world.

III

Beyond Innovation and Social Media

20

POWER IN OUR HYPERCONNECTED WORLD

A conversation with Anne-Marie Slaughter, President, New America Foundation

To view clips
from the conversation
with Anne-Marie Slaughter
scan the QR code
or visit:
http://goo.gl/YWJrK0

"Our government—any government, any organization—is the sum of the human beings who operate it, who bring with them all their faults, foibles, and frailties, and all of their creativity and cleverness," said Jake Sullivan,[1] *national security advisor to Vice President Joe Biden and formerly your successor as director of policy planning at the Department of State. Those leadership traits—faults, foibles, frailties, creativity, and cleverness—seem emphasized by the hyperconnectivity that characterized the world today. Is that just one of the characters of the digital era, or is leadership changing?*

I think it's a function of the digital era, but not just because they're more evident because that's certainly part of it—if you make a slip, everybody will know it immediately. But it's more just the speeding up of time. When you read about Washington in the 1940s, there was time for a Supreme Court justice and a secretary of state to go play tennis or to walk to work together. There was just more time to reflect, to check. The digital age has accelerated the compression of time dramatically. Now you can get e-mails all around the clock. You could do nothing but sit at your computer and answer e-mails all day long and much of the night if you're connected to people in China. I think it's much more that there are no safeguards; there are many fewer checks. People have always made mistakes, but they weren't visible immediately. There were ways of checking them and they, themselves, frankly were a little more rested and a little more balanced. When you look at people who are working in the White House or at the top of the State Department, these people are exhausted much of the time.

In terms of trust, there's no question that for a long time trust declined because people knew more. Once you got to the point where nobody trusted government to begin with, which is practically where we are now—it's around twenty-five people—then I think the availability of all these ways of speaking directly to people—tweeting directly, speaking directly, podcasting, and so on—actually allow people to seem more human. Not everybody, but there seem to be a fair number of government officials who manage to use all these tools to seem less packaged. There are ways in which when people see you make mistakes and you own up to those mistakes and you say, "Yes, I slipped up, I shouldn't have said that, I was tired or I was stupid or whatever," that actually helps people trust you more because they know more about you. That's the thing; you couldn't sell a John Kennedy to people today. I mean even if the press were the way they were with Kennedy, nobody would believe it. They would think, "That's packaged, that's spun." They're so aware that the information they get is constantly being manipulated. That earlier time was part of a whole culture, not just of trust but also of innocence, and we lost the innocence. So, now there's actually a way where you can get people to trust you more by clearly not being perfect, being far from perfect.

Mark Twain said: "History does not repeat itself, but it does rhyme."[2] *In 2011, Peter Singer and Noah Shachtman*[3] *wrote: "While applying lessons from the past can be a useful analytic tool, we frequently unearth old analogies that may not be the right fit for the new problem we face. Indeed, most often we turn to the songs we know best, the ones we hummed in our youth, when others may be more apt."[4] As the Internet and the 24/7 news cycle has brought both the past and the present out of history books and in to our everyday lives, as we Google our way to the top, as intelligence gathering is becoming more accurate than ever, as secrecy and transparency are evolving, do you think it's easier today to take risks in our leadership style?*

In one way, I think no because there's such a flood of information. You desperately need a framework or a paradigm to interpret it. In some ways, we're even more likely to cling to the paradigms we know because how else are we going to possibly make sense of all this. As a liberal from an international relations point of view and as somebody who grew up in the Cold War, I can use a Cold War lens. That's exactly where you know some of those analogies may be wrong; but I'm a liberal Cold War person, so I'll look back and think, "Wait a minute, what's happening right now with China is a security dilemma where we're doing one thing and they misinterpret it; and they do one thing and we misinterpret it." If I didn't use those frames, how on earth would I make sense of the fact that now I'm getting a hundred articles on China every week? How do I assimilate that information and digest it quickly; in many ways, I use analogies from the past, I use frameworks from my past. I'm not convinced that it doesn't actually reinforce the frames you grew up with.

As leadership is evolving, so is power—more diluted and less concentrated than ever before. How would you define power today?

Power today is about connectedness. I argue that power in a networked world is how centrally positioned you are. The more connected you are, the more central you are, the more information you have, the more contacts you have to mobilize.

Let me start with the more traditional world of foreign policy, which is the chessboard world. I, as I said before, was raised during the Cold War. That's the absolute epitome of the chessboard. There are only two principal players. In that world, as Thomas Schelling[5] argues in his book *The Strategy of Conflict*,[6] the modal relationship between the two principal actors in foreign policy is conflict. The question is how you get anything done in a world in which that is true. He said it's not zero-sum conflict. Neither the Soviet Union nor the United States wanted to blow up the world. We really didn't. We each wanted to win the conflict, but not at the price of blowing up the world. Arms control was exactly where you could see there was a common interest, even though there was a basic conflictual relationship. So, how do you deal with that? Well, Schelling basically introduced game theory—or in other words chessboard strategy. Simply put: if I do this, the other side will do that; and then I will do this; and the other side will do that. You play it out as far as you can. That's what gave rise to "tit-for-tat." If you want to change conflict to cooperation, you try cooperating and you see if they will play back. If they don't, then you get conflictual again. Those are the bargaining games that structured foreign policy in the chessboard world. It is traditional geopolitics done with now, unfortunately for strategy, 194 states.

It was a lot easier when the world was smaller or when we had bigger blocs. It's much harder to do that kind of strategy now. Our relations with Iran represent, without question, the chessboard; relations between Palestine and Israel and our trying to broker them is the chessboard again. Syria has lots of nonchessboard elements, but the way we're approaching it with negotiations in Geneva is classic chessboard. Chessboard diplomacy, chessboard foreign policy, chessboard strategy are all alive and well. The chessboard hasn't gone anywhere. It's still very much there.

The chessboard world, however, is not the world that most people look out and see today. If you were born in the 1990s, your modal relationship in the world would not be conflict; it would be connection. You had grown up in the world of globalization. You had grown up in the constant interconnectedness, what Thomas Friedman[7] calls the "hyper-connectedness" of everyone. You grew up in a world of networks, a world where everybody was networked. States themselves are networked, but of course so are different parts of states. Every different kind of government agency is networked. Then, of course, the networks of business—that is the global economy. There's either supply-chain networks or corporations themselves networked in all kinds of ways. Civil society brought us the International Criminal Court and the landmine treaty. Those were networks of civil society actors. There are networks of criminals—what are we facing? We're facing terrorism, money laundering, arms trafficking, drug trafficking—those are criminal networks. And, there are networks of individuals, increasingly in social movements.

That world isn't the chessboard. That world is the Internet. I use the Internet not as the actual Internet, but as the metaphor for the world. The Internet is a network of networks. That's what foreign policy looks like—a network of all these different networks and how they intersect. In that world, the strategy of conflict is useless. You are talking about vast networks. You need to be thinking about whom to connect and how. You start with a very different set of actors because you're not talking about states. I mean states can play in that world, but what you're really looking at are constituencies, different sectors of society. You can think about it as the private sector, the public sector, and the civic sector; or you can think about it as different constituencies. The way former Secretary of State Hillary Clinton thought about it was that there are young people, women, civil society, business, religious groups. I use those examples because she created an ambassador to each of those constituencies. Melanne Verveer[8] actually had the title of ambassador for global women's issues; Tomicah Tillemann[9] had the title of special representative to civil society; Ronan Farrow[10] had the title of special representative for youth; Kris Balderston[11] was the special representative for public–private partnerships. What she was really doing was doing diplomacy for the networked world—thinking about different constituencies and thinking critically about how we create relations with these different constituencies. When it comes to Alec Ross, for example, his job was to be part of and connect the State Department to all the people who are mixing technology and policy in all sorts of different ways. Our job—at the time I was heading policy planning at the State Department—was to connect to those communities, but also to connect them with each other.

What are the challenges in a world of networks?

We're just at the outset of foreign policy, the Internet version of foreign policy. We can see the networks, but what's the strategy? In a strategy of conflict, how do we connect young people across the Middle East in such a way that we're not just meeting with them, but we actually not only get information from them—which is the lifeblood of diplomacy— we are able to do things on the ground? We need to think of connectedness to create links and advance people's interests. That's the strategy of networks, of connection. And we're just at the outset.

Here's the deeper way of thinking about diplomacy in the networked world, in the Internet world, as opposed to the chessboard world: it's a different frame. I said chessboard versus the Internet. It's a different set of analytics. In other words, how do you analyze what's likely to happen in that world? Well, again in the geopolitical world, you know the states; you get information; you try to plot it out in terms of the security dilemma. You can plot it out. With the Internet frame, you need analytics of flows. You need the analytics of the flows of people and capitals, arms, and anything related to climate change. You need to be able to think about exactly what John Kerry highlighted at the 2014 Munich Security Conference,[12] where he talked about food security, resource scarcity, climate change, and criminal networks. However, we still don't have the tools to analyze those flows. We do have demographic tools. We can look at the number of young people in any given country; we can see how the flows from Latin America to the United States are going to be enormous in this century. But it's not the way we trained people to think in foreign policy. We certainly don't have those tools in the State Department. I do not have the ability to map the flows of people, capitals, and other kinds of instruments. That's a different set of analytics.

The last thing we need is a different set of tools. The key set of tools are digital tools. Digital diplomacy is about much, much more than communication. It is essential for communication. It's essential for engagement. It is about listening and responding. It's about ambassadors engaging in lots of ways, but it's much more important than that.

In the framework of the networked world, it's important to think about connections; how to engage all different networks; how to keep them connected and build new connections; how to monitor what's happening; how to advance your interests. Your tools are going to be digital. You're going to be creating a website more than anything else. You're going to be thinking about how to use big data. You're going to be thinking about how you then create technologies that allow people to collaborate with each other extremely easily in all sorts of ways.

We still have a foreign policy apparatus that is created primarily for the chessboard world—and that is one of the challenges. We need a foreign policy apparatus for the Internet world. That means we need a different frame to engage. We need different analytics of what's driving those networks. We need different tools of how to create them, shape them, work with them, monitor them, and ultimately figure out how to advance national interests and global interests in that world.

"We indeed face an era of digital Darwinism, a phenomenon where technology and society evolve faster than our ability to adapt," says digital analyst Brian Solis. [13] *Adaptation, however, is an ephemeral concept. It's certainly a constant in politics and foreign policy—it has always been. But the realities today's leaders are trying to adapt and respond to are going to be different from what millennial leaders and future generations will have to face. The economy is moving to a peer-economy, foreign policy is pivoting to the people while forcing itself into interacting with all players—traditional and less traditional. The peer factor—so to speak—is becoming predominant in the political and economic jargon. Is that a possible direction for the leaders of tomorrow? Are today's leaders truly adapting to the world out there to better respond to new challenges?*

There's a huge generational divide. The generational divide right now is as great as it was between the men of the 1950s and the hippies of the 1960s. You don't see it as visibly. In 1968, there were people in the streets; they dressed differently; they let their hair grow. You could identify: here's somebody from the establishment, and here's somebody from the younger generation. Today, it's less visible, but it's no less profound.

People under thirty-five to forty—I don't know where the cutoff is but somewhere there—who are "digital natives" think radically differently about the world. They think differently about human nature. They think it's much more collaborative and cooperative. They think very differently about privacy. They think differently about sharing. So, you have leaders who are from one generation, a different way of thinking, a different physical world, and a completely different analysis. When they look at the world, they see states. When young people look out at the world, they see people. That's a big difference.

Power and technology. It can be a very tricky partnership, given the increasing role played by technology companies around the world. What is their role today in the new power structure? How do you see them evolving into something less difficult to understand?

I think about this a lot because Google has improved my life immeasurably. It's very hard for me to see them not as a good force. People probably thought the same in the late nineteenth or early twentieth century. We look back and we see Andrew Carnegie, steel magnates, the railroad barons, and we think, "Oh my god, they control way too much power." But, as a citizen you might have thought of them as positive developments—for instance, railroads had made it possible for people to cross the country. They were connecting people. They were connecting physically rather than electronically, but think about what it did. The great steel magnates, the banking fortunes, these were fortunes made on technologies that empowered people.

That's true today too. In the end, power corrupts. I think history teaches that whenever competition is destroyed or severely diminished, people suffer.

One thing that is different today is that there's this culture in Silicon Valley that has a very different attitude toward government. They think they don't need government in many ways, and that's new. We are evolving toward a different relationship between government and the citizens. The social contract of the twenty-first century will be different. In some ways, you could say technology giants are delivering an empowering technology. In many cases, they're trying to solve the same kinds of problems that government is. But we're going to have to find ways to allow more competitors, and we also are going to have to redraw the lines about what we need government for.

What can we do with a combination of public and private? No matter how big Microsoft and Google might be, they can't really do things on their own. They're bigger than many governments, but they're not bigger than the big governments. This very process is going to be one of the more interesting changes to live through in the next decade or two.

NOTES

1. "Jake Sullivan Delivers Inspiring Message to 2013 Graduates," University of Minnesota's Humphrey School of Public Affairs, last updated May 21, 2013, http://www.hhh.umn.edu/features/2013_Commencement.html.

2. Attributed to Mark Twain.

3. Peter W. Singer is director, Center for Twenty-First-Century Security and Intelligence, and Senior Fellow, Foreign Policy, at the Brookings Institution in Washington, DC. Noah Shachtman is nonresident fellow, Foreign Policy, Center for Twenty-First-Century Security and Intelligence, at the Brookings Institution.

4. Noah Shachtman and Peter W. Singer, "The Wrong War: The Insistence on Applying Cold War Metaphors to Cybersecurity Is Misplaced and Counterproductive," Brookings Institution, last updated August 15, 2011, http://www.brookings.edu/research/articles/2011/08/15-cybersecurity-singer-shachtman.

5. Dr. Thomas Schelling is a distinguished professor of economics at the University of Maryland. In 2005, he was awarded the Nobel Prize in Economics for enhancing the "understanding of conflict and cooperation through game-theory analysis." He has been elected to the National Academy of Sciences, the Institute of Medicine, and the American Academy of Arts and Sciences.

6. Thomas Schelling, *The Strategy of Conflict* (Cambridge, MA: Harvard University Press, 1960).

7. Thomas L. Friedman has been the *Times*' foreign affairs columnist since 1995, traveling extensively in an effort to anchor his opinions in reporting on the ground. Friedman has won three Pulitzer Prizes: the 1983 Pulitzer Prize for international reporting (from Lebanon), the 1988 Pulitzer Prize for international reporting (from Israel), and the 2002 Pulitzer Prize for distinguished commentary. In 2004, he was also awarded the Overseas Press Club Award for lifetime achievement and the honorary title Order of the British Empire (OBE) by Queen Elizabeth II. In 2009, he was given the National Press Club's lifetime achievement award. *The World Is Flat: A Brief History of the Twenty-First Century*, his fourth book, published in April 2005 (New York: Farrar, Straus and Giroux), became a number-one *New York Times* best seller and received the inaugural Financial Times/Goldman Sachs Business Book of the Year Award in November 2005. The book has sold more than four million copies in thirty-seven languages.

8. Melanne Verveer is the executive director of Georgetown University's Institute for Women, Peace and Security. She most recently served as the first US ambassador for global women's issues (2009–2013), a position to which she

was nominated by President Barack Obama in 2009. She coordinated foreign policy issues and activities relating to the political, economic, and social advancement of women, traveling to nearly sixty countries. She worked to ensure that women's participation and rights are fully integrated into US foreign policy, and she played a leadership role in the administration's development of the US National Action Plan on Women, Peace, and Security.

9. Tomicah Tillemann was appointed by Secretary Hillary Clinton as the State Department's senior advisor for civil society and emerging democracies in October 2010. He continues his service under Secretary John Kerry. Mr. Tillemann and his team operate like venture capitalists, identifying ideas that can strengthen new democracies and civil society, and then bring together the talent, technology, and resources needed to translate promising concepts into successful diplomacy. He and his team have developed over twenty major initiatives on behalf of the president and secretary of state.

10. Ronan Farrow is the host of the *Ronan Farrow Daily* show on MSNBC. He was previously Secretary of State Hillary Clinton's special adviser for global youth issues and director of the State Department's Office of Global Youth Issues (2011–2012). He joined the Obama administration in 2009 after his appointment as special adviser for humanitarian and NGO affairs in the Office of the Special Representative for Afghanistan and Pakistan.

11. Kris Balderston currently leads FleishmanHillard's Washington, DC, office. He served as special representative for global partnerships at the US Department of State, where he led the Global Partnership Initiative within the Office of the Secretary of State (2009–2013). Balderston also has held various roles during President Clinton's term and served as Senator Hillary Clinton's legislative director (2001–2002) and then deputy chief of staff (2002–2009).

12. United States Department of State, *Remarks at Munich Security Conference*, http://www.state.gov/secretary/remarks/2014/02/221134.htm .

13. Brian Solis, "Leadership in an Era of Digital Darwinism," *Brian Solis* (blog), last updated December 16, 2011, http://www.briansolis.com/2011/12/leadership-in-an-era-of-digital-darwinism/.

A NEW SPACE FOR DIPLOMACY

A conversation with Robert Kelley, Assistant Professor,
School of International Service, American University

To view clips
from the conversation
with Robert Kelley
scan the QR code
or visit:
http://goo.gl/JBflCP

*In a 2010 essay "The New Diplomacy: Evolution of a Revolution,"
you write: "The age of diplomacy as an institution is giving way to
an age of diplomacy as a behavior."*[1] *Can you expand on that?*

My definition of the institution in diplomacy refers to the embodiment
of the exclusive world of diplomacy. It's a space for all diplomatic actions that is limited to a certain group of people that has been accorded
a series of rights and privileges in order to conduct diplomacy. It is a
physical space, but it's also a normative one, with rules, international
laws, and bilateral and multilateral treaties and conventions. This is
what I call the institution.

Where I see a shift is that you're seeing an increasing number of
actors outside that institution, outside that physical and normative embodiment that we call diplomacy. Those new players are actually being
able to impact and affect the course of politics in the world. Institutions
are reflective of a certain paradigm of diplomacy, which I call the diplomacy of status. In other words, it's through their status that diplomats

conduct diplomacy. The main criteria or qualifier is that they have the status of a diplomat and it's recognized as such. That status gives diplomats representational power and political relevance.

Outside of this space—outside of the institution—there are new and emerging external actors, which I call actors within the paradigm of the diplomacy of capabilities. Simply by accomplishing acts we usually associate with official diplomats, they become diplomatic actors in themselves—but actors of the nonstate variation that operate outside of the institution. The demonstration of those capabilities by nonstate actors is what gives them their relevance and legitimacy, and consequently their entry into the world of diplomacy—something that was not extended to them before.

Social media and digital tools are possibly the most visible representation of how diplomacy has been changing. Terms like digital diplomacy and citizen diplomacy have now entered the daily foreign policy jargon of both our government officials, including head of governments, foreign ministers, and ambassadors, as well as everyday citizens, who are now veritable foreign policy actors. Some refer to it as hyphenated diplomacy, but it's really a shift from traditional diplomacy to a diplomatic environment with multiple players, some emerging anew and—as you said—outside of government. What has been the role of technology in diplomacy in the inclusion of new players?

Clearly, technology has had a massive impact on the course of diplomatic events and international politics more broadly.

I see technology having a disruptive effect but also, in a way, the effect of revealing the power of gatekeeping in diplomatic affairs. What I mean by disruption is that technology—like many other contexts—has shaken up the way things are done. It has caused a creative disruption in diplomacy. It's a kind of innovation that is destroying how things have been done traditionally. It's a new set of tools, ideas, and approaches to getting diplomacy done. This is not certainly limited to technology, but technology has had a disruptive impact. A second effect of technology is gatekeeping: indeed, it shows how far government has become removed from its ability to control, regulate, and filter the flow of information, which allows for a much larger space for private actors, non-state actors, and civil society.

Because of the availability and supply of information, the asymmetries between government and the rest of the world, between government and nongovernment, have been reduced. When nonstate actors have so much control over the information channels—not necessarily on the information itself—and when they can regulate the flow of information, that becomes an enormous source of power for them. And that source of power is highly transferrable—it's like that conversation game where, in a room full of people, whoever is holding the orange gets to talk. Similarly, the gatekeeper is the one with the orange and the orange keeps moving around, forcing us to always check who is in control of the flow of information at any given moment. I think that's the place the government is in for the most part—it takes government time to locate where the information is, where it's coming from, and who's in control of it. If government controls that, then it can regulate the passage of that narrative to other places.

For those governments that have asserted their control over the information space, manipulation can be the next step if they are savvy and agile enough to get out front of the general public on narratives. But that's becoming increasingly hard to do. By itself the information is not powerful; it's how it's used. In order to maximize the amount of power that one can gain from information, you have to use it the right way, and the flow needs to reach certain channels, reach a large percentage of the population. Governments have been manipulating and remanipulating stories for a long time to maintain control over the narrative, and of course they could because they had the most advanced broadcasting and jamming technologies at their disposal. Those who grew up during the Cold War saw firsthand how the United States and the Soviet Union took the same stories and came at them from two different directions. One of the classic examples is what happened in the early 1980s in the struggle over the hearts and minds of Europeans over intermediate nuclear forces being placed in Europe by the United States. Russia actively manipulated European public opinion to try to only make European antinuclear weapons but also to style Russia as being in favor of nonproliferation, which was actually not the case.

The struggle over the control of information flows says a lot about power and how power by itself is highly relative. Power must have an ambition or objective beyond simply wanting to enhance power.

It's a new environment where power and influence are almost redefined. How would you define those two elements in the digital, participatory age?

I see them as connected. Influence is not power and vice versa, but they are interrelated. When it comes to exerting power, it's not just about having and amassing power. Power needs to be applied in some ways so there's a sort of return. The way that I've seen the conversation on power evolve is in how there is less importance on material power and more on controlling ideational power. Because of this shift, the evidence that you are *powerful* is the extent to which you're getting people to change their minds. That is very difficult to measure.

The way I've seen power develop—especially when you have a multiplicity of actors involved in the power game—is that you have states needing power to survive on one side, and on the other side all other actors that both need power to be relevant but also seem to be more interested in the way they apply their power to do something. The effective solving of problems is a clear indicator of applied power. You see that in many nongovernmental entities and civil society organizations that are trying to ease suffering and imbalances and tackle transnational issues.

This is quite different from what states normally do—of course states are interested in solving problems and security dilemmas to look after the welfare of their own people, but the bottom line is they have to exist. They need enough power in order to continue to exist and ward off any attempt to their sovereignty. On the opposite side, organizations that are focused on solving problems draw on the energy of a transnational constituency that shares their concerns. Once the issue they're working on is resolved, then they dissolve. This is what happened, for example, to the constituency of people that supplied the momentum toward the international campaign to ban land mines. They came together, and they had success. Once they achieved victory, they still maintain a stake in the survival of the solution to the problem—in this case the ban of land mines—but they're more dispersed than when they gained momentum. In many cases, power translates in having the issue inserted in the agenda of the international community.

Unfortunately, it seems that a lot of the nontraditional diplomatic actors that are inhabiting foreign policy at this stage don't recognize how powerful they truly are. They are finding out as they move along.

What has happened to power and influence in countries like Iran and China in which access to social media and the outside world is blocked or controlled?

With respect to China and Iran, what their behavior has shown is the degree to which they rely on tightly controlling the narrative for their regime to survive. When activity on social media, or in the mass media, contradict their narrative, you're going to experience backlash.

Interesting about China is the way that it's gone about trying to expand their influence into the English-speaking world and the launch of their CCTV brand. If you do an analysis of the content they develop and broadcast—similarly to Russia Today—it's quite remarkable to see the difference with traditional news media, the stories that they choose, the editorial decision that are made, and what is on their agenda compared to the focus on news coverage that traditional media have.

Certainly, technology has facilitated a new trend for which governments are now trying to move from monologue to dialogue when it comes to their relations with their counterparts, citizens, and audiences. However, it appears to be a long and complicated move as governments are still struggling with the nature of engagement as related to power and networks. Do you agree?

Governments are still struggling. We see a plethora of reasons why: governments are huge bureaucracies; they're not agile; they're less transparent; they suffer from a general credibility problem. I don't think governments have come to grips with those weaknesses. Governments want somehow to retain their organizational integrity, but still perform well and be an agile bureaucracy. That to me is an oxymoron. I don't see how it's going to take place. Governments are still going to be massive machines, and very little in this kind of environment can move quickly and be done quickly.

In international affairs, foreign ministries everywhere have to struggle with this very problem, with how to be responsive and how to be competitive in a marketplace where all the innovation is taking place outside.

So, what is government to do? First, government needs to realize that it cannot do all those things to the same level and expertise as private and nonstate actors can. Second, government can take stock of what it can do really well. Time and again, what we have seen government contribute in the process of political change is being a source of accountability and legitimacy. These are the two areas where nonstate actors and nongovernmental players are weak. They have to work very hard to gather that legitimacy; they don't have rule of law or a monopoly on the use of force to serve them.

In my view, government should cede the innovation; it should surrender those hopes of being as innovative as the private sector, of being on the front lines of creative disruption. Governments should realize that as bureaucracies, full innovation is out of reach for them. It does not mean that governments are then out of the game. What it means is that they need to find collaborations with entities and institutions that do innovate well. Through that collaboration you can then take the best of what's out there. You can really harness the innovative capacity of nonstate actors and the accountability and legitimacy of government. We have seen that formula work over and over again.

Governments cannot be innovative by themselves. They can be innovative in the way that they develop and implement solutions in public and foreign policy, as government has the best read on the amount of material power, money, leverage, and influence it can use to its advantage. The way forward is to locate partners out of the institution, out of that self-imposed confined space that is government itself. This is the only way to help release the creative energy that exists inside and outside of government, and draw solutions.

The paradox is highlighted by the dual-paradigm approach to foreign policy and the pursuit of diplomatic relations. States need to survive and they cannot fail; they need to protect their assets and people, social and intellectual capital, financial markets, and military strength. Losses in any of those areas would result in upheaval. It's too risky for government to stake its existence on solving problems that fall outside its interests. That's why we need nonstate actors.

In a networked world, persuasion still plays a key role. But we're still far from understanding the true dynamics of networks, outside of their values, objectives, and norms, in particular given the new nonstate players in the foreign policy. How do networks operate and how are they evolving?

I'm seeing two different kinds of conversations happening on this front. On the one side, especially in the communications camp, there's a lot of magnetism about the network idea. This is where the communication leans to network models, the power to structure an organization horizontally, where there's no top-down control. That kind of structure sounds definitely more appealing and egalitarian, where everybody can contribute. On the other side, there are those thinking that we're putting too much stock on the idea of networks, as we still don't know what networks are doing for us. It's not enough to just say that networks do a good job in putting people in contact with each other. But does that lead to anything? Does it accelerate actions? We still don't know.

The existence of networks by themselves is not enough to get excited about. I'm more intrigued by the commodity that moves through networks, and that's ideas. This is where my analysis becomes really Gramscian. Antonio Gramsci[2] was the Italian socialist who, from within his jail cell, looked around Europe in the early 1920s and said, "Why didn't the Marxist prophecy become true?" It is because of ideas finding a hegemonic space and being nurtured to the point where they find widespread acceptance and there's consent. There was no popular will to adopt socialism in Europe in the 1920s—and that's why he ended up in jail. So, let's go back to hegemony and start to think about what Gramsci calls the hegemonic bloc—the germination of an idea as it steadily grows into a dominant state of mind governing thoughts and action. In the case of networks, in order for them to grow and expand, there needs to be something that drives them. A network by itself is sort of a shell. What flows through the nodes and the links is what matters the most. That can happen on a large complex network as well as on a two-node network. For nonstate actors, they need to be as expansive as a network can be in order to achieve their goals to achieve that hegemonic bloc to one into formation; they also need to have mobilization, and massive propagation of their ideas for that to happen.

In this new environment, is the more traditional foreign policy establishment pluralizing or merely faking it?

Governments are still testing the waters with networks, but they're still struggling. One of the problems is still that due to the credibility gap, governments look disingenuous when they say you can trust them. That undermines government's participation in the network, in a natural way. Unless there is a way to enter a network environment organically, forcing it often does not work out the way you planned it. For example, when the State Department made a significant ad purchase on Facebook, it made it seem like that it was contriving the very engagement that it sought to promote naturally. Of course it boosted their numbers and, through that ad buy, it drew more people to the pages. But the authenticity of that engagement probably suffered.

When it comes to analytics and the numbers behind how networks operate, the devil in the details of quantitative research is that once you start looking at your data and you realize there's nothing there, then your data sets are useless. With technologies, apps, and social media, superficially the downloading itself and the number of users prevails over the very goal of your action. It might be a first step, but there are still several steps to go before those numbers yield a substantive return.

NOTES

1. John Robert Kelley, "The New Diplomacy: Evolution of a Revolution," *Diplomacy and Statecraft* 21, no. 2 (2010): 286–305.

2. Antonio Gramsci was an Italian Marxist theoretician and politician. He wrote on political theory, sociology, and linguistics. He was a founding member and one-time leader of the Communist Party of Italy and was imprisoned by Benito Mussolini's fascist regime. Gramsci is best known for his theory of cultural hegemony, which describes how states use cultural institutions to maintain power in capitalist societies.

22

DIGITAL BUILDING BLOCKS FOR DEMOCRACY

A conversation with Petrit Selimi, Deputy Minister of Foreign Affairs of Kosovo

To view clips
from the conversation
with Petrit Selimi
scan the QR code
or visit:
http://goo.gl/RZR7qZ

The launch of the Digital Kosovo portal digitalkosovo.org[1] in July 2013 is an important step forward for Kosovo in achieving full recognition on the World Wide Web—including a country-code top-level domain (or ccTLD)[2]—and empowering its citizens with full access to the Internet and its benefits. At the presentation of Digital Kosovo, you said:[3] "The exclusion of Kosovo from many of the biggest websites in the world means that Kosovo citizens continue to be excluded from fully utilizing online services; a right taken for granted by people around the world. It also has a detrimental knock-on effect on our economy." In other words, not being fully recognized on the World Wide Web has implications on how your citizens can access services, or even buy products online—thus impacting economic growth. But this is also a problem for your government being able to offer online services to your citizens and for them to exercise their civil rights and duties through online platforms, options that many consider a given.

How has the Digital Kosovo project developed and what are the next steps?

When Kosovo became independent in 2008, the first focus of the Ministry of Foreign Affairs was full bilateral recognition of Kosovo because we couldn't go through the UN as Russia was blocking it. Ninety-nine percent of the work of the first foreign minister and his staff was contacting missions on a bilateral level from other countries. When I came on board—I came from the corporate sector, with a public relations background, from the Internet and telecom industries—I realized that the Internet could have covered a lot of black holes in terms of Kosovo's narration. The Internet could have helped us in terms of presenting what Kosovo is and how do people know about us. It could also have helped us in terms of recognition not just on a bilateral basis, but also on other platforms. Obviously, first and foremost, a lack of ccTLD meant that Kosovo could not issue its own IP addresses; could not have its own native habitat, in which organizations and companies were able to use a specific ccTLD for creating their own internal market. It also meant that on the drop-down menus of 99 percent of websites around the world, Kosovo was just not there. Companies in other countries just don't care. They probably don't have people, time, or resources to deal with adding new countries on a drop-down list of countries. We could not go to the International Organization for Standardization (ISO)[4] because we were not a member of the UN, and ISO operates as a UN agency.

As we couldn't go straight to the source to have all websites and platforms around the world to add Kosovo on the drop-down list of countries for users to use services as citizens of Kosovo, we decided to actively promote and propagate changes page by page, platform by platform, company by company. That's how the idea behind Digital Kosovo was born. And the most successes have come directly from the citizens of Kosovo, normal people who decided to contact portals and the likes to ask for Kosovo to be added in their registration forms, users agreements, and so on. In the period 2008–2009, I was at the London School of Economics with a scholarship. Obviously Kosovo was not a choice in their website. So, I decided to write to the school and the management team of the school's website to have Kosovo added. They first responded Kosovo was indeed not an option in their scroll-down menus, but I argued that I was indeed a student from Kosovo, with a Kosovo passport and a British visa stamped on it, as the UK government, where the school is located and operates from, has recognized Kosovo as independent. My argument was, "If I'm a student here at your university as a recipient of a scholarship, based on the fact that I'm from Kosovo, why can't you manually add Kosovo?" They finally decided to add Kosovo to all their scroll-down menus. If you multiply that by a hundreds, then you have progress. When Twitter recognized Kosovo, it was thanks to the efforts of Kushtrim Xhakli, then a seventeen-year-old boy who was working for the IPKO Foundation,[5] through his appeals, emails, petitions. This is about being digital diplomats for Kosovo. Real people out there working for the good of their country.

Today, as part of our digital diplomacy strategy, designed to cover as much as possible from digital domain names to digital recognition, we decided to establish a portal, a web resource in which whoever wants to lobby or write letters can use templates, can use addresses, can use all sorts of information on steps to take. This is how Digital Kosovo was born, designed to empower people to conduct their own digital diplomacy: to send letters and e-mails to all big corporations and digital platforms out there for having Kosovo recognized as a country in their online forms. If a deputy foreign minister like me sends a letter, it's obviously the letter of a politician. If a hundred clients—or even one thousand clients—write to Lufthansa, for instance, and say, "Listen, we travel with Lufthansa all the time, but you have us in the magazine as a different map. Why don't you have us in your program card?" All of a sudden you get attention.

The intention of Digital Kosovo was to circumvent the big problem, the lack of shortcuts for Kosovo, by enabling people to do what people do best: lobby on behalf of a country they love. If you're an Internet corporation based in Silicon Valley, you don't really want to get involved in foreign policy, politicians, and diplomats. But if your users in a given area are asking you to revise the situation for the common good of your users and your company, then we might get somewhere. Digital Kosovo was meant to provide our people with the necessary tools to talk to Silicon Valley giants and companies around the world; to get their voices heard.

In terms of social media use in Kosovo, Facebook is the most popular social media platform in the country, used by approximately three-quarters of Kosovo's Internet users. While users can select Kosovo as a location, Facebook has not recognized Kosovo as an independent country. The country's lobbying efforts combined with citizen advocacy have successfully convinced websites such as Twitter, and more recently LinkedIn, to include Kosovo. What's the role of social media in Kosovo?

According to the last census, one in every four Kosovar lives in the diaspora. Kosovo is extremely intertwined and dependent on contact with the outside world. From the 1970s, 1980s, and the 1990s and during the war, basically up to five or six hundred thousand Kosovars fled a country of 1.8 million people. They live mostly in Germany and Switzerland, and they're living across the Atlantic, in the United States. My uncle lives in New Jersey where he owns and manages a restaurant; my cousins from my mother's side are all living in Staten Island where they have businesses. I have family in London, in France, in Germany; and that is typical for many Kosovars. That's when the Internet becomes the easiest way to stay connected with family members. My grandmother used to speak with her grandchildren—who she sees only once a year—through Skype. Because of our demographic structure and the diaspora, digital tools and social media platforms, like Twitter and Facebook, play a very important role. They're not just tools for social engagement and for connecting with the world, but they're increasingly important in terms of online advertising and economic growth.

We're also the youngest country in Europe by age of its citizens; we had a high birth rate for years, and this has significantly dropped as things have normalized. But we still have a very young population—around 70 percent of the population is under the age of thirty. At any given point, there are 450,000 students of Kosovo in the school system, primary, secondary—and that represents almost one-third of the entire population. Hence, there is a big engagement with social media. Also, because of the way and rapidity the Internet developed in Kosovo, around 75 percent of Kosovar households have a broadband connection at home. Whoever comes to Kosovo is surprised by the quality of Internet access.

The Norwegian ambassador to the Republic of Kosovo, Jan Braa-thu,[6] said: "Via Digital Kosovo, we can all be digital diplomats and make use of our potential influence by demanding that Kosovo is recognized by companies on the Internet. It is about more than just personal inconvenience. We see great potential in utilizing digital to support Kosovo's statehood."[7] Norway has been a great partner in the launch of your digital agenda, together with the United Kingdom and IPKO Foundation. Public–private partnerships in the creation of this initiative were key, as a full inclusion of Kosovo in the global Internet infrastructure and all online activities is beneficial not just for the country, but also for the region, companies, and education and research institutions around the world. Can you elaborate on that?

Government should be as little as possible in terms of contacts with corporations, because corporations are genuinely reluctant to deal with politicians and political issues. I think from day one, when we started our public diplomacy project, we covered a very wide scope of action from interfaith dialogue to digital diplomacy, to conferences, Fulbright scholarships, and exchanges. It was clear since the very beginning that we needed to involve civil society. We decided to partner with other governments and entities so as to create partnerships and develop a plan of action that eventually evolved into our Digital Kosovo platform. We matched up donations from the Norwegian and British governments, we partnered with entities like the British Council and the IPKO Foundation—which originates out of a telecom company, but is philanthropic in nature. We were very happy to outsource our idea to other parts of the political sphere and the civil society landscape. I think that's actually how it should be done. What's the point for me to hire additional people in my staff at the government level and balloon the budget of the Ministry of Foreign Affairs, when I simply can use the money to advocate and fund-raise with the help of other partners? For us, it was a creative way to engage as many people as possible. In this context, one Euro can take you very far; two Euros can take you even further; but two Euros and a partner who knows how to spend them can make magic happen.

Digital Kosovo is managed by a team inside IPKO Foundation, a locally operating nongovernmental organization (NGO) with the goal of seeding and supporting the development of the next generation of leaders with a digital vision for Kosovo. In addition, the portal does not reflect the policies or opinions of supporting organizations. How important is the independence of the project and what's the role of the government of Kosovo in the project?

It's very important. From day one, I was engaged in decentralizing our work without amassing and hoarding cash and people in our foreign ministry, but rather the opposite. We have been trying to find as many partners and coalitions as possible. It's not only about digital diplomacy. It's also about religious freedoms, security, economic growth.

Let's talk about Kosovo's country-code top-level domain. The last country to be assigned one by the Internet Corporation for Assigned Names and Numbers (ICANN) was Montenegro in May 2013.[8] *What would it mean for Kosovo to have its own country code on the Internet and how close you are to get one?*

A ccTLD for Kosovo would mean a new sustainable habitat for our citizens and for our companies. Because we don't have a country code, we are limited to the .coms, .orgs, and likes. That not only restricts our ability to select a proper digital name for a business or a project but also our ability to have a recognizable domain in Kosovo, to let our service industry and the media landscape grow organically in the country they operate and beyond its borders, without losing its national identity. On the other hand, there is the issue with IP codes. In terms of advertising, for example, a company is not able to determine its market in Kosovo because our IP addresses are all based outside of Kosovo. It's impossible for a company to calculate the impact of an online campaign in Kosovo—and thus the way a company grows its market within Kosovo—because there's no way to calculate the number of hits. To advertisers, our clicks, our hits are not separated from Serbian or Albanian clicks, depending on which IP addresses we use. In this IP-less landscape, Kosovo is really a loser, not only because of identity issues as there's still no ccTLD, but very practically because our companies are put in a disadvantaged position vis-à-vis other rivals in the Balkan region, which instead have the ability to track their customers, to chase their customers, to interact with their customers. That type of activity is severely hampered for Kosovo companies.

Now, because of the advent of social media tools, the market is changing, and consumers, companies, and advertisers actually chase information and products via secondary platforms. That makes it a bit better for us in Kosovo.

This is how we are presenting our case to ICANN. Kosovo is a member of the World Bank and the International Monetary Fund (IMF)—a sovereign member—we're also a member of the European Bank for Reconstruction and Development (EBRD) and the Council of Europe Development Bank (CEB).[9] There are a number of financial institutions which have Kosovo under its fold. If they want to have separate statistics on Kosovo, we need the country to be able to have its own code. It's a slow process—and, for example, we recently got a SWIFT code,[10] and by 2015 we should be able to get our own telephone country code, separate from Serbia's.

Achieving those goals—starting from an Internet country code for Kosovo to achieving standards that other countries have been enjoying for decades—is key for us as it's a way to foster international inclusion of Kosovo, strengthen our global Internet infrastructure, better regulate and evaluate our commercial activities and trade independently, and being able to conduct accurate statistics on our products and services. Statistics are an essential part of being a state, a nation.

I said in the past that digital diplomacy has been to diplomacy and foreign policy what Jane Jacobs[11] had been for urban planning in the 1960s. With her community-based approach, Jacobs inspired generations of urban planners and activists around the globe to focus more on neighborhood-centered city structures and social interactions rather than massive power structures and large-scale developments that would have undermined the development of our society. "Old ideas can sometimes use new buildings. New ideas must use old buildings," Jacobs wrote in her 1961 book **The Death and Life of Great American Cities.**[12] *What's your take?*

I went to college in Oslo. First I took theology in my first semester, and then I switched to social anthropology with a semester in urbanism. Going back to Kosovo after my studies was like I was living firsthand what I learned in school. The city landscape was changing so quickly, so rapidly. Those physical changes, the changes in the physical landscape of our cities were projected onto the changing social structures. For example, we went through what I call the Walmart-ization of Kosovo in only three years—quite more rapidly than the span of over fifty years that it took to the United States to go through the same process starting from the 1960s and 1970s. From no shopping malls, now Kosovo counts about twenty-six, and that's just around the capital of Pristina. But the same happens in many other sectors of society.

I think digital has been a big part of that same change. We have to make sure—and this is my personal conviction, I might be wrong—a lot of diplomats say that diplomacy is diplomacy, it is done behind closed doors, and the public can just damage the results of what can be achieved mano-a-mano. But government-to-people and people-to-people diplomacy can certainly reach more. We need to show to the world where we came from and where we are going; why we need to be recognized. And that can only be done now through digital means, there is no other way. If you do not become part of that digital movement, you are excluding yourself and robbing yourself of the chance of (a) saving lives, but (b) to engage in proper foreign diplomacy, which is now—unfortunately for some ambassadors—much more rooted in this massive flow of information and interaction online.

You're a very young politician in your early to mid-thirties. Over 70 percent of Kosovo's population is under the age of thirty, so Kosovo is a digitally "switched on" nation with Internet penetration and usage similar to Europe-wide and global norms; Internet penetration based on the number of users is 76.6 percent. What is the role of the new generations in Kosovo in harnessing their own future and the future of the country through technology, innovation, and new ideas?

It is very important. In a way I feel, not sorry, but that we become sometimes ageist in our public discourse. Because it's all about young, quick, and now—especially when it comes to foreign policy, because we often associate foreign policy with those who are older.

For Kosovo, our demographics are clear, a very young nation. We are dependent—and we are not there yet—on finding a model of growth that is sustainable and that can harness our resources at best, including the fact that our population is very young. In Kosovo, you can often see a lot of energy and dynamism, not always noticed elsewhere.

NOTES

1. The Digital Kosovo online portal is a new initiative by IPKO Foundation, with the support of the Republic of Kosovo Ministry of Foreign Affairs, the British Council, and the Norwegian Embassy. The initiative helps overcome the virtual barriers that currently exist in the online recognition of Kosovo by encouraging a range of Internet properties from shopping websites to travel to add Kosovo to their sites. Using Digital Kosovo advances Kosovo's digital presence across major websites around the world, so that Kosovo's citizen can take advantage of all the Internet has to offer in the same way as all global citizens.

2. Two letter domains, such as .uk (United Kingdom), .de (Germany) and .jp (Japan) (for example), are called country-code top-level domains (ccTLDs) and correspond to a country, territory, or other geographic location. The rules and policies for registering domain names in the ccTLDs vary significantly, and ccTLD registries limit use of the ccTLD to citizens of the corresponding country.

3. Kosovain.eu, "Launch of 'Digital Kosovo' Supports Kosovo Citizens to Lobby for Greater Internet Inclusion," last updated September 3, 2013, http://kosovain.eu/en/Kosova/Launch-of-Digital-Kosovo-Supports-Kosovo-Citizens-to-Lobby-for-Greater-Internet-Inclusion-24187.

4. The International Organization for Standardization (ISO) is the world's largest developer of voluntary international standards. International standards give state-of-the-art specifications for products, services, and good practice, helping to make industry more efficient and effective. Developed through global consensus, they help to break down barriers to international trade. ISO was founded in 1947, and since then has published more than 19,500 international standards covering almost all aspects of technology and business.

5. The IPKO Foundation powers the Digital Kosovo platform. IPKO Foundation is a local operating foundation in Kosovo. Its goal is to seed and support the development of the next generation of leaders with a digital vision

for Kosovo. These young leaders may come from any sector or discipline but are united in their embrace of technology, the Internet, and the information society.

6. Ambassador Jan Braathu has been Norway's ambassador to the Republic of Kosovo and the Republic of Albania since 2011.

7. Kosovain.eu, "Launch of 'Digital Kosovo.'"

8. ICANN signed an Accountability Framework agreement with the country-code top-level domain (ccTLD) manager for .ME (Montenegro), the Ministry for Information Society and Telecommunications of Montenegro, on May 13, 2013. The Accountability Framework program provides two mechanisms by which ccTLD managers can formalize their relationship with ICANN. The first is an Accountability Framework document that sets out the obligations of a ccTLD manager and ICANN. It also covers dispute resolution and termination and is designed for ccTLD managers requiring a formal document with ICANN.

9. The Council of Europe Development Bank (CEB) is a multilateral development bank with a social vocation. Established on April 16, 1956, in order to bring solutions to the problems of refugees, its scope of action has progressively widened to other sectors of action directly contributing to strengthening social cohesion in Europe. The CEB represents a major instrument of the policy of solidarity in Europe, in order to help its forty-one member states achieve sustainable and equitable growth: it thus participates in financing social projects, responds to emergency situations and, in so doing, contributes to improving the living conditions of the most disadvantaged population groups.

10. SWIFT is the Society for Worldwide Interbank Financial Telecommunication, a member-owned cooperative through which the financial world conducts its business operations with speed, certainty, and confidence. More than 10,500 banking organizations, securities institutions, and corporate customers in 215 countries use and trust SWIFT codes every day to exchange millions of standardized financial messages.

11. Jane Jacobs was an American-Canadian journalist, author, and activist best known for her influence on urban studies. Her influential book *The Death and Life of Great American Cities* (New York: Random House, 1961) argued that urban renewal did not respect the needs of most city-dwellers.

12. Jane Jacobs, *The Death and Life of Great American Cities* (Random House, 1961 edition), 188.

23

AN INCUBATOR OF IDEAS AND GROWTH

A conversation with David H. Thorne, Senior Advisor to the US Secretary of State

At the 2013 SelectUSA Investment Summit, Secretary Kerry said: "Foreign policy today is economic policy. And leaders in government need to understand that. There is a synergy and an importance to this relationship that cannot be denied." Indeed, foreign policy has many ramifications, and certainly economic growth and financial sustainability are some of the key priorities for many governments, especially in a time of crisis like the one we've been facing for the past few years, both in the United States and in Europe. Economic diplomacy can strengthen relationships—political and economic—but can also spur growth and catalyze innovation, at home and abroad. In this context, what is the role of the digital economy?

The digital economy is a key element to position economic and commercial issues more prominently within the foreign policy landscape. It is a way to promote global prosperity through the empowerment of young people and entrepreneurs. It is the recognition of the role of technology and innovation in shaping our future.

In the United States, one of our greatest economic drivers has been innovation. US government and business leaders understand that we are no longer the world's leader in many sectors and industries—and this is okay, as long as our efforts are focused on remaining the world's number-one innovator. I have seen firsthand the transforming effect of leveraging new technologies to spur innovation and growth in the United States, where social media, big data, and cloud technologies are now part of our economic landscape.

The digital economy in the United States currently accounts for around 7 percent of the gross domestic product. The figure will only grow, especially considering that the digital economy accounted for 37 percent of our economic growth in the past twenty years. If you look at the last decade, around 40 percent of new jobs in America have come from new technologies.

The digital economy represents an incredible shift that is only going to accelerate in the future, bringing promises but also challenges. In Europe, as the digital economy grows, what we call the app-economy—which revolves around the use of applications for mobile phones—will have generated 5 million jobs. Around the world, you now have young entrepreneurs and startups all over the spectrum contributing greatly to economic growth by exploring the potential of technologies like cell phone apps and building businesses from the ground up with small initial investments.

While the digital economy is a new way of helping boost growth and prosperity, I would argue that the larger theme is one of how to face challenges throughout the world. Global power is being increasingly shared among more national and transnational platforms, such as the European Union and ASEAN. In addition, the power of the individual is also on the rise, fueled by social media tools. In this increasingly globalized environment, every effort toward a stronger economic diplomacy can't help but benefit us.

Internet freedom, digital divide, access to broadband and tele-communications infrastructures. . . . What are the main challenges in our path to a sustainable and effective digital economy?

The greatest challenge for a more fluid digital economy is the ecosystem that supports it. You cannot really have a robust digital economy without building and nurturing a robust and well-functioning ecosystem around it. That includes cooperative relationships between the legal framework in which startups and entrepreneurs operate; it includes a more central focus on education and training; it includes capital. The necessary ingredients to a successful ecosystem are open systems that are fluid and able to adjust; shared information and the ability to share information easily and in real-time; a legal structure that is conducive to expanding enterprises and fostering relationships and partnerships.

When it comes to the role of government, the biggest contribution we can make to the shaping of the digital economy ecosystem is to become a facilitator between ideas, people, government agencies, and the international community. We also need to be better conveners: the goal is to have everybody involved and operate in synchronicity.

The digital economy does not belong in a large institution. It is a bottom-up enterprise, and it must be kept that way in order to keep its vitality. Government needs to understand this new dynamic and contribute to the sustainability of the ecosystem, while at the same time promoting transparency and anticorruption initiatives.

My friend Reid Hoffman, founder of LinkedIn, once said that the huge advantage of Silicon Valley right now is the ecosystem in which it operates, aimed to sustain and nurture relationships. It is about a sustainable local interplay between people, capital, and government. The ecosystem in Silicon Valley has become the primary force of technological innovation that is fueling our digital economy. Similarly, other areas and cities in the United States have focused in the past few years in local progrowth policies that can be implemented not in a top-down way, but rather at the local and municipal level. This is when the way to create business ecosystems is through local public and private leadership. The goal is to improve the quality of life of our citizens; create a probusiness environment; invest in the future; and innovation and economic transformation.

As ambassador to Italy, you launched the Digital Economy Forum, a public–private sector collaboration to catalyze innovation, entrepreneurship, and job creation. What is the experience of the Digital Economy Forum and how has it evolved to become a new, innovative ingredient in US foreign policy?

The Digital Economy Forum was about contributing to the digital ecosystem in Italy and expanding the already strong economic relationships between Italy, Europe, and the United States. It was launched to focus on the digital economy in terms of job creation and economic growth. It was a way for us to form a dialogue around digital technologies and their potential to help people grow their businesses. We ran a series of very practical workshops and events on how to use everything that is available—from online marketing platforms to social media and cloud computing—to help people empower ideas and embark in new ventures.

The Digital Economy Forum in Italy became a way for us to engage—on a lot of different levels—on policy dialogues, around economic growth, around the importance of the Internet and broadband, and the importance of young people and entrepreneurship. It was sort of a catch-all for talking about a lot of these different issues on a policy level. On a public level, it was also a way for us to work with Italian and American companies, chambers of commerce, universities, and other groups involved with entrepreneurship about why these things are important and how do we help them work together.

What we noticed right from the very beginning is how creating a dialogue helped young entrepreneurs nurture an engaging networking environment. Networking is a true bottom-up and transparent exercise that enables you to exchange information and ideas in a fluid and organic way. Thanks to the networking environment we created, the success of the initiative was instantaneous, bringing together almost ten thousand participants online and helping them become part of the economic dialogue. Being able to network needs to become part of the process for new generations, as they're not only the engine for economic growth, but they also help push the economic and creative process forward.

One of the things we tried to do in Italy with the Digital Economy Forum was to really focus on what young people have to contribute, in terms of perspectives and growth. When it comes to looking for opportunities, young people are the best at transforming challenges into opportunities as, most of the times, they have nothing to lose. Those are the people who tend to come up with the most interesting and creative ideas because they don't have the confines of a comfortable job or a family business. They have to create their own future. I think that bringing them into the discussion helps the political process, the economy, and the government, as a provider of services to its citizens.

The Digital Economy Forum was also about competitiveness, one of the themes I've raised often during my tenure in Italy. How to make Italy—as well as Europe and the United States—more competitive is a challenging question, and many have acknowledged that in order to achieve this, we require more structural reforms and investments to induce job growth and improve productivity. But underlying this talk of hitting the right numbers and drafting the right laws is a more fundamental question: how to keep leaders and citizens alike focused on a common goal, a single vision. As leaders, we should not forget that unity of purpose is the only way to truly create the necessary political will during any difficult transformation. Only with a unified vision will we have a stronger chance of pushing the economy forward. That unified vision is needed also when it comes to the digital economy.

The Digital Economy Forum showed that an important role is now played by small and medium-sized enterprises, as well as young entrepreneurs and startups. How is the foreign policy community embracing these new players?

The American foreign policy community definitely is. There has been a lot of research about the importance of small- and medium-sized companies, new businesses, and startups and what they contribute to growth and job creation. I think in the past four to five years, because there has been so much attention to those issues, there has been recognition of these companies as major players in our economy, to be embraced as much as blue chip corporations.

The benefit that comes from interacting with all economic players—large and small, startups and established traditional businesses—is also linked to the potential for the economy to prosper moving forward. Established industrial leaders could develop stronger relationships with startups and innovation hubs as a means of acquiring cutting-edge research and development. Steps such as these would reap dividends not only for individual investors, but for the entire country.

When it comes to young generations, one undeniable fact is that as the world population grows, much of that growth is going to be represented by a movement into the middle class—the estimate is around three billion people over the next twenty-five years. Around 60 percent of that growth is people under thirty years of age, alongside with the demand for the creation of seven hundred million new jobs. That is one of the biggest economic challenges the international community is going to face. Without embracing the digital economy and a culture of innovation, we are going to have instability, strife, and lack of satisfaction. Investing in young people is something governments need to do more.

As you mentioned, the digital economy relies on innovation and new creative ideas in order to harness the digital era and promote growth and global prosperity. Technology per se is not sufficient. Do you think foreign policy can function as a true incubator of ideas and open the door to policies that are better suited to respond to new challenges, including the current economic crisis?

Foreign policy can certainly be an incubator of ideas. But we need to understand that the role of government is not to be an entrepreneur. Government can move toward a culture of innovation and help build the necessary ecosystem, dialogue, and framework. It's then for the private sector to make ideas blossom and become reality.

In many countries around the world, the digital economy ecosystem I described earlier is not yet present—or it's still struggling to take shape and prosper. This is where foreign policy can play an important role. We find that everyone wants innovation, everyone wants job creation, and everyone wants economic growth. It's important to find a productive way to talk about those issues and really focus the discussion within the international communities and in our dealings with our partners bilaterally.

Certainly, our foreign policy structure, in terms of reach with embassies all over the world, is a unique attribute to how we operate. And that is something we can contribute to the ecosystem. As a large network, we are well placed to be able to pick up new ideas and act as a link between government and entrepreneurs, between capitals and infrastructures. Our embassies really need to engage more with the entrepreneurship world in each country. We understand why it's important on a whole host of different levels. Depending on the country, both in the Western world and in developing nations, entrepreneurship and the digital economy acquire different trajectories according to the local challenges specific to that area. We can have an important role in helping entrepreneurs to network with their peers in their home countries and here in the United States, but also to connect them more to the people that have power, authority, and influence in their countries.

One of the things we tried to do with the Digital Economy Forum in Italy was to encourage business leaders, high-net-worth individuals, to become more active or to become angel investors as a way to increase capital for local entrepreneurs. It is about changing the way the system operates and fostering relationships that the digital economy can benefit from. And this benefits economic growth and prosperity locally and internationally, including in terms of youth employment, an issue that is not limited to any particular geography. Entrepreneurship is critical to addressing the job gap and making opportunities for young people.

Now, I mentioned innovation. Innovation is key. It does upset the status quo because it introduces new elements that make old processes obsolete. That is why we will always encounter some resistance at the beginning, in government and in the private sector, in the Western world and in developing countries.

You said: "In the US, we have no doubt that much of the current and future strength of our economy will depend on growth and innovation stemming from digital technologies. These technologies also go beyond the business world and have penetrated deeply into American politics, entertainment, and culture."

Each country shows its specific set of dynamics. What characterizes America are the values we live by and we're most admired for: the sense of democracy, freedom, and self-determination that is America. Those values are inculcated in our trying to help and inspire people around the world. They are part of our economic engine and our way of life. This is why America has an important role in pushing the digital economy agenda and help it become a key priority for the international community in order to face economic challenges and complement the globalization process. Digital tools have not only helped bring people together, but they also exposed the power of ideas—and ideals—in a way that is energizing the policy ecosystem. As part of our focus to economics, we need to bring this dynamic new dimension of the economy in our foreign policy agenda, encouraging a large dialogue around new technologies and innovation. We need to understand how we can be effective in this new digital environment and let innovation prosper so that old government structures are not in the way in facilitating a move toward the digital economy.

24

FROM MACHIAVELLI TO THE DIGITAL AGE

A conversation with Gianni Riotta, Member of the Council on Foreign Relations and Pirelli Visitor Professor, Princeton University

To view clips
from the conversation
with Gianni Riotta
scan the QR code
or visit:
http://goo.gl/ese5fO

*In your latest book,[1] **Has the Web Brought Us Freedom? Politics and Civil Society in The Digital World** , you argue that the twenty-first century is the century characterized by a pivot to the people, as opposed to the twentieth century masses-centered.[2] "We have to look at ourselves, the very architects and artisans of technology, rather than to focus on software and hardware," you write. Governments are now trying to adapt to this new reality and use social media as a tool not only to broadcast their message, but also to listen to the people and nurture a veritable dialogue. Do you think they are successful or perhaps, as some critics say, it is only a smoke screen—a tactical maneuver—with no effect on the more traditional political rhetoric and foreign policy discourse?*

The twentieth century was a century of masses. You would go to school as a mass; you would work in the field or in an assembly line as a mass. The same mass would be changing in less than twenty-four hours. In twenty-four hours you could go from being a farmer to being a worker, to being a soldier. The mass was multifunctional. Labor, war, school, and, of course, politics were all about the masses. The leaders of the time—Stalin, Hitler, Mussolini, Roosevelt, Churchill—knew their countries were divided into one, two, three blocks. And when they talked to citizens in Italy, the United States, Germany, and Russia, they would talk to these huge masses. This is why it was okay back then to talk about mass media—because when the *New York Times* would publish an article, millions and millions of people would agree with its content. When Walter Cronkite[3] at CBS would say something, everybody in America was listening. The same was true in Europe.

It was easier to spread a message because our communities were more homogenous. Then this mold was broken. It was broken when the Catholic Church decided that instead of using one master language to talk to the masses, as for centuries they had done using Latin, each local church would start using the local language. In a way, they allowed a new access to the community, making things smoother, more direct, and smaller. The same happened with schools. All over the Western world schools were differentiated. So models that were imposed in the French empire, the British empire—models that were imposed over millions of people—were going away.

When that was broken, it became almost impossible for leaders to lead masses. Immigration had an impact as well as it was changing our society quite profoundly. The sexual revolution meant that you didn't talk to citizens any more, you talked to men and women on gender-specific issues. Then the green movements appeared, introducing another spin in the way governments were addressing its constituencies. It was incredibly difficult to deal with all this. I call it a kaleidoscopic society, where everything is fragmented. Sociologist Zygmunt Bauman[4] uses the metaphor of the liquid society, but to me is not the proper definition because any liquid assumes the shape of the vessel that contains it. Ours is not a shapeless society. It's instead a society in which each pixel, each figment, has its own very strong identity.

How do you address a society where each individual counts as a mass in itself? The medicine and the scourge is social media. Meaning that the way we can address a society that has become polarized and frag-mented is through re-creating a community within the social media sphere.

In 2013, we commemorated the quincentennial of Niccoló Machi-avelli's **The Prince.** *Since then, the structure of power in the twen-ty-first century has certainly changed. Global interconnectivity has forced governments to rethink their foreign policy priorities while at the same time acknowledge new players and engage with the world. It is a new world where Machiavellian's vertical hier-archies have been complemented with horizontal webs and net-works. "The Prince is perfect in describing even the most current events in national and foreign policy," you said at a July 2013 panel discussion at the Italian Embassy in Washington, DC. "So-cial media and digital diplomacy are the only elements missing from his analysis."[5] Indeed, for the Machiavellian Prince it would be more difficult to rule in the twenty-first century, as he'd be confronting and engaging with public opinion online. How would Machiavelli tackle the digital era?*

As a politician and a diplomat in his own time, Machiavelli was a failure, a middle-range fellow who ended up in trouble. None of his great strategies went anywhere; none of his more devious plots went any-where. He was a failure. The reason he was a failure is because very often in sixteenth-century Florence, as well as in Washington—or Beij-ing, London, Paris, Rome—in the twenty-first century, a great strategy is not the best way to go. A great strategy is trumped by big interests and intrigues, and backstabbing. But Machiavelli was really not Machia-vellian. I don't know, with the kind of keen mind that he had, how he would square the equation in the age of social media?

Machiavelli would actually find in social media, and in the public opinion steered by social media, the missing link—or the link that he missed—in order to be successful. Because when he tried to steer the interests of the ruler, he said not to trust mercenary troops, raise a national army, think of Italy as a nation and not a coalition of many cities. Why wasn't he able to raise any common consent? Because he was missing a center of where to put his strategy. Machiavelli was a great writer—a writer of plays, of history, of political philosophy, of what is called now political propaganda. If he were to use Twitter or Facebook or any other social media, he could have certainly better harnessed public opinion, as he could have gone to the ruler and said, "Look, millions of people are retweeting my tweets, millions of people are buying my prints on Kindle or on Amazon. So you better listen to me!" Today's Machiavellis, even if they lack his brain and his purity of intent—even though historians would frown on the use of the word "purity" vis-à-vis Machiavelli—use social media exactly for that. If you want to raise an issue, you go on social media. If you want to raise awareness on anything, you go on social media.

What Machiavelli would probably tell us about social media—and I hope he doesn't blast me from heaven or hell for trying to say so—is that it's important that you reach a community through any mean, digital on not, but it's so very important that you have a vision to do that; that you have the strategy; that you have the cold analysis. Often people are lacking a vision, a strategy. What's next? What do you want to build? Our gamble today is to have a solid vision and a canny practice.

In the twenty-first century, what is the role of innovation—not just technology per se?

I'm very fond of Melvin Kranzberg's[6] first law of technology,[7] which states that technology is neither good nor bad, nor is it neutral. Technology is not a positive force in itself; it's not a negative force in itself; it depends on how we use it.

At the same time, when we use a certain technology, we are forced into a certain set of communication values and ideas. The same is true with social media. For example, there's now a common consensus that the Arab Spring didn't generate on social media. Social media was not the sparkle that ignited the Arab revolution, not at all. But today, in countries like Turkey, China, and Egypt—even in Syria—you see social media playing a role. It is not a one-dimensional environment. In China for example, the government decides what access to allow its citizens. It's a game of cat and mouse, because social media has a tremendous potential for liberation and emancipation, and for spreading knowledge.

And at the same time, companies use it for getting data. It is used by governments to check on each other and on their own citizens, as the NSA scandal proved it to be the case. Is this a surprise? No, it's normal.

Churchill spied on De Gaulle; De Gaulle tried to spy on Churchill; Roosevelt would routinely spy on Churchill; Churchill would try to spy on the Americans.

We must also remember that a tweet—a message on social media—is not just a stone that is cast and then is forgotten. Instead, it is cast and recast, and recast again. Don't think of it as a stone that you have to throw, but rather a brick that you lay building a wall. You have to be aware—as a diplomat especially, as a politician, as somebody representing a government who is tweeting or posting blogs—that you're building a palace with your single statements. After your palace is finished, you're building another palace; then you're building a city; then you're building a few cities; then you're building roads and bridges connecting those cities. People tend to think what I say today, stays today. No. You're producing bricks that will last forever. With social media, you put your wisdom there today and it stays there for a long time. You had better be aware of that.

Your book illustrates all facets of the so-called digital revolution framing it into your own personal experience. You write: "Today, all aspects of our life, our loved ones and our family, the job market and the economy, education and research, politics and society, culture and literature, consumerism and money, love and eroticism, and even faith and religion, keep us glued to a computer monitor, the black mirror of a tablet, the kaleidoscopic lights of a smartphone."[8] I certainly can relate to that. That said, has the web brought you freedom?

I don't think that as an individual I am free of the general condition that the human race enjoys and suffers. I'm not a great believer in the individual who finds happiness on his own—or freedom on his own; or even wealth on his own. I was brought up during the Cold War, and as such I was a son of the Cold War. Very few people nowadays realize that, given the numbers of theaters of war and international tensions in the world compared to how many human beings are living on earth, never in human history have so few of them been involved in actual war. The war in Congo, the war in Rwanda, killed at the end of the last century millions of people. Yet, they are completely out of the personal and political and diplomatic radar of the European public. And I was amazed at how fast and how completely painless for the European public opinion the Balkan war was. I expected that in Europe, to see again concentration camps, ethnic cleansing, private revenge, bombs, would shake everybody out of their hinges. It did not. And to realize why, you have to challenge the common wisdom. Europeans are peaceful. They don't believe in war because they were so shaken by World War II that they renounced war. Europeans fell in love with the status quo, because never had they had it so good and never in human history had people had it so easy. Europeans today do not believe in war and do not believe in changing the status quo.

So do you expect the web to make yourself free? I say yes. Yes, because I expect the web to make myself more contemporary. As a son of the Cold War—as somebody who will die with his personality shaped under the Cold War—I do believe in strong identities. I do believe that you have to be contemporary in order to engage the world. If you're not somebody, if you're not rooted somewhere, you cannot engage the world. We live now in an age of weak identities that pass like ghosts over earth and don't leave any kind of impression. But as a son of the Cold War, I'm deeply aware that identity can be a set of wings that can carry you far away. It can also be a cage that can lock you in forever. When I see what happened in the Balkans, what is still going on in the Middle East or in Afghanistan—or when I see how slowly India is freeing itself from bureaucratic rules and bureaucratic traditions—I see identity as a very good thing, but also as a very bad thing. The web is a mirror, and looking yourself in a mirror is always very tricky. There are days where you like what you see very much and there are days where you dislike what you see *very* much, especially when time passes and you are not as young as you used to be. But the mirror has a very strong role in identity. The mirror obliges you and forces you to deal with reality. And this is something that we're not doing enough. When I see my friend Evgeny Morozov[9] saying that the web is the well of all evil, that it is a Pandora vase that will damage human civilization, of course I think that he's exaggerating. Now, Marx, who lived before the digital revolution, might have been wrong when he tended to believe that materialistic economic interests were the only interests that move mankind, but he was certainly right when he suggested that in order to understand what people are doing, you need to have a little peek at what goes on in their wallets. This is true for critics and apologists of the web revolution as well.

The battle on the web today is about values. Values should be implemented on the web. It is a battle against the generation of relativism. For over twenty years, we have discussed about the clash of civilizations:[10] us versus them. If you open up a newspaper or a website, it's still filled up with Syria. Is Syria us versus them? No, it is them versus them. Shias versus Sunnis. Secular Islam versus religious Islam. Democratic Islam versus autocratic Islam. It is an Islamic civil war, and it is something that actually started over a century ago. Islam that engages modernity versus Islam that doesn't want to engage modernity. Were we good in supporting the Islam that is engaging modernity? We were terrible—and we still are terrible. And we pay the price now. But the real civil war is not Islam versus the Western world, the real civil war that we are fighting now is tolerance versus intolerance. What is the web and how can digital diplomacy help? Diplomacy can stir up these values, and dialogue, and community. The web is the perfect place to do it.

NOTES

1. The book, published in Italian by Einaudi Editori, is originally titled *Il web ci rende liberi? Politica e vita quotidiana nel mondo digitale* (Milan: Einaudi Editori, 2013).

2. Gianni Riotta, *Il web ci rende liberi? Politica e vita quotidiana nel mondo digitale* (Milan: Einaudi Editori, 2013), 176.

3. Walter Cronkite was the host of CBS' *Evening News* for nineteen years, from 1962 to 1981. During the heyday of CBS News in the 1960s and 1970s, he was often cited as "the most trusted man in America" after being so named in an opinion poll.

4. Zygmunt Bauman is professor emeritus of sociology at the University of Leeds, England. He is one of the world's most eminent social theorists writing on issues as diverse as modernity and the Holocaust, postmodern consumerism, and liquid modernity.

5. Andreas Sandre, "Statecraft and Foreign Policy from Machiavelli to Digital Diplomacy," *BigThink*, last updated July 23, 2013, http://bigthink.com/experts-corner/statecraft-and-foreign-policy-from-machiavelli-to-digital-diplomacy.

6. Melvin Kranzberg was a professor of history at Case Western Reserve University from 1952 until 1971. He was a Callaway professor of the history of technology at Georgia Tech from 1972 to 1988.

7. Melvin Kranzberg's six laws of technology state: (1) Technology is neither good nor bad; nor is it neutral. (2) Invention is the mother of necessity. (3) Technology comes in packages, big and small. (4) Although technology might be a prime element in many public issues, nontechnical factors take precedence in technology-policy decisions. (5) All history is relevant, but the history of technology is the most relevant. (6) Technology is a very human activity—and so is the history of technology.

8. Riolta, *Il web ci rende liberi?*, 3.

9. Evgeny Morozov is a writer and researcher of Belarusian origin who studies political and social implications of technology. He is currently a senior editor at *The New Republic*. In January 2011, Morozov published his first book: *The Net Delusion: The Dark Side of Internet Freedom* (Public Affairs, 2011). In addition to exploring the impact of the Internet on authoritarian states, the book investigates the intellectual sources of the growing excitement about the liberating potential of the Internet and links it to the triumphalism that followed the end of the Cold War. In March 2013, Morozov published a second book, *To Save Everything, Click Here* (Public Affairs, 2013) in which he critiques "technology solutionism," the idea that technology as a way to fix any problem is timely and potentially valuable.

10. The Clash of Civilizations is a theory, developed by political scientist Samuel P. Huntington, that states that people's cultural and religious identities will be the primary source of conflict in the post–Cold War world. It was proposed in a 1992 lecture by Huntington at the American Enterprise Institute (AEI), and later developed in his 1993 essay "The Clash of Civilizations?" which appeared in *Foreign Affairs*.

25

TECHNOLOGY AND FREEDOM

A conversation with Marietje Schaake,
Member of the European Parliament

You've been called the most wired politician in Europe. You're referred to by many as one of the few members of the European Parliament who really understands what is going on in terms of Internet, net freedom, and digital innovation. You yourself candidly admitted: "I think I was elected because of the Internet. I had no budget. I had no master plan, but I did have different networks of people. I was in contact with young entrepreneurs and I was already on Facebook and Twitter."[1] This being said, do you think we are paying too much attention to social media as a tool for politics when we should be looking at how social media, technology, and the Internet are reshaping the world in which we live?

Too often the focus in discussions around technology and democracy is on how social media can be used as campaign tools. Meanwhile, a lot of policies should be made or updated to meet the revolutionary impact technology has on our societies. In the absence of relevant policies, there is a vacuum that is leading to a lack of guarantees of competition, of fundamental rights and of security. There is a need for more focus on how to ensure our laws keep up to speed with technological developments.

Five years ago, the lack of knowledge about the working of tech-
nology in the European Parliament was such that you organized a
series of workshops called "Nerds in the EU Parliament"[2] *to cover*
a range of topics, from what happens when you click "send" to
transmit your e-mail, to copyright issues, to Internet freedom and
the blocking of websites and platforms. What happened since then
and how is the European Parliament tackling technology and
Internet freedom today?

The workshops were a way to involve my colleagues and to introduce
them to experts from the tech community. Since then I have focused
more on seminars, hearings, and other parliamentary work to ensure
people's rights and freedoms are ensured.

What are the most pressing issues Europe should address in order
to tackle Internet freedom and become a truly digital continent
with a functioning digital economy?

That is a long list! Net neutrality, data privacy, copyright reforms, export controls, Internet governance, access and knowledge, and ensuring
security is not used as a blanket argument to compromise fundamental
rights: the two can and must go hand in hand.

Let's talk about Europe and the United States in the debate on the
future of the Internet in the wake of the Edward Snowden revela-
tions about the NSA. Where's the debate now and where is it head-
ing?

The revelations have meant a wake-up call for those who needed that. I
believe it has helped the development of a broad political coalition that
seeks to strengthen EU laws to protect people's fundamental rights, and
that looks more critically at the consequences of unchecked power by
either governments or companies in the context of the digital environment. Still, there has not been enough of a response to truly make sure
the overreach by secret services is curbed, and that judicial and democratic oversight is in place.

At the National Democratic Institute's International Leaders Forum in September 2012, you said:[3] *"In the decisions I make, I think it's important to keep in mind what impact they have across borders." You spoke of a "paradox between our legal and political structures, grounded in jurisdiction and the laws of nation-states, and the seemingly borderless global environment or constituency—as you referred to it—that we find in the 'Internet public,'" global citizens connected by new communications technologies. Can you define the new "Internet public" and how governments—both at a national and at a regional level like in the EU—look at their responsibilities across borders?*

I believe the global context is often forgotten by companies and governments alike, when it is not in their immediate interest. So, for example, companies are eager to enter new markets, even if it means signing up to abiding by, and acting according to, laws that violate universal human rights. On the other hand I see increasingly empowered networks of people who manage to influence decision makers in other countries too. The movement to fight SOPA,[4] PIPA,[5] and ACTA[6] is exemplary, as well as the technical support that was shared with activists in the Middle East in the middle of the peaceful uprisings against authoritarian regimes.

The "multistakeholder" model, in which all stakeholders informally decide on norms for governing the Internet, requires reforms and improvements. Can you expand on that?

I believe the term "risks" is becoming very empty. Just because there are different people at the table does not mean everyone relevant is at the table, or that they are proportionately present in relation to who they represent. So the meetings must become more inclusive, and companies and governments should be held accountable somehow; the informal nature of the multistakeholder model should not get in the way of ensuring checks and balances.

What's the role of market players—like Internet companies, telecoms, social media platforms—in the debate around Internet freedom, open Internet, and net neutrality?

All of these actors have made their voices heard, but have pushed for different outcomes. The lobby has been quite intense, and while I believe we need to enshrine net neutrality in EU law, it is still easier to prevent reform than to accomplish it. The Council of Ministers is up next in putting their position forward, and I urge them to take the example of the European Parliament, which pushed for strong net neutrality guarantees.

When it comes to Internet freedom, the risk for legislators and government is overregulation. Indeed, controlling and regulating software and technology is not an easy task. Where's the balance, especially understanding that some technology is not only harmful and dangerous, but can really be used as virtual weapons?

In many cases we do not need new laws, we just need to make sure that agreed principles, as aspects of open societies and open economies, are applicable in new contexts. When it comes to export controls specifically, it is not so much about regulating the technology, as it is about regulating the transactions. Companies that sell surveillance and intrusive systems to governments of countries with very poor rule of law and human rights standards should be subject to licensing requirements. It allows for more transparency and accountability, and also provides more clarity for companies.

We must ensure that the public interest of the open Internet and the position of Internet users are kept high on the priorities list. Otherwise, at the hands of companies seeking maximum profit at any price, and at the hands of governments that seek maximum control over their citizens, the Internet user and the open Internet are compromised.

NOTES

1. Ben Rooney, "Europe's Most Wired Politician," *Wall Street Journal*, last updated, June 17, 2011, 8:01 a.m. GMT, http://blogs.wsj.com/tech-europe/2011/06/17/marietje-schaake-europes-most-wired-politician/.

2. Marietje Schaake, "Europe Needs an Ambitious Digital Agenda," *Euractiv*, last updated, June 4, 2014, http://www.euractiv.com/sections/infosociety/europe-needs-ambitious-digital-agenda-302565.

3. National Democratic Institute, "Democracy Spotlight: Marietje Schaake," *YouTube*, accessed August 22, 2014, https://www.youtube.com/watch?v=WEPckXL8Pfo.

4. The Stop Online Piracy Act (SOPA) was a United States bill (H.R. 326) introduced in the US House of Representatives by Lamar S. Smith (R-TX) to expand the ability of US law enforcement to combat online copyright infringement and online trafficking in counterfeit goods. The bill was introduced on October 26, 2011, in the 112th session of Congress, but was not enacted. It authorizes the Attorney General to seek a court order against a US-directed foreign Internet site committing or facilitating online piracy to require the owner, operator, or domain name registrant, or the site or domain name itself if such persons are unable to be found, to cease and desist further activities constituting specified intellectual property offenses under the federal criminal code including criminal copyright infringement, unauthorized fixation and trafficking of sound recordings or videos of live musical performances, the recording of exhibited motion pictures, or trafficking in counterfeit labels, goods, or services. The full text is available here: https://www.govtrack.us/congress/bills/112/hr3261/text.

5. The Protect IP Act (Preventing Real Online Threats to Economic Creativity and Theft of Intellectual Property Act, or PIPA) was a US bill (S.968) introduced in the US Senate as by Patrick Leahy (D-VT) on May 12, 2011, during the 112th session of Congress with the stated goal of giving the US government and copyright holders additional tools to curb access to "rogue websites dedicated to the sale of infringing or counterfeit goods," especially those registered outside the United States. The bill was not enacted. The full text is available here: http://thomas.loc.gov/cgi-bin/query/z?c112:S.968.

6. The Anti-Counterfeiting Trade Agreement (ACTA) was signed in 2011 by Australia, Canada, Japan, Morocco, New Zealand, Singapore, South Korea, and the United States. The text of the ACTA Agreement can be found here: www.mofa.go.jp/policy/economy/i_property/pdfs/dcta1105_en.pdf.

26

THE POTENTIAL OF BIG DATA

A conversation with JR Reagan, Principal, Deloitte & Touche

To view clips
from the conversation
with JR Reagan
scan the QR code
or visit:
http://goo.gl/hf9jYO

Global interconnectivity and the Internet have changed how governments and businesses function, how the media industry operates, and how people live. According to the June 2013 issue of **Foreign Affairs** *, however, "a new, less visible technological trend is just as transformative: 'big data.'"*[1] *Indeed, as the magazine points out, there is a lot more information floating around than ever before, and both the public and private sectors are trying to put it to extraordinary new uses. The idea is to use big data not just as a communication tool, but a way to learn from a large body of information things that we could not comprehend when we used only smaller amounts. What is big data and how are governments trying to harness it?*

Big data is the data you own and the data that you don't. Governments have a lot of information they've collected over the years—census data, health data, safety data, all sorts of things. However, when we start to combine that with data you don't own—for example, data from the social media sphere—then you really have contextual types of problems that you can address.

Let's not forget that what we call big data is big; really big. The number of mobile devices that constantly broadcast location and other data is projected to exceed the entire population of the Earth, according to the most current Cisco Visual Networking Index (VNI).[2] The forecasts are that the world will create four times more data in 2015 than it did in 2011. Users of these devices upload more than 350 million photographs to social media sites every day, on average. Planes, trains, and automobiles sense and relay information, as do many homes, lawns, lights, factories, packages, and stores—to name just a few of the residents of the Internet of Things in which we all now reside.

Turning big data's gigantic, seemingly amorphous cloud of bits and bytes into valuable information will be as transformative in the coming decade as the Internet and mobile technologies were in the previous one.

Citizens continue to benefit when the public sector puts big data to use, too. Governments are able to quickly pinpoint areas of potential civil unrest, and nongovernmental organizations deploy better solutions to poverty and health care problems. Communities respond more quickly to everything from potholes to hurricanes, and amateur sky gazers help scientists analyze massive datasets to find new planets.

But big data can go beyond that. Organizations, for example, can use data visualizations to identify areas of vulnerability before a crisis hits, and to map out responses to potential risks. By looking at data from numerous sources, a utilities company may be able to see an impending cyber attack and stop a breach before it occurs.

It's this combination of data—an organization's own, joined with relevant, publicly available datasets—that offers a glimpse of what is possible with big data.

"The benefits to society will be myriad, as big data becomes part of the solution to pressing global problems like addressing climate change, eradicating disease, and fostering good governance and economic development," Viktor Mayer-Schönberger[3] and Kenneth Cukier[4] write in their book titled **Big Data: A Revolution That Will Transform How We Live, Work, and Think.** *What are the limits of the so-called datification of our world and lives?*

It all depends on who you are and the circumstances in which you're viewing a particular issue. A lot of people have no problem giving out their date of birth, for example. They think they might get some benefit from it. But in another context, you might not even realize that your date of birth is being farmed. This hyperdata really depends on the situation that people are in. Probably without even knowing it, most people are going to be more comfortable with more information being known about them than they realize. And that is because all around them, there's a huge information flow that they benefit from: from coupons and opportunities, to what the government can do for them, including municipal, state, and federal services that you get just by releasing your geolocation or your contact information. We always complain for example, "Why do I have to keep giving the same information over and over again?" That gets solved through big data.

Where the limits come are on what we call the atomic problem. Let's use the example of my date of birth: it might be fine for me to release it in some circumstances, but not in others. But who does determine that, and when they can use it, and how? We can't have a finger on a button, a mouse click, every time to make that decision. I think that's where we're pushing the boundaries of big data.

Big data is even bigger—so to speak—or have the potential or growing at an accelerated speed if we consider the mobile and smartphone market around the world, one of the main sources for data crunchers. Are mobile technologies changing the way governments function, impacting on all sectors of activity, from commerce to foreign policy?

Big data is driving governments to really think they can operate at the same speed of companies. But that's a really challenging process for a government.

Now, in terms of interactions between citizens and government, on one side, big data has changed everybody's expectations of what can and can't be done in our own personal lives, including our life as citizens. On the other side, it has changed the way we think of our interactions with both the public and private sectors.

Those interactions happen at any point during the day with a myriad of devices, without us realizing it. That's where it gets even more challenging in the Internet of Things. It's not just a human being with a mobile phone anymore. It's about all those things that we're interfaced with and through—our car, our television, our refrigerator, our watch, and so on. Now, they all assume our identity. I think that's really the next frontier.

Isn't the hypergrowth of data also increasing the risks relating to security and cyber attacks?

Absolutely. But I think there are ways to deal with the risk of hyperconnectivity just as we've dealt in the past with every other technological problem. First, we need to stop thinking about the problem in terms of how it was created—or in terms of data silos and data warehouses. Data is pretty much everywhere, and that is why we need to think about it in terms of the user experience and the user context. Users should be able to have some kind of control on those key elements of personal information that are really important—things like health records and all personal identifiable information. Those are important. Once the user is able to get a handle on those things—just as we have a handle on them in the physical world—then the rest becomes about the benefits, the upside of having it that much easier to spread that information around. The result is about us achieving a comfort factor with big data.

Creating a comfort level with big data will certainly not solve all social problems. It can help ease some of the issues. Government in this case will probably end up following the lead of industry, more than the other way around, with industries following government. It's about the government showing you the value of using your information before you let it have it. But once they do that, your comfort level grows. Social media tools like Facebook and Twitter do this all the time. We don't realize how much information we give out on social networks, but we're very comfortable using them. Advertisers are now getting into that same mode. The government still needs to pick up a little bit.

Now, in terms of government, we could certainly see an increased emphasis on cyber security. Protecting sensitive information is paramount. There's also a clear shift to continuous monitoring from the traditional certification and accreditation process. Again, as data collection, storage, and analytics improve, so should the ability to predict and counteract threats.

Social media and mobile communications are certainly one of the main sources for big data miners. But they're also becoming the main sources for governments to learn from and listen to their audiences both at home and abroad. Do you think governments now have learned how to use social media to engage with the world and not just to broadcast or collect data?

The really interesting horizon opportunity for government is exactly that. As a government, if you understand that your citizens are telling you lots of things about their personal lives, about their likes and dislikes, about how they view government services, then it becomes more about listening than broadcasting messages. This represents a new set of skills for government. Being able to bring together conversations that they wouldn't have done before is also something that can be very revealing. In some ways, if they learn to operate in this new environment, governments have the potential to move from reactive to proactive, to preemptive, to even predictive.

As big data and mobile technologies are becoming part of the day-to-day operations of many governments, innovation is now something everybody talks about. Innovation, however, is mostly seen a prerogative of the private sector, rather than of governments and public administrations. What is innovation and how can a government be innovative?

For me, innovation is not about doing different things but doing things differently. When you put it in that way—thinking about it differently—then you get a whole new range of how to think about it. You also get a whole new range of who can be the really innovative people. Sometimes we subscribe that to a particular department or an individual as opposed to really knowing that everyone has these really great "aha" moments. It's about big ideas; or even a single big, great idea. Well, what do you do with it? In order to be able to capture it, it's important to have more a grassroots innovative culture that does not kill ideas before they even germinate. We cannot risk to have them go through a gauntlet where we try to kill them all as we search for justifications and a return on investment. We need to point ourselves toward a discovery process, in which we are able to reimagine problems and cocreate solutions. This is really where we need to head as governments.

As we're getting much more into a crowdsourcing, cocreation environment, government is learning to listen to more people, running contests, involving more of the citizens in the problem-solving process. That gives really a great extension of government in times when government has less resources. It's important to implement the process onto the existing organization. It's a fascinating process to watch what happens, because that new approach, the new ideas, and seeing those ideas coming to life. We start to see government kind of change.

In 2011, US President Barack Obama said: "The first step in winning the future is encouraging American innovation. None of us can predict with certainty what the next big industry will be or where the new jobs will come from. Thirty years ago, we couldn't know that something called the Internet would lead to an economic revolution. What we can do—what America does better than anyone else—is spark the creativity and imagination of our people."[5] Creativity, I believe, is key when it comes to innovation. Do you agree?

Absolutely. There's a great video that I love to show to my students. It's Emily Pilloton's TEDGlobal 2010 talk[6] in Oxford, England, on teaching design for change. Emily moved to Bertie County, North Carolina, to engage in a bold experiment of design-led community transformation and turn around the school system. What she says is that being able to contribute creative capital to a community that didn't have it before— we talk a lot about intellectual and social capital, but creative capital is not something we normally give to a community—can bring new opportunities to some of the poorest areas in the country. Creative capital was for the Bertie County community what was needed to help turn things around, to reimagine their problems.

Indeed, creativity is something we're seeing more of. It is something necessary—and desired—to actually have a meaning and help spread opportunities around communities.

I think that the most valuable advice I could give to future genera-tions of leaders is to not abdicate innovation to anyone else. We all have great ideas. It's what you do with them, how you use your creativity. It's about, "Small enough to win, big enough to matter." Proceed with small ideas because when you string these together, then it lights a fire. Peo-ple want above all the notion that what they say and do really matters. Once you start that flywheel turning and you show that you can make a difference with some really great ideas, other people get on board too. You get others involved even as citizens.

Now, we've got a great engine started, and we haven't had to do a lot to start it. But we had to start it with some small spark, and the spark starts with you.

NOTES

1. Kenneth Neil Cukier and Viktor Mayer-Schoenberger, "The Rise of Big Data: How It's Changing the Way We Think about the World," *Foreign Af-fairs*, May–June 2013, http://www.foreignaffairs.com/articles/139104/kenneth-neil-cukier-and-viktor-mayer-schoenberger/the-rise-of-big-data.

2. According to the Visual Networking Index (VNI) report, by 2018, there will be twenty-one billion networked devices and connections globally, up from twelve billion in 2013.

3. Viktor Mayer-Schönberger is the professor of internet governance and regulation at Oxford University's Oxford Internet Institute. His research fo-cuses on the role of information in a networked economy. He is the coauthor of *Big Data: A Revolution That Will Transform How We Live, Work, and Think* with Kenneth Cukier in 2013, which was a *New York Times* best seller and translated into twenty languages. The book won the National Library of Chi-na's Wenjin Book Award, and was a finalist for the FT Business Book of the Year. In 2014 they published a follow-on work, *Learning with Big Data: The Future of Education*.

4. Kenneth Cukier is the data editor of *The Economist*. From 2007 to 2012 he was the Tokyo correspondent, and before that, the paper's technology correspondent in London, where his work focused on innovation, intellectual property, and Internet governance.

5. The White House, "Remarks by the President in State of Union Ad-dress," accessed June 26, 2014, http://www.whitehouse.gov/the-press-office/2011/01/25/remarks-president-state-union-address.

6. Emily Pilloton, "Teaching Design for Change," TED.com, last updated July 2010, http://www.ted.com/talks/emily_pilloton_teaching_design_for_change.

BIBLIOGRAPHY

Videos of some of the interviews can be accessed at: http://goo.gl/gNHpww.

Agoada, Joe. "Entrepreneurs in Institutions: Why Intrapreneurs Are So Valuable to International Development." *TechChange* (blog). Last updated June 14, 2013. http://techchange.org/2013/06/14/entrepreneurs-in-institutions-why-intrapreneurs-are-so-valuable-to-international-development/.

American Presidency Project, The. Electronic Mail Message to Prime Minister Carl Bildt of Sweden. February 5, 1994. Accessed July 25, 2014. http://www.presidency.ucsb.edu/ws/?pid=49664.

Anderson, Chris. "How Web Video Powers Global Innovation." TED.com. Last updated July 2010. https://www.ted.com/talks/chris_anderson_how_web_video_powers_global_innovation.

Aspen Institute, The. *Aspen Institute Dialogue on Diplomacy and Technology*. Accessed June 23, 2014. http://www.aspeninstitute.org/policy-work/communications-society/dialogue-on-diplomacy-and-technology.

Athar, Sohaib. Twitter post. May 1, 2011, 3:58 p.m. https://twitter.com/ReallyVirtual/status/64780730286358528 .

———. Twitter post. May 1, 2011, 4:09 p.m. https://twitter.com/ReallyVirtual/status/64783440226168832.

———. Twitter post. May 1, 2011, 4:44 p.m. https://twitter.com/ReallyVirtual/status/64792407144796160.

———. Twitter post. May 1, 2011, 4:48 p.m. https://twitter.com/ReallyVirtual/status/64793269908930560.

———. Twitter post. May 1, 2011, 5:02 p.m. https://twitter.com/ReallyVirtual/status/64796769418088448.

———. Twitter post. May 1, 2011, 5:10 p.m. https://twitter.com/ReallyVirtual/status/64798882332278785.

———. Twitter post. May 1, 2011, 5:16 p.m. https://twitter.com/ReallyVirtual/status/64800262354763776.

———. Twitter post. May 1, 2011, 11:24 p.m. https://twitter.com/ReallyVirtual/status/64892915167657984.

Barzun, Matthew. "Diplomacy in the Cloud." *Matthew Barzun* (blog). Last updated February 10, 2014. http://matthewbarzun.tumblr.com/post/76233037602/diplomacy-in-the-cloud.

Beckstrom, Rod. "Build a Safer Internet for a Safer World." *The World Economic Forum* (blog). Last updated June 14, 2013. http://forumblog.org/2013/06/build-a-safer-internet-for-a-safer-world/.

Bildt, Carl. *Statement of Government Policy in the Parliamentary Debate on Foreign Affairs.* Stockholm: Regeringskansliet, 2013.

———. Twitter post. August 9, 2013, 4:21 a.m. https://twitter.com/carlbildt/status/365749692673425412 . http://www.government.se/content/1/c6/20/90/53/c7791e9a.pdf.

Blight, Garry, Sheila Pulham, and Paul Torpey. "Arab Spring: An Interactive Timeline of Middle East Protests." *Guardian.* Last modified January 5, 2012. http://www.theguardian.com/world/interactive/2011/mar/22/middle-east-protest-interactive-timeline.

Braconier, Henrik, Giuseppe Nicoletti, and Ben Westmore. "Shifting Gear: Policy Challenges for the Next 50 Years." OECD Economics Department Policy Papers N. 9. Paris: OECD Publishing, 2014.

Brookings Institution. *Noah Shachtman.* Accessed June 26, 2014. http://www.brookings.edu/experts/shachtmann.

———. *Peter W. Singer.* Accessed June 26, 2014. http://www.brookings.edu/experts/singerp.

Carvin, Andy. LinkedIn profile. Accessed June 24, 2014. https://www.linkedin.com/in/andycarvin.

Chan, Margaret. "Best Days for Public Health Are Ahead of Us, Says WHO Director-General." World Health Organization (WHO). Last updated May 21, 2012. http://www.who.int/dg/speeches/2012/wha_20120521/en/.

Cisco. *Visual Networking Index (VNI).* Accessed June 26, 2014. http://www.cisco.com/c/en/us/solutions/service-provider/visual-networking-index-vni/index.html.

Clarallo, Joe. "So What Do You Do, Pete Cashmore, Mashable Founder and CEO?" Mediabistro. Last updated August 19, 2009. http://www.mediabistro.com/So-What-Do-You-Do-Pete-Cashmore-Mashable-Founder-and-CEO-a10600.html.

Clinton, Hillary. *Hard Choices.* New York: Simon and Schuster, 2014.

———. "Remarks on Internet Freedom." Washington, DC: United States Department of State, January 21, 2010. http://www.state.gov/secretary/20092013clinton/rm/2010/01/135519.htm.

———. Twitter post. June 10, 2013, 12:44 p.m. https://twitter.com/HillaryClinton/status/344132945122054144.

———. Twitter profile. Accessed June 23, 2014. https://twitter.com/HillaryClinton.

CNN. "CNN Heroes: Everyday People Changing the World." Accessed June 24, 2014. http://www.cnn.com/SPECIALS/cnn.heroes/2013.heroes/kakenya.ntaiya.html.

Code for America. *About Us: Who We Are.* Accessed June 24, 2014. http://codeforamerica.org/about/.

Commons and Lords Hansard. *Debate on the Address: HC Deb 29 November 1944 vol. 406 cc9-56.* Accessed October 4, 2013. http://hansard.millbanksystems.com/commons/1944/nov/29/debate-on-the-address#S5CV0406P0_19441129_HOC_52.

Conrad, Tom. "BarCampBlock." *Tom Conrad* (blog). Last updated August 19, 2007. http://tomconrad.net/2007/08/19/barcampblock/.

Council of Europe Development Bank. *The CEB's Mandate.* Accessed June 26, 2014. http://www.coebank.org/Contenu.asp?arbo=74&theme=1.

Council of Foreign Relations. *Book: The New Digital Age.* Accessed June 1, 2014. http://www.cfr.org/technology-and-foreign-policy/new-digital-age/p30507.

Cukier, Kenneth. *Kenneth Cukier Biography.* Accessed June 26, 2014. http://www.cukier.com/knccv.html.

Cukier, Kenneth Neil, and Viktor Mayer-Schoenberger. "The Rise of Big Data: How It's Changing the Way We Think about the World." *Foreign Affairs* (May/June 2013).

Dartmouth College. *Faculty Directory: Chris Trimble.* Accessed May 20, 2014. http://www.tuck.dartmouth.edu/faculty/faculty-directory/christopher-r-trimble.

Dartmouth College. *Vijay Govindarajan.* Accessed May 20, 2014. http://www.tuck.dartmouth.edu/people/vg/.

Democratic National Committee. The "romneytaxplam.com." Accessed June 23, 2014. http://www.romneytaxplan.com/.

Digital Kosovo. *About Digital Kosovo.* Accessed June 26, 2014. http://www.digitalkosovo.org/about/.

Dorsey, Jack. Twitter post. October 1, 2013, 11:00 a.m. https://twitter.com/jack/status/385056531269427201.

———. Twitter post. October 1, 2013, 6:34 p.m. https://twitter.com/jack/statuses/385170855380000769.

Eaton, Joshua, and Ben Piven. "Timeline of Edward Snowden's Revelations." Al Jazeera. Accessed June 9, 2014. http://america.aljazeera.com/articles/multimedia/timeline-edward-snowden-revelations.html.

Ericsson. *Ericsson Mobility Report.* Accessed July 22, 2013. http://www.ericsson.com/mobility-report.

European Commission. Speech by Neelie Kroes, Vice-President of the European Commission responsible for the Digital Agenda, at Digital Venice on Italian Leadership for a Connected Continent. Accessed July 10, 2014. http://europa.eu/rapid/press-release_SPEECH-14-534_en.htm.

Fast Company. "MIT Media Lab guru Joi Ito says we need to be all four of these people to make innovation happen. #iusf13." *Fast Company* (blog). Last updated November 6, 2013, 7:31 p.m. http://blog.fastcompany.com/post/66231797770/mit-media-lab-guru-joi-ito-says-we-need-to-be-all.

FleishmanHillard. *Kris Balderston.* Accessed June 26, 2014. http://fleishmanhillard.com/profile/kris-balderston/.

Foreign and Commonwealth Office. *Digital Diplomacy: The FCO's Digital Work.* Accessed May 29, 2014. http://blogs.fco.gov.uk/digitaldiplomacy/.

Fried, Jason, and David Heinemeier Hansson. *Rework.* New York: Crown Business, 2010.

Friedman, Thomas. *Thomas L. Friedman Official Biography.* Accessed June 26, 2014. http://www.thomaslfriedman.com/about-the-author.

Georgetown University. *Georgetown Institute for Women, Peace and Security: Meet the Team.* Accessed June 26, 2014. http://giwps.georgetown.edu/about/staff.

Ghattas, Kim. *The Secretary: A Journey with Hillary Clinton from Beirut to the Heart of American Power.* New York: Times Books, 2013.

Gold, Rich. *The Plenitude: Creativity, Innovation, and Making Stuff,* foreword by John Maeda. Cambridge, MA: The MIT Press, 2007.

Google Developers. *Public DNS.* Accessed June 9, 2014. https://developers.google.com/speed/public-dns/.

Graham, Mark, and Stefano de Sabbata. *Age of Internet Empires.* Oxford: Oxford Internet Institute's Information Geographies, 2013. http://geography.oii.ox.ac.uk/?page=age-of-internet-empires.

Gray, Rosie. "How Carne Ross Created a New Kind of Diplomacy." *BuzzFeed.* Last updated July 9, 2013, 11:47 a.m. http://www.buzzfeed.com/rosiegray/how-carne-ross-created-a-new-kind-of-diplomacy.

Gustin, Sam. "Google Unveils Tools to Access Web from Repressive Countries." *TIME.* Last updated October 21, 2013. http://business.time.com/2013/10/21/google-digital-rebels/.

Ha, Anthony, Kim-Mai Cutler, and Ingrid Lunden. "Twitter Buys MoPub for $350M to Up the Ante in Mobile Advertising." Last updated September 9, 2013. http://techcrunch.com/2013/09/09/twitter-said-to-acquire-mopub/.

Hague, William. Twitter post. August 9, 2013, 4:45 a.m. https://twitter.com/WilliamJHague/status/365755800951599104.

Haque, Umair. "Is Your Innovation Really Unnovation?" *Harvard Business Review* (blog). May 27, 2009, 11:26 a.m. http://blogs.hbr.org/2009/05/unnovation/.

Harf, Mary. Daily Press Briefing. Washington, DC: United States Department of State. March 26, 2014. Accessed May 29, 2014. http://www.state.gov/r/pa/prs/dpb/2014/03/223978.htm.

Harvard University. *Innovations in American Government Awards.* Accessed June 24, 2014. http://www.ash.harvard.edu/Home/Programs/Innovations-in-Government/Awards.

Hudson, David. "U.S. to Help Nigeria in the Search for Kidnapped Girls." *The White House* (blog). Last updated May 7, 2014, 3:34 p.m. http://www.whitehouse.gov/blog/2014/05/07/us-will-send-military-and-law-enforcement-officials-nigeria-help-rescue-missing-girl.

Huntington, Samuel P. "The Clash of Civilizations?" *Foreign Affairs* (Summer 1993): 22–51.

ICANN. *Glossary*. Accessed June 16, 2014. https://www.icann.org/resources/pages/glossary-2014-02-03-en.

ICANN. "ICANN Signs an Exchange of Letters with ccTLD Manager for Montenegro (.ME)." ICANN. Last updated June 17, 2013. https://www.icann.org/news/announcement-2013-06-17-en.

ICANN. *Welcome to the Global Community*. Accessed June 24, 2014. https://www.icann.org/get-started .

ICT for Disaster Risk Reduction. Incheon City: United Nations Asian and Pacific Training Centre for Information and Communication Technology for Development (UN-APCICT/ESCAP), 2010. http://www.preventionweb.net/files/14338_14338ICTDCaseStudy21.pdf.

International Finance Corporation, The. *About IFC*. Accessed May 20, 2014. http://www.ifc.org/wps/wcm/connect/corp_ext_content/ifc_external_corporate_site/about+ifc.

IPKO Foundation. *About Us*. Accessed June 20, 2014. http://ipkofoundation.org/about.

ISO. *About ISO*. Accessed June 26, 2014. http://www.iso.org/iso/home/about.htm.

Italian Presidency of the Council of the European Union. Twitter post. July 9, 2014, 9:35 a.m. https://twitter.com/IT2014EU/status/486866175021056000.

Ito, Joi. "The Internet, Innovation and Learning." *Joi Ito* (blog). Last updated December 5, 2011, 9:56 p.m. http://joi.ito.com/weblog/2011/12/05/the-internet-in.html.

———. "Ito to Finally Get a Degree." *Joi Ito* (blog). Last updated March 18, 2013, 4:17 p.m. http://joi.ito.com/weblog/2013/03/18/ito-to-finally.html.

Jacobs, Jane. *The Death and Life of Great American Cities*. New York: Random House, 1961.

Jublia. *About Jublia*. Accessed June 24, 2014. http://jublia.com/about.html.

Kail, Eric G. "Don't Make Assumptions about the Next Generation; Invest in It." *Harvard Business Review* (blog). Last updated January 25, 2013, 1 p.m. http://blogs.hbr.org/2013/01/dont-make-assumptions-about-the-next-generation-invest-in-it/.

Kakenya Center for Excellence, The. *About Us*. Accessed June 24, 2014. http://www.kakenyasdream.org/about-us/.

KantarSprt. *2010 FIFA World Cup South Africa: Television Audience Report*. London: FIFA, July 2011. http://www.fifa.com/mm/document/affederation/tv/01/47/32/73/2010fifaworldcupsouthafricatvaudiencereport.pdf.

Kelley, John Robert. "The New Diplomacy: Evolution of a Revolution." *Diplomacy and Statecraft* 21, 2 (2010): 286–305.

Kelly, Sanja, Mai Truong, Madeline Earp, Laura Reed, Adrian Shabaz, and Ashley Greco-Stoner. *Freedom of the Net*. Washington DC: Freedom House, 2013. http://freedomhouse.org/sites/default/files/resources/FOTN%202013_Full%20Report_0.pdf.

Kemp, Simon. "Social, Digital and Mobile Worldwide in 2014." *We Are Social* (blog). January 9, 2014, 4:09 p.m. http://wearesocial.net/blog/2014/01/social-digital-mobile-worldwide-2014/.

Kerry, John. "Remarks on Syria." Washington, DC: United States Department of State, 2013. http://www.state.gov/secretary/remarks/2013/08/213503.htm.

———. Twitter post. February 11, 2014, 5:12 p.m. https://twitter.com/JohnKerry/status/433362824413200384.

King, John. "Bush: Join 'Coalition of Willing.'" CNN.com. Last updated November 20, 2002, 6:13 p.m. http://edition.cnn.com/2002/WORLD/europe/11/20/prague.bush.nato/.

Kohut, Andrew, Richard Wike, Juliana Menasce Horowitz, Katie Simmons, Jacob Poushter, Cathy Barker, James Bell, Bruce Stokes, and Elizabeth Mueller Gross. *Social Networking Popular across Globe: Arab Publics Most Likely to Express Political Views Online*. Washington, DC: Pew Research Center, 2012. http://www.pewglobal.org/files/2012/12/Pew-Global-Attitudes-Project-Technology-Report-FINAL-December-12-2012.pdf.

Kosovain.eu. "Launch of 'Digital Kosovo' Supports Kosovo Citizens to Lobby for Greater Internet Inclusion." Last updated September 3, 2013. http://kosovain.eu/en/Kosova/

Launch-of-Digital-Kosovo-Supports-Kosovo-Citizens-to-Lobby-for-Greater-Internet-Inclusion-24187.

Kunju, Bhas. "Bring Back Our Girls Campaign Makes World Cup Appearance." Goal.com. Last updated June 23, 2014, 12:14 a.m. http://www.goal.com/en-sg/news/3999/world-cup-2014/2014/06/23/4904548/bring-back-our-girls-campaign-makes-world-cup-appearance.

Machiavelli, Niccoló. *The Prince*. Translated by W. K. Marriott. Salt Lake City: The Project Gutenberg, 2006. Kindle e-book.

Manyika, James, Armando Cabral, Lohini Moodley, Suraj Moraje, Safroadu Yeboah-Amankwah, Michael Chui, and Jerry Anthonyrajah. "Lions Go Digital: The Internet's Transformative Potential in Africa." McKinsey and Company. Last updated November 2013. http://www.mckinsey.com/insights/high_tech_telecoms_internet/lions_go_digital_the_internets_transformative_potential_in_africa.

Martin, Clifton, and Laura Jagla. *Integrating Diplomacy and Social Media: A Report of the First Annual Aspen Institute Dialogue on Diplomacy and Technology*. Washington, DC: The Aspen Institute, 2013. http://csreports.aspeninstitute.org/documents/IntegratingDIPLOMACY.pdf.

Mayer-Schönberger, Viktor, and Kenneth Cukier. *Big Data: A Revolution That Will Transform How We Live, Work, and Think*. New York: Eamon Dolan/Houghton Mifflin Harcourt, 2013.

McNeil, Donald, "Car Mechanic Dreams Up a Tool to Ease Births." *New York Times*. Last updated November 13, 2013. http://www.nytimes.com/2013/11/14/health/new-tool-to-ease-difficult-births-a-plastic-bag.html.

Mergel, Ines. "Assessing the Impact of Government Social Media Interactions." Brookings Institution. Last updated June 10, 2014. http://www.brookings.edu/blogs/techtank/posts/2014/06/23-government-social-media-interactions.

Messina, Chris. "Groups for Twitter; or a Proposal for Twitter Tag Channels." *Factory City* (blog). Last updated August 25, 2007. http://factoryjoe.com/blog/2007/08/25/groups-for-twitter-or-a-proposal-for-twitter-tag-channels/.

———. Twitter post. August 23, 2007, 3:25 p.m. https://twitter.com/chrismessina/status/223115412.

Ministry of Foreign Affairs of Russia (MFA Russia). Twitter post. April 23, 2014, 12:44 p.m. https://twitter.com/mfa_russia/statuses/459009929227931648.

———. Twitter post. February 6, 2012, 6:35 a.m. https://twitter.com/mfa_russia/statuses/166485247180017664.

MIT Media Lab. *Yo-Yo Ma and the Hypercello*. Accessed March 15, 2014. http://web.media.mit.edu/~joep/SpectrumWeb/captions/Cello.html.

The MIT Press. *Rich Gold*. Accessed June 24, 2014. http://mitpress.mit.edu/authors/rich-gold.

National Democratic Institute. "Democracy Spotlight: Marietje Schaake." *YouTube*. Accessed August 22, 2014. https://www.youtube.com/watch?v=WEPckXL8Pfo.

Ntaiya, Kakenya. "A Girl Who Demanded School." TED.com. Last updated October 2012. https://www.ted.com/talks/kakenya_ntaiya_a_girl_who_demanded_school.

Nye, Joseph S. *Soft Power: The Means to Success in World Politics*. Cambridge, MA: PublicAffairs, 2004.

Nyren, Ron. "Public Private Partnership Outlook." UrbanLand. Last updated May 3, 2013. http://urbanland.uli.org/economy-markets-trends/public-private-partnership-outlook/.

Obama, Barack. "Remarks by the President in Address to European Youth." Brussels: The White House, March 26, 2014. Accessed May 29, 2014. http://www.whitehouse.gov/the-press-office/2014/03/26/remarks-president-address-european-youth.

Obama, Michelle. Twitter post. May 7, 2014, 5:03 p.m. https://twitter.com/FLOTUS/statuses/464148654354628608.

Okpamen, Ehidiamhen, Niyi Aderibigbe, Temitope Bolade, Douglas Imaralu, and Chinedu Agbatuka. "#AFRICA–Inside the Continent's New $14bn Social Media Industry." Ventures. Last updated June 20, 2014. http://www.ventures-africa.com/2014/06/africa-inside-the-continents-new-14-billion-social-media-industry/.

Oxford University, Oxford Internet Institute. *Professor Viktor Mayer-Schönberger*. Accessed June 26, 2014. http://www.oii.ox.ac.uk/people/?id=174.

Page, Scott E. *The Difference: How the Power of Diversity Creates Better Groups, Firms, Schools, and Societies*. Princeton, NJ: Princeton University Press, 2008.

Phillips, Macon. "Change Has Come to WhiteHouse.gov." *The White House* (blog). Last updated January 20, 2009 (12:01 p.m.). http://www.whitehouse.gov/blog/2009/01/20/change-has-come-whitehousegov.

Pilloton, Emily. "Teaching Design for Change." TED.com. Last updated July 2010. http://www.ted.com/talks/emily_pilloton_teaching_design_for_change.

Qian, Haiyan, and Vincenzo Acquaro, *United Nations e-Government Survey 2014*. New York: United Nations, 2014.

Regeringskansliet (Government Offices of Sweden). *Carl Bildt*. Accessed May 29, 2014. http://www.government.se/sb/d/7505/a/70396.

———. *Stockholm Initiative for Digital Diplomacy*. Accessed May 29, 2014. http://www.government.se/sb/d/18138.

Rice, Condoleezza. *Transformational Diplomacy*. Washington, DC: United States Department of State, January 18, 2006. http://2001-2009.state.gov/secretary/rm/2006/59306.htm.

Rice, Susan. Twitter post. February 4, 2012, 12:49 p.m. https://twitter.com/AmbassadorRice/status/165854588216414208.

———. Twitter post. February 6, 2012, 4:36 p.m. https://twitter.com/AmbassadorRice/status/166636416216997889.

Ries, Brian. "Michelle Obama: It's Time to Bring Back Our Girls." Mashable. Last updated May 7, 2014. http://mashable.com/2014/05/07/michelle-obama-nigeria-bring-back-our-girls/.

Riotta, Gianni. *Il web ci rende liberi? Politica e vita quotidiana nel mondo digitale*. Milan: Einaudi Editori, 2013.

Rojas, Fabio. "How Twitter Can Predict an Election." *Washington Post*. Last updated August 11, 2013. http://www.washingtonpost.com/opinions/how-twitter-can-predict-an-election/2013/08/11/35ef885a-0108-11e3-96a8-d3b921c0924a_story.html.

Rooney, Ben. "Europe's Most Wired Politician." *Wall Street Journal*. Last updated June 17, 2011, 8:01 a.m. GMT. http://blogs.wsj.com/tech-europe/2011/06/17/marietje-schaake-europes-most-wired-politician/.

Ross, Carne. *The Leaderless Revolution: How Ordinary People Can Take Power and Change Politics in the 21st Century*. New York: Simon and Schuster, 2011.

———. Twitter post. January 9, 2013, 12:47 p.m. https://twitter.com/carneross/status/289065873749196800.

———. Twitter post. January 9, 2013, 3:23 p.m. https://twitter.com/carneross/status/289105069964664832.

Rouhani, Hassan. Twitter post. October 1, 2013, 4:24 p.m. https://twitter.com/HassanRouhani/status/385138174822850560.

Rowan, David. "Open University: Joi Ito Plans a Radical Reinvention of MIT's MediaLab." *Wired UK*. Last updated November 15, 2012. http://www.wired.co.uk/magazine/archive/2012/11/features/open-university.

Royal Academy of Arts Archive. *Transcripts of Annual Dinner Speeches 1953*, RAA/SEC/25/5/4.

Sandre, Andreas. "Diplomacy 3.0 Starts in Stockholm." *The Huffington Post*. Last updated May, 17, 2014. Posted January 15, 2014. http://www.huffingtonpost.com/andreas-sandre/digital-diplomacy-stockholm_b_4592691.html.

———. "Statecraft and Foreign Policy from Machiavelli to Digital Diplomacy." BigThink. Last updated July 23, 2013. http://bigthink.com/experts-corner/statecraft-and-foreign-policy-from-machiavelli-to-digital-diplomacy.

Sarukhan, Arturo. Twitter post. November 12, 2009, 5:58 p.m. https://twitter.com/Arturo_Sarukhan/status/5662543976.

Schaake, Marietje. "Europe Needs an Ambitious Digital Agenda." *Euractiv*. Last updated, June 4, 2014. http://www.euractiv.com/sections/infosociety/europe-needs-ambitious-digital-agenda-302565.

Scott, Ben. "#WhyHashtagActivismMatters." *The Weekly Wonk* (blog). Last updated May 15, 2014. http://weeklywonk.newamerica.net/articles/whyhashtagactivismmatters/.

SEACOM. *Our Company.* Accessed May 21, 2014. http://seacom.mu/our-company/.

Seeking Alpha. "Twitter Management Discusses Q4 2013 Results—Earnings Call Transcript." Last updated February 6, 2014, 8:40 a.m. http://seekingalpha.com/article/1998991-twitter-management-discusses-q4-2013-results-earnings-call-transcript.

Shachtman, Noah, and Peter W. Singer. "The Wrong War: The Insistence on Applying Cold War Metaphors to Cybersecurity Is Misplaced and Counterproductive." Brookings Institution. Last updated August 15, 2011. http://www.brookings.edu/research/articles/2011/08/15-cybersecurity-singer-shachtman.

Slaughter, Anne-Marie. "America's Edge: Power in the Networked Century." *Foreign Affairs.* January/February 2009. http://www.foreignaffairs.com/articles/63722/anne-marie-slaughter/americas-edge.

———. "A Pivot to the People." Project Syndicate. Last updated March 20, 2012. http://www.project-syndicate.org/commentary/a-pivot-to-the-people.

———. "Remarks, The Big Picture: Beyond Hot Spots and Crises in Our Interconnected World." University Park: Pennsylvania State University's *Journal of Law and International Affairs* 286 (2012). http://elibrary.law.psu.edu/jlia/vol1/iss2/5.

———. "Why Women Still Can't Have It All." *The Atlantic.* Last modified June 13, 2012. http://www.theatlantic.com/magazine/archive/2012/07/why-women-still-cant-have-it-all/309020/.

Smith, Adam, and Stacy Lamb. "Texts from Hillary." *Texts from Hillary* (blog). Accessed June 23, 2014. http://textsfromhillaryclinton.tumblr.com/.

Solis, Brian. "Leadership in an Era of Digital Darwinism." *Brian Solis* (blog). Last updated December 16, 2011. http://www.briansolis.com/2011/12/leadership-in-an-era-of-digital-darwinism/.

Sreenivasan, Sree. "Social Media Talk @DISummit #disummit." Digital Innovators' Summit. Accessed June 24, 2014. https://docs.google.com/presentation/d/16ZL2_o19ZZ3i_s4A5sZELuBtKh5_b9TuFNVsFWyCIpE/present#slide=id.i0.

———. Twitter post. June 8, 2013, 11:27 a.m. https://twitter.com/sree/status/343388813843910656.

Stanford University. *James S. Fishkin.* Accessed June 24, 2014. http://comm.stanford.edu/faculty-fishkin/.

Stop TEDx Ummayad 2014. Facebook page. Accessed June 24, 2014. https://www.facebook.com/pages/Stop-TEDx-Ummayad-2014/518126811616756.

SWIFT. *About SWIFT.* Accessed May 3, 2014. http://www.swift.com/about_swift/index.

TED.com. *TEDGlobal.* Accessed June 24, 2014. https://www.ted.com/attend/conferences/tedglobal.

———. *The TEDxChange Scholarship.* Accessed June 24, 2014. http://www.ted.com/about/programs-initiatives/tedx-program/tedx-in-the-developing-world/tedxchange-scholarship.

TEDxAmsterdam. *TEDxAmsterdam.* Accessed June 24, 2014. http://www.tedxamsterdam.com/.

TEDxBaghdad. *TEDxBaghdad.* Accessed June 24, 2014. http://tedxbaghdad.com/.

TEDxKhartoum. *TEDxKhartoum.* Accessed June 24, 2014. http://www.tedxkhartoum.com/site/.

TEDxMogadishu. *TEDxMogadishu.* Accessed June 24, 2014. http://tedxmogadishu.com/.

TEDxRamallah. *TEDxRamallah.* Accessed June 24, 2014. http://www.tedxramallah.com/.

TEDxRiodelaPlata. "Jorge Odón: Del taller mecánico a la sala de partos." Last updated August 18, 2012. http://www.tedxriodelaplata.org/videos/del-taller-mec%C3%A1nico-sala-partos.

———. *TEDxRiodelaPlata.* Accessed June 24, 2014. http://www.tedxriodelaplata.org/.

TEDxTeheran. *TEDxTeheran.* Accessed June 24, 2014. http://www.tedxtehran.ir/.

Tor Project. *Tor Overview.* Accessed May 29, 2014. https://www.torproject.org/about/overview.html.en.

Toyama, Kentaro. *Kentaro Toyama.* Accessed June 24, 2014. http://www.kentarotoyama.org/profile/default.htm.

———. "Twitter Isn't Spreading Democracy—Democracy Is Spreading Twitter." *The Atlantic*. Last updated November 11, 2013, 4:59 p.m. http://www.theatlantic.com/technology/archive/2013/11/twitter-isnt-spreading-democracy-democracy-is-spreading-twitter/281368/.

Traywick, Catherine. "Passport Google Imperialism: Mapping the World's Most Popular Websites." *Foreign Policy*. Last updated October 3, 2013, 1:50 p.m. http://blog.foreignpolicy.com/posts/2013/10/03/google_imperialism_mapping_the_world_s_most_popular_websites.

Tsu, Sun. *The Art of War*. Translated by Lionel Giles. Salt Lake City: The Project Gutenberg, 1994. Kindle e-book.

Twitter. "Twitter Reports First Quarter 2014 Results." Twitterinc.com. Last updated April 29, 2014. https://investor.twitterinc.com/releasedetail.cfm?releaseid=843245.

United Nations. "Deputy UN Chief Calls for Urgent Action to Tackle Global Sanitation Crisis." *UN News Center*. Last updated March 21, 2013. http://www.un.org/apps/news/story.asp?NewsID=44452.

United States Department of State. *Bureau of International Information Programs*. Accessed May 29, 2014. http://www.state.gov/r/iip/.

———. *Remarks at the Clinton Global Initiative*. Accessed December 20, 2013. http://m.state.gov/md198094.htm.

———. *Remarks at Munich Security Conference*. Accessed December 20, 2013. http://www.state.gov/secretary/remarks/2014/02/221134.htm.

———. *Tomicah S. Tillemann*. Accessed June 26, 2014. http://www.state.gov/r/pa/ei/biog/160354.htm.

———. *21st Century Statecraft*. Accessed June 12, 2014. http://www.state.gov/statecraft/.

United States Department of State, Office of the Historian. *Chiefs of Mission from France*. Accessed June 20, 2014. http://history.state.gov/departmenthistory/people/chiefsof mission/france.

———. *Benjamin Franklin (1706–1790)*. Accessed June 20, 2014. http://history.state.gov/departmenthistory/people/franklin-benjamin.

———. *Biographies of the Secretaries of State: Thomas Jefferson*. Accessed June 20, 2014. http://history.state.gov/departmenthistory/people/jefferson-thomas.

University of Maryland. *Thomas C. Schelling: Distinguished University Professor Emeritus*. Accessed June 26, 2014. https://www.econ.umd.edu/faculty/profiles/schelling.

University of Michigan. *Scott E Page*. Accessed May 20, 2014. http://vserver1.cscs.lsa.umich.edu/~spage/.

University of Minnesota, Humphrey School of Public Affairs. "Jake Sullivan Delivers Inspiring Message to 2013 Graduates." Last updated May 21, 2013. http://www.hhh.umn.edu/features/2013_Commencement.html.

USAID. *Who We Are*. Accessed June 20, 2014. http://www.usaid.gov/who-we-are.

USC Annenberg, School for Communications and Journalism. *Philip Seib*. Accessed June 1, 2014. http://annenberg.usc.edu/Faculty/Communication%20and%20Journalism/SeibP.aspx.

Ushahidi. *Mission*. Accessed June 24, 2014. http://www.ushahidi.com/mission/.

US Small Business Administration. *Small Business Innovation Research*. Accessed March 15, 2014. http://www.sba.gov/content/small-business-innovation-research-program-sbir.

Venema, Vibeke. "Odon Childbirth Device: Car Mechanic Uncorks a Revolution—Vibeke Venema." BBC News. Last updated December 3, 2013, 7:32 a.m. http://www.bbc.co.uk/news/magazine-25137800.

Voice of Russia, The. "Russia Surprised by US, Ukraine Misinterpreting Geneva Agreement." The Voice of Russia. Last modified April 23, 2014. http://voiceofrussia.com/news/2014_04_23/Russia-surprised-by-US-Ukraine-misinterpreting-Geneva-agreement-Moscow-0981/.

Walker, Alice, "TEDxRamallah—Alice Walker آليس ووكر—How I Learned to Grow a Global Heart." TED.com. Last updated July 6, 2011. http://tedxtalks.ted.com/video/TEDx Ramallah-Alice-Walker-How-I;search%3Atag%3A%22palestine%22.

Ward, Jon. "Republican Party Path Back from 2012 Election Requires Shift in Culture, Not Just Tactics." *Huffington Post*. Last updated January 11, 2013. http://www.huffingtonpost.com/2013/01/10/republican-party-election-2012_n_2443344.html.

Warzel, Charlie. "Twitter Hints That At-Replies and Hashtags Are About to Be Streamlined." *BuzzFeed*. Last updated March 19, 2014, at 12:41 p.m. http://www.buzzfeed.com/charliewarzel/is-twitter-phasing-out-hashtags-and-at-replies.

Washington Post. "NSA Slides Explain the PRISM Data-Collection Program." Last modified July 10, 2013. http://www.washingtonpost.com/wp-srv/special/politics/prism-collection-documents/.

White House, The. Facebook post. Last updated May 7, 2014, 6:24 p.m. https://www.facebook.com/photo.php?fbid=10152473948824238.

———. *Operation Iraqi Freedom: Coalition Members*. Accessed June 23, 2014. http://georgewbush-whitehouse.archives.gov/news/releases/2003/03/20030327-10.html.

———. "President Bush, President Havel Discuss Iraq, NATO." Office of the Press Secretary. Last updated November 20, 2002. http://georgewbush-whitehouse.archives.gov/news/releases/2002/11/20021120-1.html.

———. "Remarks by the President in Address to the Nation on Syria." Office of the Press Secretary. Last updated September 10, 2013. http://www.whitehouse.gov/the-press-office/2013/09/10/remarks-president-address-nation-syria.

———. "Remarks by the President in State of Union Address." Accessed June 26, 2014. http://www.whitehouse.gov/the-press-office/2011/01/25/remarks-president-state-union-address.

———. "Remarks by President Barack Obama at Town Hall Meeting with Future Chinese Leaders." Office of the Press Secretary. Accessed December 20, 2013. http://www.whitehouse.gov/the-press-office/remarks-president-barack-obama-town-hall-meeting-with-future-chinese-leaders.

———. "We The People: Your Voice in Our Government." Accessed June 23, 2014. https://petitions.whitehouse.gov/.

———. "White House Announces We The People." Office of the Press Secretary. Accessed September 1, 2013. http://www.whitehouse.gov/the-press-office/2011/09/01/white-house-announces-we-people.

Wikipedia contributors, "Alice Walker." Wikipedia, The Free Encyclopedia. Accessed June 24, 2014. http://en.wikipedia.org/wiki/Alice_Walker.

———. "Al-Shabaab (militant group)." Wikipedia, The Free Encyclopedia. Accessed June 24, 2014. http://en.wikipedia.org/wiki/Al-Shabaab_(militant_group).

———. "Antonio Gramsci." Wikipedia, The Free Encyclopedia. Accessed June 26, 2014. http://en.wikipedia.org/wiki/Antonio_Gramsci .

———. "Clash of Civilizations." Wikipedia, The Free Encyclopedia. Accessed June 26, 2014. http://en.wikipedia.org/wiki/Clash_of_Civilizations.

———. "Evgeny Morozov." Wikipedia, The Free Encyclopedia. Accessed June 26, 2014. http://en.wikipedia.org/wiki/Evgeny_Morozov.

———. "Jane Jacobs." Wikipedia, The Free Encyclopedia. Accessed June 26, 2014. http://en.wikipedia.org/wiki/Jane_Jacobs.

———. "Mitt Romney." Wikipedia, The Free Encyclopedia. Accessed June 23, 2014. http://en.wikipedia.org/wiki/Mitt_Romney.

———. "Melvin Kranzberg." Wikipedia, The Free Encyclopedia. Accessed June 26, 2014. http://en.wikipedia.org/wiki/Melvin_Kranzberg.

———. "Melvin Kranzberg's Laws of Technology." Wikipedia, The Free Encyclopedia. Accessed June 26, 2014. http://en.wikipedia.org/wiki/Kranzberg's_laws_of_technology.

———. "M-Pesa." Wikipedia, The Free Encyclopedia. Accessed May 20, 2014. http://en.wikipedia.org/wiki/M-Pesa.

———. "Penn and Teller." Wikipedia, The Free Encyclopedia. Accessed June 24, 2014. http://en.wikipedia.org/wiki/Penn_%26_Teller.

———. "Pete Cashmore." Wikipedia, The Free Encyclopedia. Accessed June 24, 2014. http://en.wikipedia.org/wiki/Pete_Cashmore.

———. "Ronan Farrow." Wikipedia, The Free Encyclopedia. Accessed June 26, 2014. http:/
/en.wikipedia.org/wiki/Ronan_Farrow.
———. "Viktor Yanukovych." Wikipedia, The Free Encyclopedia. http://en.wikipedia.org/
wiki/Viktor_Yanukovych. Accessed May 28, 2014.
———. "Virtual Private Network." Wikipedia, The Free Encyclopedia. Accessed May 29,
2014. http://en.wikipedia.org/wiki/Virtual_private_network.
———. "Walter Cronkite." Wikipedia, The Free Encyclopedia. Accessed June 26, 2014.
http://en.wikipedia.org/wiki/Walter_Cronkite.
———. "Wikileaks." Wikipedia, The Free Encyclopedia. Accessed May 28, 2014. http://en.
wikipedia.org/wiki/WikiLeaks.
———. "Yo-Yo Ma. Wikipedia, The Free Encyclopedia. Accessed June 24, 2014. http://en.
wikipedia.org/wiki/Yo-Yo_Ma.
———. "Zygmunt Bauman." Wikipedia, The Free Encyclopedia. Accessed June 26, 2014.
http://en.wikipedia.org/wiki/Zygmunt_Bauman.
World Bank, The. Current President: Dr. Jim Yong Kim. Accessed May 20, 2014. http://
www.worldbank.org/en/about/president/about-the-office/bio.
———. International Bank for Reconstruction and Development. Accessed May 20, 2014.
http://web.worldbank.org/WBSITE/EXTERNAL/EXTABOUTUS/EXTIBRD/0,,menu
PK:3046081~pagePK:64168427~piPK:64168435~theSitePK:3046012,00.html.
World Economic Forum, The. Global Risks 2014 Report. Accessed June 24, 2014. http://
www.weforum.org/reports/global-risks-2014-report.
World Forum for Ethics and Business. World Forum for Ethics and Business. Accessed May
20, 2014. http://www.wfeb.org/about_us.html.
Yong, Hu, and Takeshi Natsuno. "Asia Loves Facebook, Latin America Loves WhatsApp."
World Economic Forum (blog). June 18, 2014. http://forumblog.org/2014/06/social-
media-worldwide/.

INDEX

BIOGRAPHIES

ALAIN BRIAN BERGANT

Alain Brian Bergant is the Secretary General of the Bled Strategic Forum, an international platform organized by the Government of the Republic of Slovenia for high-level strategic dialogue among leaders from the private and public sectors on key issues facing Europe and the world in the twenty-first century. Bergant was previously Slovenia's Ambassador to the Republic of Macedonia (2007–2012). He is a career diplomat and held posts at his country's embassies in Finland, Sweden, and Hungary. At the Ministry of Foreign Affairs, he worked as political director and assistant to the State Secretary. Bergant graduated with a degree in international law from the Faculty of Law at the University of Ljubljana, Slovenia.

CLAUDIO BISOGNIERO

Claudio Bisogniero is the ambassador of Italy to the United States. He presented his credentials to US President Barack Obama on January 18, 2012. He was previously NATO's deputy secretary general (2007–2012), responsible for a variety of security and strategic issues on the alliance's agenda. At NATO he also followed the alliance's Summits in Bucharest, Strasbourg/Kiel, and Lisbon, and worked actively in the preparatory phase for the 2012 NATO Summit in Chicago. Bisogniero is a career diplomat. He entered the Italian Foreign Service in May 1978 after graduating with a degree in political science from the University of Rome in 1976. He was posted in Beijing; Brussels; Washington, DC; and New York. In Rome, he served in the Office of the

Diplomatic Adviser to the president of the republic and in the Office of the Secretary General of the Ministry of Foreign Affairs. In February 2002, he was appointed deputy director general for political multilateral affairs and deputy political director, responsible for issues concerning NATO, the United Nations, the G7/G8, disarmament, OSCE, antiterrorism, and human rights. In June 2005, he was named director general for the Americas, with responsibility for the relations of Italy with the United States and Canada, as well as with all the countries of Latin America.

VINCENZO COSENZA

Vincenzo Cosenza is a social media strategist and head of the Rome office of BlogMeter, a company specialized in social media monitoring, analytics, and management platforms to agencies and businesses. Before joining the team of analysts and researchers at BlogMeter in 2013, Cosenza worked at Hill+Knowlton Strategies in Italy and at Microsoft Italia. His research activity on social media has been featured around the world. In 2009, he created the first World Map of Social Networks, which he updates twice a year with the most popular social media sites by country, according to Alexa traffic data. Cosenza is the author of *Social Media ROI* (2012) and La società dei dati (2012). He is a frequent contributor to newspapers and magazines in Italy, and his work has been featured around the world in *Newsweek*, *Le Monde*, *The Economist*, BBC, and *Wired*. Cosenza studied economics and marketing and holds a master's degree in innovation management from the Scuola Superiore Sant'Anna in Pisa, Italy.

STEPHANE DUJARRIC

Stéphane Dujarric was appointed by United Nations Secretary-General Ban Ki-moon as his spokesperson in March 2014. Dujarric had previously served as spokesperson for UN Secretary-General Kofi Annan from 2005 to 2006 and then as deputy communications director for Secretary-General Ban Ki-moon from 2006 to 2007. Just prior to his current appointment, Dujarric was the director of news and media for the United Nations Department of Public Information and previously, director of communications for the United Nations Development Programme (UNDP). In the private sector, Dujarric worked for ABC News television for close to ten years in various capacities in the network's New York, London, and Paris news bureaus. He traveled extensively on assignment to cover major stories throughout Europe, Africa, and the Middle East. He is a graduate of Georgetown University's School of Foreign Service.

CHARLES FIRESTONE

Charles M. Firestone is executive director of the Aspen Institute Communications and Society Program. Since his appointment in December 1989, this program has focused on the implications of communications and information technologies for leadership, the impact of new technologies on democratic and social institutions, and the development of new communications policy models and options for the public interest. He was also the institute's executive vice president for policy programs and international activities from 1997 to 2000. Prior to his positions with the Aspen Institute, Firestone was director of the Communications Law Program at the University of California at Los Angeles and an adjunct professor of law at the UCLA Law School. He was also the first president of the Los Angeles Board of Telecommunications Commissioners. Firestone's career includes positions as an attorney at the Federal Communications Commission, as director of litigation for a Washington, DC, public interest law firm, and as a communications and entertainment attorney in Los Angeles. Firestone is the editor or coauthor of seven books, including *Digital Broadcasting and the Public Interest* (The Aspen Institute, 1998) and *Television and Elections* (The Aspen Institute, 1992), and has written numerous articles on communications law and policy. He holds degrees from Amherst College and Duke University Law School and resides with his wife, sculptor Pattie Porter Firestone, in Chevy Chase, Maryland.

TOM FLETCHER

Tom Fletcher was appointed Her Majesty's ambassador to the Lebanese Republic in August 2011. Tom was born in Kent, and studied at Harvey Grammar School (Folkestone) and Oxford University (Hertford College), graduating with a first-class degree in modern history. He has an MA in modern history, and is a senior associate member of St. Anthony's College for International Studies, Oxford. Fletcher was awarded the Companion of St. Michael and St. George (CMG) in the 2011 New Year's Honours, for services to the prime minister. In 2010, he was named foreign policy adviser to Prime Minister David Cameron. He was previously private secretary for foreign affairs, security, and development to Prime Minister Gordon Brown (2007–2010). A career diplomat, Fletcher served in Paris and Nairobi.

KIM GHATTAS

Kim Ghattas is a BBC correspondent based in Washington covering international affairs. She was the BBC's State Department correspondent from 2008 until 2013, and traveled regularly with the secretary of state. She is the author of the New York Times bestselling book, *The Secretary: A Journey with Hillary Clinton from Beirut to the Heart of American Power*. Ghattas was previously a Middle East correspondent for the BBC and the *Financial Times*, based in Beirut. She was part of an Emmy Award-winning BBC team covering the Lebanon–Israel conflict of 2006. Her work has also been published in *TIME* magazine, the *Boston Globe*, the *Philadelphia Inquirer*, and the *Washington Post*. She appears regularly on NPR and American television shows as a commentator on foreign policy.

TEDDY GOFF

Teddy Goff is a partner at consulting firm Precision Strategies. Goff was previously the digital director for President Obama's reelection campaign, leading the president's digital strategy and managing the 250-person nationwide team responsible for the campaign's social media, e-mail, web, online advertising, online organizing, front-end and product development, design, and video presences. Under Goff's leadership, Obama for America raised more than $690 million over the Internet, registered more than a million voters online, built Facebook and Twitter followings of more than 45 and 33 million people respectively, earned more than 133 million video views, ran more than 100 million dollars in online media spend (the largest such program in political history). As a member of the campaign's leadership, he also played a seminal role in shaping and executing the broader campaign's strategy for communications, fundraising, and organizing. Before joining the campaign, Goff served as associate vice president for strategy at Blue State Digital, overseeing the company's creative. On President Obama's 2008 campaign, Goff was responsible for state-level digital campaigns, managing everything from email and social media programs to online organizing strategies in more than twenty-five battleground states. He also oversaw the creation and launch of the Obama administration's new WhiteHouse.gov website as a member of the Presidential Transition Team. Goff, a graduate of Yale University, has been featured in *TIME*'s list of the "30 people under 30 who are changing the world," Bloomberg *Businessweek*'s list of "The Most Eligible Hires in Techdom," AdAge's "Wish List" of the top four Obama campaign officials, BusinessInsider's list of the hottest people in online politics, and the *AdWeek* 50.

ALEXANDER B. HOWARD

Alexander B. Howard is a writer and editor based in Washington, DC. Currently, he is a columnist at TechRepublic and a contributor to TechPresident, among other fine publications. Howard has been recognized by The Washingtonian Magazine as one of Washington's "TechTitans," calling him a "respected trend-spotter and chronicler of government's use of new media." He has appeared on-air as an analyst for NPR, WHYY, WAMU, Al Jazeera English, Al Jazeera America, Washington Post TV, WJLA, and a guest on The Kojo Nnamdi Show. Howard is a member of the Government of Canada's independent advisory panel on open government. Previously, he was a fellow at the Tow Center for Digital Journalism at Columbia Journalism School and a fellow at the Networked Transparency Policy Project in the Ash Center for Democratic Governance and Innovation at the Kennedy School of Government at Harvard University. From April 2010 to May 2013, he was the Washington correspondent for Radar at O'Reilly Media. Prior to joining O'Reilly, he was the associate editor of SearchCompliance.com and WhatIs.com at TechTarget, where he wrote about how the laws and regulations that affect information technology are changing, spanning the issues of online identity, data protection, risk management, electronic privacy and IT security, and the broader topics of online culture and enterprise technology. Howard has also contributed to WIRED, the National Journal, PBS Mediashift, The Daily Beast, NextGov, Forbes, Buzzfeed, Slate, The Atlantic, Huffington Post, Govfresh, ReadWriteWeb, Mashable, TechPresident, CBS News' What's Trending, Govloop, Governing People, and the Association for Computer Manufacturing, among others.

JOI ITO

Joi Ito is the director of the MediaLab at the Massachusetts Institute of Technology, which he's been heading since 2011. He is a leading thinker and writer on innovation, global technology policy, and the role of the Internet in transforming society in substantial and positive ways. A vocal advocate of emergent democracy, privacy, and Internet freedom, Ito has served as both board chair and CEO of Creative Commons, and sits on the boards of Sony Corporation, Knight Foundation, the John D. and Catherine T. MacArthur Foundation, the *New York Times* Company, and The Mozilla Foundation. In Japan, he was a founder of Digital Garage, and helped establish and later became CEO of the country's first commercial Internet service provider. He was an early investor in numerous companies, including Flickr, Six Apart, Last.fm, littleBits, Formlabs, Kickstarter, and Twitter. Ito's honors include *TIME* magazine's "Cyber-Elite" listing in 1997 (at age thirty-one) and selection as one of the "Global Leaders for Tomorrow" by the World Economic Forum (2001). In 2008, *BusinessWeek* named him one of the "25 Most Influential People on the Web." In 2011, he received the Lifetime Achievement Award from the Oxford Internet Institute. In 2013, he received an honorary DLitt from The New School in New York City.

ROBERT KELLEY

Robert Kelley is an assistant professor at the School of International Service, American University. Kelley's involvement in the study of public diplomacy over the last decade has coincided with a sharp increase in interest in the field, in which he has been an active contributor. He completed studies on the state of US public diplomacy since 9/11 earning the degree of doctor of philosophy in international relations at the London School of Economics. He subsequently developed this research while a Hayward R. Alker postdoctoral fellow at the USC Center for International Studies. Notable publications include the article "US Public Diplomacy: A Cold War Success Story?" in the *Hague Journal of Diplomacy* (2007), "Between 'Take-Offs ' and 'Crash Landings'": Situational Aspects of Public Diplomacy" in *The Public Diplomacy Handbook* edited by Nancy Snow and Philip M. Taylor (Routledge, 2008), "The New Diplomacy: Evolution of a Revolution" in *Diplomacy and Statecraft* (2010), and "Advisor Non Grata: The Dueling Roles of US Public Diplomacy" in *Trials of Engagement: The Future of US Public*

Diplomacy, edited by Ali Fisher and Scott Lucas (Brill, 2011). In recent years, Kelley's research has shifted toward the power and activities of nonstate actors in diplomatic affairs, the subject of his forthcoming book *Agency Change: Diplomatic Action beyond the State* (Rowman and Littlefield, 2014). In 2012–2013, Kelley directed the Intercultural Management Institute at American University setting a new course for the training and consulting of diplomatic corps around the world. Prior to entering academia, he worked at the US Department of State.

MATTHIAS LÜFKENS

Matthias Lüfkens leads the digital practice of Burson-Marsteller across Europe, the Middle East, and Africa (EMEA). Before joining Burson-Marsteller, Lüfkens was head of digital media at the World Economic Forum (WEF) where he designed and implemented the digital strategy. As a digital expert, he has advised a wide range of Fortune 500 companies as well as non-profit organisations on the benefits of using social media as a strategic communication tool. He is a specialist in combining traditional media outreach with innovative on-line outreach campaigns. Lüfkens has become an authority about "digital diplomacy," namely the use of social media by world leaders. He has authored the Twiplomacy study which looks specifically at the use of Twitter and social networks by heads of state and government and the the interconnections between them. Previously a journalist, he was Baltic States correspondent for Agence France Presse, *Libération*, and the *Daily Telegraph* in the early nineties (1991–1996) when the Baltic countries regained their independence. From 1996 to 2004, he was deputy editor-in-chief of EuroNews television in Lyon, France.

NICK MARTIN

Nick Martin is the cofounder and president of TechChange. As resident, he oversees all strategy and programming for the organization. Martin is an educator, technologist, and social entrepreneur with significant international peacebuilding and development expertise. He currently teaches courses at the United Nations University for Peace (UPEACE), and has given a number of guest lectures and speeches on the role of technology in peacebuilding, development and humanitarian work. He is the founder of two innovative and award-winning digital media and conflict transformation programs: DCPEACE and Peace-

Rooms. In 2009, Martin was selected as a global fellow by the International Youth Foundation and as a Washington, DC, Humanities Council Scholar for his leadership in launching the programs and his track record as a young social entrepreneur. Martin received his BA with honors from Swarthmore College and an MA in peace education from UPEACE.

CHRIS MESSINA

Chris Messina is a designer and advocate for the open web. He is best known as the "godfather" of the hashtag as he was the first to suggest (in August 2007) the use of the pound symbol for organizing groups on Twitter. Messina is also the cofounder of the BarCamp and coworking communities and sits on the boards of the OpenID and Open Web Foundations. Messina was most recently head of community and growth at NeonMob (2013). He was previously at Google as a developer advocate (2009–2011) and later as a UX Designer (2012–2013). At Google he worked on the Google+ Profiles, Pages, and Platform team, and helped create the Google Developers (developers.google.com) brand, website, and product vision. Before Google, Messina worked at Mozilla and later cofounded Citizen Space and Citizen Agency.

ADRIAN MONCK

Adrian Monck is managing director and head of public engagement at the World Economic Forum, where he was previously head of communications and media. From 2005 to 2009, he headed the Department of Journalism at City University London, where he was also a professor, and a member of the forum's first Global Agenda Council on Journalism. Monck has a background in journalism having worked at ITN, Sky News, and CBS News. Monck studied modern history at Oxford University and holds an MBA from the London Business School. He was the president of Britain's Media Society from 2005 to 2006. He is a member of the British Academy of Film and Television Arts (BAFTA), the Royal Television Society, and the Media Society. Monck is the coauthor of *Crunch Time: How Everyday Life Is Killing the Future* (Icon, 2007), and *Can You Trust The Media?* (Icon, 2008).

MACON PHILLIPS

Macon Phillips is coordinator for the Bureau of International Information Programs at the US Department of State, a position he assumed in September 2013. His first role in the Obama administration was at the White House, as a special assistant to the president and director of digital strategy (2009–2013). In this role, Phillips developed and managed the Obama administration's online program, including White-House.gov and the petition platform We The People. Prior to the White House, Phillips ran the new media program for the Presidential Transition Team (Change.gov) and served as the deputy director of the Obama campaign's new media department (BarackObama.com). Before the campaign, Phillips led Blue State Digital's strategy practice, working with clients like the Democratic National Committee and Senator Ted Kennedy. A proud AmeriCorps VISTA alum, the Huntsville, Alabama, native is a graduate of Duke University.

JR REAGAN

JR Reagan is a principal at Deloitte and Touche. In this role, he's Deloitte's lead client service partner for the National Protectorate Programs Directorate of the US Department of Homeland Security (DHS NPPD). He is an advisor to the US Greenhouse, which offers locations across the United States to provide an advanced, immersive environment designed to accelerate breakthroughs. He has led innovation initiatives within the firm including acting as federal chief innovation officer, leading the Center for Federal Innovation and the Deloitte Analytics HIVE. Reagan's clients come from the commercial and government sectors in more than twenty countries worldwide. He currently serves as a US eminence fellow and a member of the US Social Media Working Group. He also serves as senior professional faculty teaching innovation and creativity at Johns Hopkins University's Carey Business School and holds a doctorate in organizational leadership from Shenandoah University. He holds a master's in management information systems from Bowie State University; a BA in sociology from the University of the State of New York; and a graduate certificate in advanced international affairs from Texas A and M (Bush School of Government and Public Service). He has guest lectured on innovation and analytics at Harvard University, Northwestern, and Notre Dame.

GIANNI RIOTTA

Gianni Riotta is an Italian journalist and writer. He's a member of the Council of Foreign Relations and a columnist for foreign policy and the Italian daily *La Stampa*. He is a visiting professor at Princeton University and at the Institute of Advanced Studies (IMT) in Lucca, Italy, where he focused on the impact of new media and social networks in cultural, political, and academic contexts. He collaborates with the School of Journalism at Columbia University. Riotta has an extended background in journalism, having been the New York correspondent for several Italian publications, including *La Stampa*, *L'Espresso*, and *Il Corriere Della Sera*. He was the editor-in-chief of Italy's financial daily *Il Sole 24 Ore* and earlier the editor-in-chief of TG1, Italy's national television news channel. He started his career as a reporter at the age of seventeen at *Il Manifesto* and *Il Giornale Di Sicilia*. Riotta graduated with a BA in philosophy from the University of Palermo and with a master's of science from Columbia University's School of Journalism.

ALEC ROSS

Alec Ross served as senior advisor for innovation to Secretary of State Hillary Clinton from 2009 to 2013. In this role he was tasked with maximizing the potential of technology and innovation in service of America's diplomatic goals and stewarding Secretary of State Clinton's Twenty-First Century Statecraft agenda. Ross helped ensure America's leadership and advances the State Department's interests on a range of issues from internet freedom to disaster response to responding to regional conflicts. Previously, he served as the convener for Obama for America's Technology, Media, and Telecommunications Policy Committee and served on the Obama-Biden Presidential Transition Team. In 2000, he and three colleagues cofounded the nonprofit organization One Economy and grew it from modest origins in a basement into the world's largest digital divide organization, with programs on four continents. He was named the 2010 Middle East/North Africa Technology Person of the Year, cited by *The Huffington Post* as one of "10 Game Changers in Politics," named a "game changer" as one of Politico's "50 Politicos to Watch" in 2010, and named one of forty under forty leaders in international development. In 2011, he was named one of the "Top 100 Global Thinkers" by *Foreign Policy* magazine. Since 2014, Ross has served as senior fellow at the School for International and Public Affairs of Columbia University. He has served as a guest lecturer at numerous institutions including the United Nations, Harvard Law School, Stanford Business School, the London School of Economics, and a number of parliamentary bodies. His writing has appeared in publications including the *SAIS Review of International Affairs*, the *NATO Review*, and the *Hague Journal of Diplomacy*. Ross, who's currently writing a book to be published by Simon and Schuster about the industries and businesses of the future, started his career as a sixth-grade teacher through Teach for America in inner-city Baltimore.

CARNE ROSS

Carne Ross founded Independent Diplomat (ID) in 2004 to address the "diplomatic deficit" created by a diplomatic system that all too often excludes or marginalizes many governments and groups most affected by the decisions made within it, and usually those who are suffering the most. As executive director of ID, he plays an integral role in each client project and in guiding the organization. He has over fifteen years of diplomatic experience in the British Foreign Office and the United Nations, working on a wide range of issues and regions including Europe, the Middle East, Africa, the global environment, terrorism, and postconflict reconstruction. He is experienced in bilateral and multilateral diplomacy and familiar with major international institutions, in particular the United Nations. Between 1997 and 1998, he served as the speechwriter to the British Foreign Secretary. He then spent four and a half years in the UK delegation on the UN Security Council. Ross resigned from the British foreign office in 2004. He is a trained negotiator and economist. He is also a playwright (*The Fox* enjoyed a short run in New York in early 2001) and author. His latest book, *The Leaderless Revolution*, was published in 2011 by Simon and Schuster (UK) and Blue Rider Press, an imprint of Penguin (US). His first book, *Independent Diplomat: Dispatches from an Unaccountable Elite*, was published in 2007 by Hurst and Co. (UK) and Cornell University Press (US).

ANDREAS SANDRE

Andreas Sandre is a Press and Public Affairs Officer at the Embassy of Italy in Washington DC, where he focuses on public and digital diplomacy. He was previously at the Italian Permanent Mission to the United Nations in New York, as a Public Affairs Officer for the Italian

Delegation to the UN Security Council. Andreas is the author of Twitter for Diplomats (Italian Ministry of Foreign Affairs and DiploFoundation, February 2013) and *Digital Diplomacy: Conversations on Innovation in Foreign Policy* (Rowman & Littlefield, January 2015). Sandre has contributed articles on foreign policy and digital diplomacy to numerous publications, including the Huffington Post, the London School of Economics' Global Policy Journal, DiploFoundation, and BigThink. He's often part of panels and conferences on digital communications, including TEDxStockholm, the Stockholm Initiative on Digital Diplomacy, the Washington Diplomats's Copuntry Promotion Strategies Conference, Berlin's International Conference on Political Communications, and the Diplomatic Courier +SocialGood conference on the Future of Diplomacy.

ARTURO SARUKHAN

Arturo Sarukhan is a nonresident senior fellow in the Foreign Policy and Metropolitan Policy programs at Brookings Institution, where he focuses on hemispheric issues, Mexico–US relations, immigration policy, new security threats, and the role of cities in the twenty-first century. The grandson and son of conflict refugees in Mexico, he served as a career diplomat in the Mexican Foreign Service for twenty years and received the rank of career ambassador in 2006. In February 2007, he was appointed ambassador of Mexico to the United States, where he served until 2013. Sarukhan held numerous positions in his diplomatic career and served as chief of policy planning at the Foreign Ministry. In 2006, he joined the presidential campaign of Felipe Calderón as foreign policy advisor and international spokesperson. He then became coordinator of the foreign policy transition team for then President-elect Calderón. Sarukhan has also been a member of several organizations, including the Mexican Council on Foreign Relations (COMEXI), the Foreign Policy Association in New York City and the International Institute for Strategic Studies in London. He studied history at the National Autonomous University of Mexico (UNAM), and has a BA in international relations from El Colegio de Mexico. He earned an MA in American foreign policy at the Johns Hopkins School of Advanced International Studies (SAIS), where he was a Fulbright scholar and Ford Foundation fellow.

MARIETJE SCHAAKE

Marietje Schaake is a Dutch politician and an elected member of the European Parliament, where she's a member of the Committee on International Trade and the Delegation for relations with the United States. She's also a substitute member of the Committee on Foreign Affairs, the Subcommittee on Human Rights, and the Delegation for relations with Iran. Beyond her work in the European Parliament, Schaake is a member of the European Council on Foreign Relations, serves on the Board of the Iran Human Rights Documentation Center, sits as a commissioner in the Global Commission on Internet Governance, and is a member of the Investment Committee of the Digital Defenders Partnership. She is also the vice president of the Supervisory Board of Free Press Unlimited, serves on the Board of Governors of the European Internet Foundation, the Board of Advisors of the Tahrir Institute for Middle East Policy, on the Board of Directors of the Flemish-Dutch House deBuren, the Advisory Board of the Dutch section of the Internet Society, and on the Board of Recommendation of the Dutch Model European Parliament. Before joining the European Parliament, she worked as an independent advisor to governments, diplomats, businesses and NGOs, on issues of transatlantic relations, diversity and pluralism, and civil and human rights.

PETRIT SELIMI

Petrit Selimi has been deputy minister of Foreign Affairs of Republic of Kosovo since June 2011. He is also a member of the special State Commission on Religious Freedoms and has been appointed as national coordinator for implementation of regional cooperation agreement with Serbia. Selimi has launched a host of innovative programs in public diplomacy, interfaith dialogue and has launched the National Strategy on Digital Diplomacy. Before joining the Government of Kosovo, Selimi ran for an MP seat for the governing Democratic Party of Kosovo at 2010 National Elections. Prior to this, he worked as a private public relations and political risk consultant. He was one of the founders and the first executive director of the daily *Express*, an independent newspaper published in Prishtina, and previously worked as media and democratization advisor at the OSCE Mission in Kosovo. In the 1990s, Selimi was a children's and youth rights activist and was one of the founders of Postpessimists, the first network of youth NGOs in former

Yugoslavia, recipient of the UN Peace and Tolerance Award. He has in recent years served in the Board of Directors of Soros Foundation in Kosovo and Executive Board of President Ahtisaari's Balkan Children and Youth Foundation. Selimi holds a BA in social anthropology from the University of Oslo, and studied media and communications at the London School of Economics, as a recipient of the Chevening Scholarship.

DEBORAH SEWARD

Deborah Seward was appointed director of the Strategic Communications Division in the United Nations' Department of Public Information in February 2011. In that role, she has responsibility for the oversight of the UN's sixty-three Information Centers around the world. She also oversees the Communications Campaign Service, which provides guidance on a wide variety of priority UN issues, including peace and security, development, and human rights. Before joining the UN, she spent more than twenty years with the Associated Press, serving in Moscow, Paris, Warsaw, Berlin, and New York, where she was international editor from 2003 to 2005. Her assignments have taken her to more than thirty countries in Europe, the Middle East, and Latin America. She also served as director of the Central Newsroom at Radio Free Europe/Radio Liberty in Prague, Czech Republic in 2006 to 2007. She is a graduate of the University of North Carolina at Chapel Hill, studied at L'Institut d'études politiques in Paris, and was a Nieman fellow at Harvard University.

ANNE-MARIE SLAUGHTER

Anne-Marie Slaughter is the president and CEO of the New America Foundation, a public policy institute and idea incubator based in Washington and New York. She is also the Bert G. Kerstetter '66 University Professor Emerita of Politics and International Affairs at Princeton University. From 2009 to 2011, she served as director of Policy Planning for the United States Department of State, the first woman to hold that position. Upon leaving the State Department, she received the Secretary's Distinguished Service Award for her work leading the Quadrennial Diplomacy and Development Review, as well as meritorious service awards from USAID and the Supreme Allied Commander for Europe. Prior to her government service, Slaughter was the Dean of Princeton's

Woodrow Wilson School of Public and International Affairs from 2002 to 2009 and the J. Sinclair Armstrong Professor of International, Foreign, and Comparative Law at Harvard Law School from 1994 to 2002. Slaughter has written or edited six books, including *A New World Order* (2004) and *The Idea That Is America: Keeping Faith with Our Values in a Dangerous World* (2007), and over one hundred scholarly articles. In 2012, Slaughter published the article "Why Women Still Can't Have It All," in *The Atlantic*, which quickly became the most read article in the history of the magazine and helped spawn a renewed national debate on the continued obstacles to genuine full male–female equality. *Foreign Policy* magazine named her to their annual list of the Top 100 Global Thinkers in 2009, 2010, 2011, and 2012. Slaughter received a BA from Princeton University; an MPhil and DPhil in international relations from Oxford University, where she was a Daniel M. Sachs Scholar; and a JD from Harvard University.

TIMOTEJ ŠOOŠ

Timotej Šooš is special adviser to the minister of foreign affairs and deputy prime minister of the Republic of Slovenia. In this capacity, he also acts as digital diplomacy coordinator/lead at the Ministry of Foreign Affairs of Slovenia and director of the Young Bled Strategic Forum, the young-leader platform of the Bled Strategic Forum. Before joining the Office of the Minister of Foreign Affairs and Deputy Prime Minister in February 2012, Šooš was an adviser to the state secretary and previously as a development cooperation communication expert. In March 2014, Šooš was selected by the German Marshall Fund of the United States as a Marshall Memorial fellow. In 2013, he was selected as a One Young World Ambassador. He graduate Summa Cum Laude from the Vanguard University of Southern California with a BA in political communication.

LARA STEIN

Lara Stein is founder and former director of TEDx and the TED Prize, having overseen the strategy, creation, development, and implementation of the TEDx program at TED. Through Stein's leadership TED expanded from two annual conferences into a global community of nine thousand TEDx events in 1,200 cities taking place in 133 countries. Over her six-year tenure from 2007 to 2013, the TEDx platform grew to include the "TEDx in a Box" program, which allows people in developing countries to more easily hold TEDx events, the TEDx corporate event platform, enabling corporations to hold TED-like events inside their organizations for free and TEDxWomen. Stein also expanded the TED platform to include a youth audience with the creation of the TEDxYouth program, TEDxYouthDay, and TEDYouth. She was also director of the TED Prize, annually granting an individual one million dollars and a "wish to change the world." Prior to TED, Stein was a consultant to numerous media, art, and technology companies, including Microsoft, Marvel Comics, Lifetime Television, and PBS. Stein's achievements have earned her recognition in several leading industry trade publications, including the *Silicon Alley Reporter*'s "Top 100 Executives," Alley Cat News' "Top Women of Silicon Alley" in Alley Cat News, and The Elite's "Who's Who Among Outstanding Female Executives."

DAVID THORNE

Ambassador David Thorne was named senior advisor to the Secretary of State in August 2013. Among other duties, Secretary Kerry has asked Thorne to lead a department-wide effort to position economic and commercial issues more prominently within the US foreign policy landscape. Ambassador Thorne is also working to elevate the importance of entrepreneurship, technology, and innovation in the State Department's promotion of global prosperity. Thorne brings a wealth of public and private sector experience to Foggy Bottom. Most recently, he served from 2009-2013 as the U.S. Ambassador to Italy, following in the footsteps of his father, Landon Thorne Jr., who was administrator of the Marshall Plan for Italy (1953–1956). Ambassador Thorne bolstered U.S.-Italian relations, strengthening partnerships with the leaders of three consecutive Italian governments. On the economic development and technology front, he launched the embassy-sponsored Digital Economy Forum, a public-private sector collaboration to catalyze innovation, entrepreneurship, and job creation. Prior to his service with the Department of State, Thorne co-founded Adviser Investments, one of the nation's most highly regarded investment advisory firms specializing in Vanguard and Fidelity mutual funds and exchange-traded funds. He has been an investor and entrepreneur in a wide variety of business ventures, including marketing consulting, real estate, publishing, and financial services.

LANCE ULANOFF

Lance Ulanoff is chief correspondent and editor-at-large at Mashable. Lance acts as a senior member of the editing team, with a focus on defining internal and curated opinion content. He also helps develop staffwide alternative storytelling skills and implementation of social media tools during live events. Prior to joining Mashable in September 2011, Ulanoff served as editor-in-chief of PCMag.com and senior vice president of content for the Ziff Davis, Inc. While there, he guided the brand to a 100 percent digital existence and oversaw content strategy for all of Ziff Davis's websites. His long-running column on PCMag.com earned him a Bronze award from the ASBPE. Winmag.com, HomePC.com, and PCMag.com have all been honored under Ulanoff's guidance. He makes frequent appearances on national, international, and local news programs including Fox News, "The Today Show," "Good Morning America," "Kelly and Michael," CNBC, CNN, and the BBC. Ulanoff has been an invited guest speaker at numerous technology conferences including SXSW, Think Mobile, CEA Line Shows, Digital Life, RoboBusiness, RoboNexus, Business Foresight, and Digital Media Wire's Games and Mobile Forum.

ALEEM WALJI

Aleem Walji is the director of the World Bank Institute's Innovation Labs. He oversees Open Government, Transparency, and Accountability initiatives with particular interest in leveraging technology to increase social accountability and improve service delivery. He oversees the Development Marketplace program, which provides social entrepreneurs access to growth financing with a focus on South Asia, East Africa, and the Middle East. Walji also serves on the Global Advisory Council on the Future of Government at the World Economic Forum. Prior to joining the World Bank Institute, Walji served as a head of Global Development Initiatives at Google.org, with a focus on eastern Africa. He led efforts related to increasing transparency and accountability in government and supporting the growth of small- and medium-size enterprises in Africa. He was also the first CEO of the Aga Khan

Foundation in Syria. He is a graduate of Emory University and the Massachusetts Institute of Technology. He completed his bachelor's degree in Near Eastern studies and anthropology and his master's degree in international development and regional planning.